D0754153

PRACTICAL PSYCHIC
SELF-DEFENSE

Also by Robert Bruce

Astral Dynamics

PRACTICAL PSYCHIC SELF-DEFENSE

Understanding and Surviving Unseen Influences

ROBERT BRUCE

HAMPTON ROADS
PUBLISHING COMPANY, INC.

Cover design by Marjoram Productions
Cover photo by Marjoram Productions

Hampton Roads Publishing Company, Inc.
1125 Stoney Ridge Road
Charlottesville, VA 22902

434-296-2772
fax: 434-296-5096
e-mail: hrpc@hrpub.com
www.hrpub.com

If you are unable to order this book from your local
bookseller, you may order directly from the publisher.
Call 1-800-766-8009, toll-free.

Library of Congress Catalog Card Number: 2001099306
ISBN 1-57174-221-2
10 9 8 7 6 5 4 3 2 1
Printed on acid-free paper in the United States

Dedication

No, I cannot go yet
While winter holds in thrall
New promises of spring:
Waiting for fulfillment
Under bare limbed trees.

No, I cannot go yet
For spring has now arrived
And there are daffodils:
Newly minted chalices
Golden, bright and green.

No, I cannot go yet
As the sealed poppies blow
Among the ripening corn
And the nightingale sings
In the night darkened wood.

But when these dear things
Have passed me by
Call me again
And I'll go.

Poem by Wynne Bruce, 2001

Acknowledgements

Romero Lourenço da Cunha: for your profound friendship, invaluable contributions, and shared hermetic wisdom.

Benjamin Bruce: for your insightful contributions and Herculean efforts during the edit from hell.

Nita Hickock: for your friendship, support, and invaluable contributions and advice.

Aaron Nathaniel Sabolch: many thanks for the research.

Donni Hackanson: many thanks for the early edit and critique.

Frank Demarco: for being so Frank during this book's conception.

Richard Leviton: for your invaluable critique and editing acumen.

Jesse Bruce (my young artist son): many thanks for the illustrations!

Wynne Bruce: for your input, critique, and a lifetime of encouragement.

Ginny and David Eldridge and Teresa and Bill Smith: for your continuing help and encouragement.

James and Kathlene Bruce: for being such wonderful children.

John Takeuchi Turner, MD: for your invaluable advice and contributions.

Michael Ross: thanks for your help and support.

Mitch, Greg, and Tracy Kibblewhite: thanks for believing in me!

Steve Hurst, David Kitson, Adrian Cooper, and Zufo: for all your many kindnesses and professional support.

Keith Alderslade: for the insane sanity breaks and refined devil's advocacy.

My thanks to the staff of Hampton Roads, for your kind professional support.

A big hug to all my friends, fans, helpers, and volunteers!

Table of Contents

Part III
Psychic Self-Defense Countermeasures:
How to Protect Yourself against
Unseen Spirit Influences 163

I n t r o d u c t i o n :

Why You Need Psychic Self-Defense

If these pages could speak, they might whisper to you of strange noises heard in the dead of night, of scuttling shadows at the edge of vision, of children paralyzed by fear, of goose bumps, evil spirits, and ghosts, and of the thick, cloying darkness from which all nightmares spring. But they would also regale you with tales of hope and wonder, of rescue and bright courage. They *will* teach you how to understand and survive a thousand terrible things that I pray might never happen to you or to anyone you love.

Psychic attack, evil spirits, haunting, and possession are uncomfortable subjects to consider, let alone to experience. Whether you believe in dark supernatural problems or not depends greatly upon your personal experience with them. But if only a few grains of truth exist in these matters, then this book is justified. Think of it as a supernatural exposé for the uninitiated, as a survival guide for those living the nightmare of being influenced by unfriendly Spirit beings.

We all have a natural tendency to deny or downplay the importance, or even existence, of anything dangerous or distasteful—death, disease, accidents, possession that cannot be easily controlled or avoided. This is human and understandable. It fosters psychological security and helps us avoid obsessing over unpleasant things that cannot be controlled. Unfortunately, this means that most of us have to experience psychic attack or other such dark spiritual problems before we begin accepting them as possibilities.

Only then do we begin trying to understand and do something about it. But given the vast amount of often confusing and/or conflicting information available on this subject, much time must be spent trying to make sense of it all. Then comes the difficult task of trying to find something practical to use to help matters. This book overcomes these problems by making metaphysical knowledge accessible, understandable, and practical to the general reader.

This book was first conceived during a lengthy discussion with my publishers over the matter of dark spiritual problems, something with which I have extensive personal experience. It is written especially for the person with no occult knowledge or experience. It deals candidly with unusual circumstances that, on the surface, might seem bizarre—that is, unless that person happens to be living under those circumstances.

My goal is to give practical advice and effective countermeasures that can be used by the novice, that is, by the average parents who suddenly find they have a weird problem on their hands. No experience, knowledge, prior skills, or psychic abilities are required to apply what is offered. Everything is explained and taught as simply as possible.

Psychic attack and possession are age-old supernatural problems that often require supernatural solutions. Many new solutions are offered here, and some relate to applied metaphysics (the practical application of magic). I have lived through everything I describe in this book and have spent decades searching for ways to survive and create spiritual peace and quiet for myself. This book derives from my experience-based understanding and success in countering the forces of darkness.

Unseen spiritual forces affect humanity in many subtle and not-so-subtle ways. There are both positive and negative spiritual forces, with a great range between them. While understanding the dynamics and motivations of these forces is often beyond ordinary understanding, they can be observed, and even studied, to some extent. The field of parapsychology is a good example of human intelligence working to make sense of paranormal phenomena. While many people choose to not openly acknowledge the supernatural (especially the forces of darkness), the evidence cannot be explained away without generous doses of irrational denial and wishful thinking.

To many people, if a thing cannot be dissected in a laboratory, it cannot exist, even though the evidence of their own eyes and senses repeatedly demands otherwise. A lack of viable scientific alternatives leads to claims of mass hallucination, hysteria, and mental disorders to explain the effects of unseen spirit influences. This is understandable when inexperienced, materialistic minds attempt to grasp what is often beyond conventional comprehension at the physical level of existence. Although it can help, denial is not enough to drive back the darkness that has plagued the hearts, minds, and dreams of humanity since our beginnings.

The situation is now much worse, supernaturally speaking, than it was in the days of our ancestors. Prior to the twentieth century, most people had substantial religious beliefs and lived simpler lives. Organized religion gave them community and spiritual support, and something to fall back upon when they encountered supernatural problems. Many of their beliefs and practices today we call superstitions. But some, no matter how illogical they might appear to be on the surface, are effective countermeasures against negative supernatural influences.

Whether one is comfortable believing it or not, the empirical evidence suggests that spirit beings of many different types, of both a positive and negative nature, exist in unseen subtle realms just beyond the physical realm. One cannot point to these realms or even describe where they are; yet these dimensions exist all around us, occupying the same space as the physical universe. Quantum physics has long supported the existence of dimensional levels beyond the physical. Originally out of science fiction, concepts like black holes, antimatter, hyperspace, and parallel universes today are very real possibilities. Though the existence of these things can be scientifically supported and modeled, it is still difficult for the average person to grasp the existence of subtle dimensional realms.

I have spent a significant part of my life searching for reasonable explanations and practical methods to help counter the influences of dark spirit beings. In my childhood and early adult life, this was for me a matter of personal survival. Later, it evolved into a quest to help the many people I encountered who had similar problems. Some people might gasp here and wonder what I have been doing wrong that has attracted so much negative attention, but you might also wonder what I have been doing right.

Just as it is in the nature of angels and other such positive spiritual beings to oppose evil, so it is in the nature of evil- or negative-minded spirits to oppose good in any way they can. Regardless of their type, I class all unwholesome spirits as Negatives, or Negs, for short. All spiritual beings that have a negative effect upon humans I call Negs. Any contact with Negs is detrimental to human existence to a greater or lesser extent, sometimes in the extreme. Negs spread unhappiness, disease, and spiritual pollution, and they interfere with humans more frequently and comprehensively than most people suspect.

Experience and reasoning led me to speculate that, for a variety of complex metaphysical reasons, doorways sometimes crack open between dimensions. These doorways in the dimensional structure of the universe allow Negs to approach the physical dimension and interact or interfere with humans. This closeness often leads to some form of psychic attack or interference. Once Negs move close to the physical dimension, they cannot stay long unless they absorb life energy from living organic beings, human or animal. Sometimes, they attach to living beings who provide them with anchors to stay here in the physical dimension. These factors may explain the seeming urgency of some types of psychic attacks; it also helps explain the sinister phenomena usually associated with psychic attacks. Such attacks seem designed to unbalance and thereby weaken victims, possibly to make them more susceptible. Everything about psychic attack revolves around gathering life energy and gaining control over victims, with the human energy body always being the center of attention for the Negs.

But psychic attacks and other such maladies do not have to be endured meekly. All Negs have innate weaknesses that can be exploited. Much can be done to avoid and/or counteract Neg-related problems. By and large, this does not involve doing anything too outlandish. For example, you might be surprised to hear that direct Neg attacks can be broken instantly just by walking across a water main or garden hose or by hopping into the shower and doing a visualization. This may sound too simplistic but the underlying principles of these countermeasures are sound.

Keep in mind that by opening this book you are reading the words of a mystic. My knowledge does not come from the dusty pages of old books, but from a lifetime of active spiritual and metaphysical exploration. Although I strive for objectivity and use a scientific method wherever possible, I speak from hands-on, real-life experience. I also have the psychic senses to see and perceive things that most people cannot and usually would rather not even know about. This book tells it like it is, according to my experience and reasoning and as objectively as possible.

My sole motivation for writing this book is to help people with problems, but not by conforming with popular knowledge. The countermeasures and protocols I offer have been used under a variety of field situations (during actual attacks by a wide variety of Neg types). All have been thoroughly "road-tested" for their effectiveness and reliability.

In this book, I deal with the most common types of psychic attacks, Neg influences, and Neg manifestations. Also offered are chapters dealing with specific children's issues and family matters. Children are far more at risk than adults. Many choose to believe children are constantly watched over and guarded by angels, but the shocking fact is that, because children are mentally and emotionally weaker than adults, plus more psychically delicate and sensitive, they are extremely vulnerable to unseen psychic interference.

Of course, angels and good spirits do exist; let me assure you of this. I have had several major encounters with angels during my life. But these exalted Messengers of God seem to have a limited intervention policy when it comes to human affairs, even concerning Neg/human interactions. While direct angelic or divine intervention is always possible, in my experience, it is something of a rarity. This is understandable because we live in the physical dimension, the realm of hard life experience. Too much direct angelic intervention would obviously be contrary to the reasons underlying physical incarnation. If God wanted to wet-nurse us humans and keep us in total physical and spiritual security, He would not have put us down here in the first place. Life is a learning experience in every sense of the word.

In the world today, those with paranormal troubles are often blamed for attracting and/or creating their own problems. Myriad explanations abound, but they generally hold that victims do something wrong or have "bad karma," often involving past lives. However, philosophy and spiritual finger-pointing are not of much practical help, and while I believe karma, choice, and free will are involved with all aspects of life, it is not only demoralizing but unfair to blame victims for their troubles. They surely have enough to deal with. Helpful advice and practical solutions are needed, not blame-based philosophies.

The previous discussion could be extended to include the nature of evil and the existence of evil spirits in general. These subjects are denied in many schools of spiritual thought today. Some traditions believe there are no such things as demons or evil spirits, only poorly evolved or misguided spirits. At a high level this may be true, but it is a moot point if one is inflicted with dark spiritual problems. Those sharing this above opinion would quickly change their minds the first time they encounter a seriously evil spirit or demon face to face. If I had listened to other people and/or adhered to the popular new-age spiritual model (which does not credit full-blown possession at all) I would most certainly have died from this darkest of maladies.

I pray to Almighty God that none of the dark supernatural maladies discussed in the book shall ever happen to you or anyone you love. But if something ever does happen, the information I present will help you roll back the darkness and make the nightmare go away.

PART 1

The Negatives:
The Relationship of Unseen
Spirit Beings and Humans

An Overview of Part 1

We begin with a frank discussion on bad or negative spirit beings (called Negs throughout the book), and historical and experiential perspectives, as well as case histories, are given in support. Some common bad spirits are discussed, especially those the author has experienced, including human and non-human spirits, poltergeists, incubi, astral snakes and spiders, and demons.

I give an explanation of the mind-split effect (bilocation or duality phenomena associated with astral projection) and this leads to an explanation of the real-time astral dimension (the spirit environment closest to the physical dimension). I follow this with speculation on the underlying mechanisms associated with life, consciousness, human bio-incarnation, sleep, dreaming, and out-of-body experiences and how these are likely exploited by bad spirits to attack, influence, and even possess sensitive humans.

Then, we move on to the origins and motivations of bad spirits; why they are drawn to interfere with humans, and the methods most likely employed. Next, there is a speculation on the spread of bad spirits and information on how natural barriers limit their travel capabilities in the real-time astral environment (which has a direct geographical relationship with the physical universe). It is essential to understand the nature and limitations of bad spirits, especially while they are manifesting close enough to the physical dimension to affect humans. This is important when analyzing problems and deciding on appropriate counter-measures.

1

The Negatives: An Introduction to Unfriendly Spirit Beings and Their Agenda

Accepting the existence of negative spirit beings—Negs—understandably can be difficult for many people. One way around this is to consider Negs as nothing more than dense patterns of negative energy. Another is to consider them as manifestations of one's own subconscious mind or the minds of others; or you can consider them to be independent, sentient thought-forms. Exactly how you understand Negs depends greatly on your experiences and beliefs and what you are prepared to accept. However, regardless of what they are, if they *exist* at all, they must be *dealt* with—which is the focus of this book.

It is difficult to describe what Negs are and where they come from. To start with, they are of many varieties. Experiencing the astral dimension through wakeful out-of-body projection can provide you with firsthand experience with other dimensions, but this will not give you an understanding of the complexities of interdimensional spirit beings and their relationships with humans. Inorganic or spirit beings—that is, beings not living as biological organisms—come from dimensions outside of the physical. Sometimes doorways open that allow these beings to cross over into areas close to the physical, and this results in manifestations that can be sensed and at times even seen by humans.

Types of Inorganic Beings

Researching the field of parapsychology reveals many documented cases of spirit manifestations, such as poltergeists, hauntings, and other phenomena. This provides more evidence of interactions between humans and spirit beings down through the ages. Added to this, the historical and religious evidence of the reality of this is overwhelming.

Any attempt to categorize inorganic beings is difficult. Often I suggest regarding anything with a negative disposition as a Neg and leaving it at that. Simplifying things this way helps avoid a lot of the confusion inherent to analyzing Neg-related problems; it also helps reduce fear levels when dealing with Negs. That said, this chapter will review the main types of Negs most likely to cause you trouble.

Some types of spirit beings exist naturally in a level of the astral dimension I call the real-time zone (see my *Astral Dynamics,* Hampton Roads, 1999). The real-time zone is the lowest part of the astral plane, the part closest to and, thus, most in tune with, our physical dimension. It's a direct reflection of the physical universe.

Many people having out-of-body and near-death experiences find themselves in the real-time zone, witnessing real-life events as they happen. During these experiences, they share many of the qualities of spirit beings. Like spirit beings, they can pass through solid matter and are invisible to other people in the physical dimension.

Earthbound Spirits: Earthbound spirits are popularly said to be involved with most supernatural manifestations including hauntings and psychic attacks. People shy away from using words like entity, evil spirit, or demon when discussing the actions of unseen beings. It's easier to relate to the concept of earthbound or mischievous spirits, no matter how evil and harmful these spirits might in fact be.

In my experience, given the number of people dying on our planet every day, true earthbound spirits are not that common. While death and immediate-afterlife processes can happen in a variety of ways, most human spirits move on and lose contact with the Earth plane within a week or two of physical death. But during that time, many spirits will attempt to contact their friends and loved ones for sentimental reasons. For this reason, most common supernatural phenomena are related to recently deceased human spirits, not earthbound ones.

The existence of "astral shells" adds to the confusion. Because astral shells appear to be earthbound spirits, this leads people to conclude earthbound spirits are involved in many manifestations. But astral shells are not true spirits because they do not contain the essence, or soul of the person represented.

An astral shell is a type of thought-form that can be likened to a common optical afterimage. While an astral shell is more complex and enduring, the principles of operation are similar. Through the act of living, people generate enduring reflections of their self-image in the astral dimension. These contain full copies of memory and personality, but lack the soul essence. After death, like old photographs, astral shells slowly fade away, but this can take many years, depending on the strength of the mind that generated it.

As mentioned previously, recently deceased spirits cannot be classed as true earthbound spirits because they will soon pass on to the next level of existence and are therefore not bound to the Earth plane. It's only when they refuse to leave the Earth plane, and find ways of staying close to it, that problems arise. The only way for deceased spirits to stay close to the Earth plane is through life-energy vampirism. They must continually replace their fading energy resources by feeding on the energies of the living. Most earthbound spirits do not seem to realize they are dead; they are confused, living in a surreal dream-like world they do not understand.

Energy vampirism is a common factor shared by the majority of troublesome Neg types. It's a matter of necessity for all spirits wishing to exist for any length of time close to the physical plane that they replenish their energy. Accidental vampirism can happen through close contact between spirits and humans. The living humans involved are often unaware this is happening because the amount of energy lost is usually insignificant. In the typical scenario, recently deceased spirits try to hug or get close to loved ones and unintentionally absorb their energy. If it's understood that close contact like this can cause problems, the possibility of a spirit becoming accidentally earthbound can be avoided.

With no physical brain for memory storage, in time earthbound spirits tend to lose their memories and identities and become confused ghosts. There are different types of these ghosts. The most common are bound to particular areas or buildings; *trapped* might be a better term. They cannot easily cross running water (rivers, streams, water mains, and pipes) unaided. To cross running water, earthbound spirits must attach themselves to susceptible living beings (human or animal) and piggyback a ride. As most typical human ghosts are not aware of this factor, they find themselves unexplainably stuck inside buildings; this can result in a house or area becoming haunted.

Only a small number of ghosts are true earthbound spirits. This state can result from a difficult or sudden death, or from an inability to accept the finality of death, often compounded by a lack of belief in spiritual matters. Such spirits maintain their earthly existence through unintentional vampirism and find themselves inexplicably bound to particular places. Alternatively, they might find themselves hitchhiking about, moving from one person to another, with little or no control over their geographical movements.

Perverted and Addicted Spirits and Ghosts: Some human ghosts linger after physical death due to their earthly cravings, perversions, and addictions, for example, to sex, drugs, alcohol. These types of ghosts tend to frequent areas and places where they can best "feed" their addictions. For example, alcoholic earthbound spirits will frequent bars and other such drinking places. They soon learn to enter, hitchhike, and overshadow drinkers, and through this method experience alcohol and drunkenness again.

Addiction-motivated human spirits soon learn how to latch onto and control susceptible people. More experienced spirits may condition and pressure susceptible people into following lives of substance abuse. Many new substance abusers are created in this way, as a person whose only weakness is that he is sensitive and susceptible to such influences becomes addicted.

Sexual perversions and addictions can have the same results and cause human spirits to become earthbound. Perverted spirits roam until they find suitably weak, susceptible hosts. They will then invade, hitchhike, overshadow, and influence their new hosts into becoming involved with their (the overshadowing spirit's) old perversions. Technically, this is a type of possession.

Deranged Ghosts: Deranged human ghosts are different from most common ghosts. They already may be deranged at the time of their death or become deranged through living unhappy earthbound afterlives. Deranged ghosts are unpredictable, and hence more troublesome, than other human ghosts. If channeled or questioned by psychics, many of this type will not remember they were once human, and if they do, their memories of earthly life will often be clouded with fantasy.

It is likely that deranged ghosts can, given enough time, permanently identify with their psychosis as madness overcomes what is left of their rational mind. When this happens, they become whatever they believe or feel themselves to be. In the fluid, astral environment, strong creative abilities are the norm, so deranged ghosts can choose any delusional form that suits them. However, when delusion overcomes them, they can permanently take on these created forms which can result in the creation of pseudo-demons. In time, in this new form, all vestiges of humanity are lost and replaced by a completely new identity. As delusional identity changes happen to many insane people, it's logical this can also happen after death.

Incubus and Succubus: Unseen astral lovers are not uncommon even today, but they have a long history going back thousands of years. Unseen lovers are often incubus or succubus beings. An incubus is the male version of an inorganic being that preys on living female humans, while the succubus is the fema' version that preys on living male humans. These are probably one and the same entity, as inorganic entities are gender-less, so I will use the term incubus hereafter to refer to both. This type of entity is capable of taking on the appearance of either male or female when manifesting. They are not normally seen, only felt, but they are very good at providing the *illusion* of a solid physical body of the appropriate gender to suit a victim's sexual preference.

Incubus entities, technically, are demonic, but they are of a low order and not evil like other types of demons. They "feed" by forcing victims to release sexual energy during orgasm. The approach of an incubus is different from most other types of psychic attacks and Neg sexual assaults in that fear is not used, and victims are seduced and/or pleasured into becoming semi-willing participants. Some incubi will try to form steady relationships with susceptible victims, visiting regularly.

This may seem like a harmless oddity, but if a person becomes sexually addicted to an incubus, he will be steadily drained of vitality. This can be debilitating, causing fatigue and illness; if continued, it could even cause death. There are many records depicting this type of relationship and the effects it can have on people.

In the early stages of incubus approach, a form of semi-waking paralysis will often be induced to disable victims while the incubus carries out its feeding attacks. Often, a beautiful face and body will be seen and/or felt by victims. However, if a victim succumbs to the charms of an incubus, these devices are no longer used. Once enamored, a victim will often deliberately summon the incubus each night by wishing it back.

I have experienced incubus attack several times over the years, including attacks involving semi-waking paralysis. One such experience, twenty years ago, gave me a rare glimpse of an incubus in its natural form. My description has since been supported by several independent observers.

I awoke late at night to waking paralysis and intense sexual arousal. It was almost pitch dark, with only a little moonlight soaking through curtains. A heavy weight was on my chest and I had difficulty breathing. The weight and outline of a young woman's body was writhing on top of me in a sexual way. Suspecting this was an attack,

I fought to break the paralysis by concentrating on moving one big toe. I broke the paralysis, but still had difficulty moving, and the sexual stimulation intensified. Rolling out of bed, I glimpsed a glowing cloud backing away from me. I rolled onto the floor, bumping my head on the bedside table and becoming wide awake in the process.

Struggling to my knees, I leaned on the bed and looked at the strange being. I felt drained but awake. Across the room from me floated a glowing, torpedo-shaped entity, about three feet long and eighteen inches wide. It was crystalline, transparent, and full of tiny sparkling motes of light. It looked much like a cellular life form, as seen under a microscope. It pulsed faintly.

At one end, inside the blunt tube-like structure, was something like a cross between a daisy flower and a propeller. This did not spin, but sparkled and pulsed with a red glow whenever it moved. It floated to the far corner of the room, hovering near the ceiling. When it moved, its movements were jerky and sudden. I sensed it was waiting for me to fall back to sleep. I stood up to get a better look and it reacted, contracting and shimmering slightly, before moving quickly through the wall and vanishing from sight.

This was a spectacular sighting of a beautiful being, whatever its coarse nature and intentions. This is not how one might imagine a Neg to look. The incubus is technically a Neg because its effects on people are negative, yet its true appearance is anything but frightening.

While involvement with incubus-type entities can happen through random encounters, they can also be attracted. This generally involves the sexual lusting of one person after another. In by far the most common scenario, one person becomes enamored with another and creates sexual fantasies based on him/her and acts on them during dreams and masturbation. This broadcasts sexual energies that can attract a roaming incubus. In this case, the incubus will often pretend to be the focus of the person's affection. You will see some of the dynamics of human-incubus relations in the following case, related by the victim herself:

"Near midnight, my husband and I had sex, after which he went to watch TV. I stayed in bed and did some energy work and meditation.

"The room was dark. I was relaxed and had a nice energy body-buzz going. Suddenly, I sensed a presence and opened my eyes. A faint comet-shaped being (like an elongated faintly glowing blob) came through the closed bedroom window. The entity appeared to be about two feet long and about nine inches wide. It seemed to be pushing its way through the air, or through the energy surrounding it, more like swimming than flying. The being had myriad pinpoints of colored light within it, with lots of red clustered more thickly around one end. It quickly circled the ceiling above me. I remember thinking, 'And who are you?' but got no noticeable response.

"Suddenly I felt a strong whooshing sensation—that's the only way I can describe it—rising up between my legs through my genital area. I was startled but not frightened, as I did not sense anything evil.

"What I felt next was nothing like normal sexual arousal. It was a sudden, intense physical need for urgent sexual release. All I can compare this to is how one feels after drinking lots of liquid, and the liquid burns to be urgently released. An intense orgasm occurred in a matter of moments. After this, the 'comet' left the room by the same window it came in by. The next day I began a very unusual menstruation.

"The period was like an intense purge. My period usually lasts about five days and is painful at times. This one was not painful, came two weeks early and lasted only one-and-a-half days. I had to stay near the bathroom all the first day. There was a lot of expelled tissue, including some gelatinous sheets about four inches long by two-and-a-half inches wide. This could not have been a miscarriage, as my husband had a vasectomy several years ago and we are faithful to each other."

I have had similar reports to the preceding from many different types of people over the years, both male and female, including two elderly women, one in her late eighties. Some encounters involve beautiful faces and bodies being seen and/or felt; other encounters involve glowing, blob-like energy beings; some involve a powerful type of forced sexual stimulation. All cause intense sexual arousal and orgasm, sometimes against the nature and will of the victims.

Elementals and Nature Spirits: On the matter of elementals and nature spirits, my experience is limited. The elemental beings and nature spirits are complex subjects and beyond the scope of this book. What I have to say concerning these beings should be considered only as basic rule-of-thumb.

Pure elementals relate to an element of nature, such as air, fire, water, or earth. But some elementals are related to more than one element. All elements and elemental beings are dualistic, having two sides: positive and constructive, negative and destructive. The four classical elemental spirit types are fire spirits (salamanders), earth spirits (gnomes), air spirits (sylphs), and water spirits (undines).

Nature spirits are best known as the fairy beings of Celtic mythology, as wild spirits involved with the forces and processes of nature and creation. Some nature spirits are intelligent, sophisticated beings, for example, the leprechauns of Ireland.

If one approaches elementals or nature spirits carefully and with respect, they can at times prove helpful. But if one approaches them carelessly or disrespectfully, they may be unhelpful or even antagonistic. Elementals and nature spirits are powerful beings that should always be treated with respect and should never be underestimated.

In my experience, human problems with elementals and nature spirits are rare. They are no real threat to humans, if left undisturbed; these spirits actively avoid human contact and will only cause problems under two circumstances. The first is when humans move into areas occupied by elemental or nature spirits and disturb them. In this case, they may cause problems, and ways must be found to placate them or the area should be vacated. The second circumstance is when elemental spirits are used as part of magical attacks by practitioners of black magic. Elementals are powerful beings and experienced help should be sought when dealing with them.

The only elemental being I have observed closely was a salamander. Like a cross between a rat and a lizard, it had burning red eyes, and overall it was the size of a small cat. My best observation was made with real-time astral sight (my eyes were open) during a morning meditation in a dimly lit room in front of a fire.

The salamander strobed, flickered, and moved in a jerky way, although it did not move far. A small black cloud surrounded and highlighted it. I had the impression that this blackness was some kind of dimensional hole possibly connecting to where it came from. I watched it from several feet away for half an hour, and it seemed to watch me also. I have no idea why it was there. My attempts to communicate with it failed. It did nothing but watch and I did not sense any threat. But I did sense it was ancient and powerful, emanating an energy different from what I am used to sensing.

Astral Snakes and Spiders: Some of the most troublesome types of Negs I have encountered are astral snakes and spiders. This is exactly what they look like when observed clairvoyantly or when seen in dreams and out-of-body experiences (OBEs). These are probably best classed as evil nature spirits. I have seen this type of being only rarely in the lower astral planes. I have only seen this type of Neg during periods of Neg attack on myself and during the "core-image removal process" (described later in the book). However, while I have sighted them during OBEs, I have never actually been attacked by them while out of body.

As far as I can ascertain, astral snakes and spiders work mainly through telepathic, hypnotic manipulation and through dream intrusion. Most cultures and religions have some kind of mythology depicting a serpent as representing evil, like the serpent in the Garden of Eden. Astral snakes and spiders will sometimes intrude on the dream state and will often cause nightmares. Many people suffering psychic attacks and/or serious Neg interference will see snakes and spiders in their dreams.

Astral spiders, of course, look different from astral snakes, although they share the same basic color (black) and have a similar look and feel to them (ugly and creepy). The most common dream-sign indicating astral spiders may be at work, apart from seeing dream spiders, are high-rise cranes (the tall cranes used on high-rise buildings); or sometimes impossibly long wires are seen to be hanging from the sky. These cranes and wires may be symbolic representations of Neg attachments, created by the subconscious mind during dreams. Another common dream-sign, associated with both astral snakes and spiders, is a black octopus and squid-type marine life forms.

Columns: This type of Neg looks like an animated column of thick black smoke, often several feet or more tall. I do not know what class of being these are, but the ones I have encountered have been extremely dangerous. It is possible that the columns I have seen are simply manifestations of very strong Negs. Here is an example from my experience.

A friend with a serious Neg problem was visiting, staying in my bedroom on a spare mattress. We retired for the night, but as soon as I lay down, I began experiencing spinal and abdominal cramping and cold shivers. I did my best to relax out of these, but I was very tired and soon slipped into a semi-trance state despite the pain. I soon developed real-time astral sight (seeing through my closed eyelids) and noticed a column of dense, black smoke as thick as a man's leg building up over my sleeping friend. Fascinated, I watched this, even though all my senses told me it was a strong Neg presence.

The column swayed back and forth several times and then struck at me like a snake. It bit my leg and searing pain coursed through my left calf muscle. I was temporarily paralyzed and felt a strong sucking sensation on my left leg. A few seconds later I managed to break the paralysis and rolled out of bed. I staggered outside, crossed running water, applied garlic (which has a repellant effect on all Negs), and slept on the couch in the living room for the rest of the night.

The next day I found a large, puffy swelling at the bite area on my left leg. This stayed with me for several months; thick blue veins appeared around the swelling. I experienced particularly strong Neg attacks and influences during this time. When I finally broke this attachment, the swelling disappeared completely along with the swollen blue veins.

Angels and Fallen Angels: The Bible (King James Version, Family Edition, 1974) is a useful place to get an orientation on angels. For example, it says: "Angel (Messenger), an order of beings, superior to men, who are employed in the service of God. In the Old Testament they are sometimes represented as men or manlike 'messengers'." They are frequently called angels of the Lord; the throne of God is represented as being surrounded by hosts of them.

Originally angels were morally neutral, but Saul was troubled with an evil spirit from God, and later they sometimes assumed the form of lying spirits. During and after the Egyptian captivity Satan appeared as prince of the evil angels. Another late development is the arrangement of angels into ranks or orders including seven archangels and the ascribing of names to them. In the scriptures, for example, only two are named, Michael, the prince of Israel, and Gabriel, though the Apocrypha names, in addition, Raphael and Uriel.

The New Testament represents angels as glorious in appearance, innumerable in number; their function is to minister to the saints. The Son of God is surrounded by hosts of them, and Satan is the leader of Fallen Angels.

Demons and Demonic Spirits: First, let's consider the views of the Bible (King James Version) on the subject of demons: Usually translated as "Devil" in the Bible. In the New Testament, it denotes a spiritual being at enmity with God, having the power to afflict men with disease and spiritual pollution. The power of demons is thought to be limited. They recognized their true status before God. They recognized Christ as the son of God and dreaded the approach of the final judgment. Beelzebub was their chief. They appeared to be the angels of the devil, or of the dragon, destined for ultimate destruction.

"Demon" is the common term used to describe the higher orders of non-human Negs. These are unlike other Negs in that they are far more ancient, intelligent, powerful, and evil. In a way, true demons are dark angels. Some demons are simply demons, but some are fallen angels. Therefore, demons are of the same level (in a negative sense) as angels, but demons are the opposite of angels. Like angels, demons have a hierarchical ranking, including archdemons and a demonic "aristocracy" in which strong demons rule as princes of darkness and command all the lesser demons.

The most widely agreed-upon hierarchical ranking for demons goes like this: kings, dukes, princes and prelates, marquises, presidents, earls and counts, knights. Below there are hosts of lower infernal demons, much like common soldiers with no particular ranking order; these are often called legionnaires.

Fortunately, like nature spirits, true demons will not attack humans at random or for no reason. That is, not unless they are interfered with or unless they are coerced into attacking someone by practitioners of black magic, or are attracted by karmic reasons. I have only encountered a handful of real demons over the years, including the one that possessed me; all have been memorable experiences, to say the least.

Many lesser Negs, especially egregors, can appear to be demonic, while not actually being true demons. The traditional demonic form is the most frightening of all to humans, and because of this, illusory demonic forms are widely used to terrify humans in nightmares and other Neg-related manifestations.

Demons versus Angels: Angels and demons, and the host of lesser beings aligned with each hierarchical side, represent two great opposing forces of the spiritual universe: good and evil. These positive and negative forces provide an infinitely graduated contrast that makes life what it is. Between them, these two warring forces generate a universal equilibrium.

Demons and bad spirits (Negs) tempt and test humankind. They also vex and punish people if they become spiritually polluted. They exert varying degrees of negative influence over everyone with whom they come into contact, and they provide life-path resistance, an activity set by karma and universal law. While we may not like it, this resistance (the difficulty level for each life) forces us to evolve as spiritual beings, life after life.

Angels and all the good spirits beneath them provide strong, positive life influences. They oppose the negative influences exerted by demons and bad spirits, and they protect us and steer us away from evil towards a positive, spiritual existence. But this does not mean that we have to put up with Neg influences meekly. It is natural to resist them in all ways.

Negs that Resemble ETs: Some spirits, both positive and negative, may *resemble* various types of ETs (extraterrestrials), while some may take on popular illusory ET forms. Some spirits may

17

have originally been ETs. In the case of Negs, just because an alien race may be technologically and metaphysically advanced, it does not necessarily follow that it is spiritually evolved. Some Negs may be former ETs, much like Negs can be former humans.

I vividly remember during my early childhood being interfered with and paralyzed by ET entities. The one I remember the best looked much like a man-sized praying mantis; it had huge eyes, a triangular head, a small mouth, and long, slender arms and legs. I woke up paralyzed many times, always enveloped in a heavy, fizzy, white noise that sapped my strength.

I have seen various alien-looking entities that were involved in haunting and poltergeist problems. One case involved three-year-old twins. I was called in because the mother and grandmother had simultaneously come under a psychic attack combined with poltergeist activity. The center of activity focused on the twins. I sat in the living room and did a trance viewing to see if I could perceive things clairvoyantly. I saw two small beings with small, slender, delicate-looking bodies and large heads and big eyes. Their skin was translucent gray and veins were apparent all over them. Their bodies and faces looked half-formed, as if they were in the middle of some kind of metamorphosis; they were about the same size as the human twins.

Based on my observations, I now call these Negs *symbiotic parasites*. They slowly take on the physical appearance of their hosts, usually small children, after they are firmly attached to them. They integrate and slowly become a part of them. Those with this condition undergo marked changes, becoming more selfish and controlling. The end result seems to be a forced type of shared physical incarnation for these astral parasites.

For the twins, I arrived just in time, before the Negs were firmly entrenched. Both children had recently undergone several weeks of night terrors and marked personality changes, according to their mother. These are predictable Neg-induced problems, and children's night terrors are the first sign of trouble.

As this was in my early days of this work, several weeks of experimenting with countermeasures ensued. I installed passive countermeasures in that house, including a skylight, and performed healing exorcisms on the twins. These were unpleasant affairs as both fought violently, with the Negs manifesting strongly through them. I am glad the children were so small, as the rage and physical strength exhibited when they were brought to me made them difficult to handle. Fortunately, both responded to healing and no one was injured. The symbiots were removed and banished from the house. The passive countermeasures kept them away and the children quickly reverted to their original sweet selves. This was over a decade ago and they are now in their mid-teens, having had no recurrence of Neg problems.

Poltergeists: Poltergeists are the most well known spirit manifestation. While they have been studied for many years and theories about them abound, little is known about them apart from the wide range of noisy physical disturbances and property damage for which they are notorious. This activity sets poltergeists apart from other spirit manifestations. If you have never experienced poltergeist activity, it can be hard to grasp the fact that non-physical beings are capable of affecting, moving, and even damaging objects in the physical realm. But the evidence that they do, no matter how one explains it away, is overwhelming.

The milder aspects of poltergeist phenomena involve audible taps and knocks and other unexplainable noises, while the stronger aspects involve the movement and levitation of physical objects, often heavy ones. This can be dangerous as solid objects can sometimes be thrown about, often at high speed. Light and appliance switches can be turned on and off and doors and cupboards repeatedly opened and slammed shut, often in view of multiple witnesses.

Poltergeists can manifest repeatedly in particular areas (haunted houses) or around particular persons or families (haunted people). They have been known to follow people from town to town, even from country to country, but most well-documented poltergeist activity involves haunted houses.

Many reasons have been given to explain poltergeist activity, such as earthbound spirits, thought-forms, and childlike mischievous spirits. Parapsychologists generally find children living in houses affected by poltergeists; the age of these children can range from infancy to puberty, but sometimes poltergeist activity involves emotionally disturbed teenagers. The presence of a child is a key ingredient in poltergeist activity in that the child provides the energy necessary for manifestations to occur.

In my experience, poltergeists usually attach themselves to children and, once they do, these spirits can be said to run amok with their newfound energies and bodies. Because of this, I have found the best way to treat poltergeist problems is to focus on the child, especially the child's bedroom, applying countermeasures as necessary. I have found this to be more effective than treating the house as a whole.

Psychokinesis (PK), the ability to affect matter with the mind, is the term that most succinctly describes the force poltergeists use. PK is a psychic ability to move physical objects or levitate them; PK is also known to start otherwise unexplainable fires. In cases in which physical objects are suspended or floated in midair by poltergeists, PK is used to manipulate or overcome gravity in some way. It has often occurred to me that if enough study were done on PK and poltergeist phenomena, some form of antigravity theory might be discovered.

I lived through an example of poltergeist activity about fifteen years ago when I stayed at a friend's house. Susan had a three-year-old son and had been experiencing haunting and poltergeist activity for several months. I stayed in the house to study the problem firsthand, but the poltergeist involved did not like me being there.

About half an hour after we retired for the night, an ashen-faced Susan came into the guestroom and woke me. She was experiencing psychic interference (experienced as cold shivers and an atmosphere of dread) and she had heard strange noises and footsteps in the house. I sensed the atmosphere, and her concerns were soon validated as more loud noises came from the other end of the house. We turned on the overhead light and went to investigate and found her son was sleeping peacefully. More loud noises soon came from the kitchen area; cupboard doors were opening and slamming shut. The phenomena settled down after a while so we tried to get some sleep. We awoke a couple of hours later as the noises started up again. We lay there for some time, listening. One noise we could not identify was a regular loud thumping that sounded like someone was pounding on the kitchen counter with a heavy weight. There were a dozen or so heavy blows a few seconds apart, but the last one had a tinkling overlay to it like the sound of splintering glass.

The following morning we found the house messy, though there was little actual damage. An hour later I noticed something odd. A heavy glass jar, full of cookies, stood on top of the highest kitchen cupboard; its top was only a couple of inches from the ceiling. It was about twelve inches high and weighed several pounds. From where I was sitting, it appeared to sag to one side as if partly melted. Closer examination revealed the cookie jar had been shattered into hundreds of pieces, yet its heavy lid was holding it together. We tried to get it down in one piece, but it fell apart as soon as we tried to move it. This was the source of the heavy pounding and splintering glass sound we had heard the night before.

On my advice, Susan and her son moved out of that house shortly after these events. Unfortunately, the poltergeist followed them and continued to hound them for some time; but the phenomenon was never again as strong as the night I stayed with them. I never discovered the true cause of Susan's problems, as she moved out of state and we lost touch. But knowing what I know, I suspect it was her son who was attracting the Negs.

It is helpful to talk for a moment about haunted houses in light of poltergeists and the other Negs I've described. A haunted house is best defined as a place in which paranormal phenomena regularly occur. Earthbound spirits with afterlife problems and/or unfinished business in the physical world are the most popular reasons given today to explain haunted houses. This type of information is usually gathered by psychics called in to investigate. Evidence and information is usually vague and sketchy, but a haunting spirit's first name, age, and some basic details of a traumatic event that happened there will often be pieced together by the psychic.

Haunted houses usually contain cold spots at which paranormal activity is centered. This can be likened to an interdimensional flow or doorway, or something like a static core image. A core image is a subconscious trauma image memory that generates negative energy, and Negs use these to influence people. The cold spots exist independently of people and occupy particular geographical locations and parts of buildings situated over them. The cold spots—there are often several—in haunted houses can result from traumatic or high-energy events experienced by people who used to live there. For example, persons may have been murdered, had their heart "broken," or committed suicide in that place. These events formed an interdimensional link strong enough to cause a haunting.

Yet interdimensional doorways do not always form, even in places where the worst types of murders have occurred. This indicates there is more to the haunted house equation than meets the eye. Other factors must be involved, such as the location of the house, power line and electrical wiring configurations, and other natural anomalies like gravity fluctuations, geological stress points, or underground streams.

Common apparitions often involve innocuous scenes from everyday life, such as ghostly figures carrying out mundane tasks. When contacted by psychics, the ghosts are always extremely vague about who they are and why they are there; it's possible many of these so-called spirits are actually astral shells left behind after death. Astral shells are thought-forms, not earthbound spirits, that do not contain the spirit essences or souls of the persons they once belonged to. The energy anomalies in haunted houses animate these shells and cause them to manifest.

The repetitious phenomena observed in the haunted house often can be a repeat of the original event involved in creating the interdimensional doorway, like an echo of the past event caught in a repeating loop. For example, a ghostly face might be frequently seen peering down from an upstairs window. The ghost's physical self may have died in that room, or something traumatic may have happened to her in that part of the house.

However, a repeating haunting apparition of a ghostly woman who was brutally murdered in the haunted house is probably not the actual earthbound spirit of that woman. It's more likely an energy pattern, a recording or imprint of her, echoing in the substance of the astral dimension, close to the physical universe. This echo has enough energy to cause it to repeatedly manifest, to haunt that house, in other words. The same thing can happen at the scene of a battle or other traumatic high-energy event, causing areas with no houses or structures to become haunted. However, in the former example, the echo of this woman and the interdimensional links associated with her can then attract spirit beings. When investigated by psychics, these beings may masquerade as the woman to hide their true identities.

The random phenomena, strange atmospheres, and psychic attacks common to haunted houses can result from the activities of Negs operating through interdimensional doorways. These can be thought of as rips in the dimensional veil through which spirit beings are able to manifest. Just as a core image can be generated inside a person's mind by a traumatic life experience, the trauma can also affect the place where it happens. This can cause a thought-form or echo to be generated and impressed on that location in the astral real-time zone. This in turn can generate dimensional holes through which Negs can gain access to the physical dimension. The larger the hole and the more energy involved, the stronger will be any resulting manifestation.

Why and How Negs Attack

Now that we've seen some of the more common Negs, we need to look at why they attack humans, and how they do it. The question of why Negs interfere with and torment humans is complex. Many of these beings seem driven to do this, in much the same way as wild animal predators instinctively prey on weaker animals, culling the sick and weak. Negs naturally seem to prey on spiritually vulnerable humans. They are also attracted to, and may even feed upon, negative emotions such as fear, anger, anxiety, and lust. Let's look first at what may motivate them to attack humans.

Life Energy = Food: Food is a powerful motivator for all species, including humans. Without it we starve and die. This factor also applies to Negs, whatever their origins. Like all beings, living or otherwise, they need some form of energy to exist. They must get this energy from somewhere. All Negs, including earth-bound spirits, are vampiristic of life energy and feed upon their victims in some way. Therefore, if you consider "food" to be a primary motivator for Neg-related psychic attacks, you have a reasonable assumption for what motivates Negs.

More-experienced Negs seem to feed off emotional energy. Fear is the most common emotion used because by inducing fear in victims, a large amount of emotional energy is generated. The mere presence of Negs induces natural fear in most humans, and the closer a Neg gets the more fear is induced. If contact occurs, waves of revulsion and many other symptoms are caused. The stronger and more evil the Neg, the more fear its presence causes. In fact, it's possible that some cases of waking paralysis are caused by nothing more than close contact with Negs. Great fear, after all, is known to cause paralysis.

Aids to Mobility: Most Negs cannot cross running water when they manifest close enough to the physical dimension to affect it. They cannot travel freely for long distances because of water mains, rivers, and streams. To move about, most Negs need to "hitchhike" rides with living beings, animal or human. Neg travel is thus limited by the availability of susceptible humans and animals with whom they can hitchhike rides. Thus a psychic attack and implantation is a way to aid Neg mobility.

Proximity to the Physical World: Some Negs require close human contact to stay close to the physical dimension. This factor causes parasitic relationships between Negs and humans to form, and can lead to a type of symbiosis in which Negs integrate with humans and share their lives. Negs are extremely long lived, and some will have coexisted with a great number of humans down through the ages. Because humans are short-lived compared to Negs, this necessitates a chain of susceptible human hosts for the Negs. This requires such Negs to regularly invade and form attachments with living humans to ensure their ability to stay in proximity to the physical world.

Vengeance and Curses: In my experience, most Negs are petty, vindictive beings. They seem to bear long-term grudges, not only against each other but against humans who trouble them. A human might harm a Neg by exorcising it or by killing its living human host. This scenario can get complex, involving grudges, curses, and persecutions and feuds, life after life.

A good example of this is the infamous witch-hunts of the Spanish Inquisition. Imagine a witch using all her skill in black magic to lay a powerful curse upon all those who convicted her and were about to burn her at the stake. The demons associated with this witch would carry out this curse, inflicting harm upon the families of these people through many succeeding generations. The families would experience continual suffering and misfortune for (to them) no discernible reasons.

Just for Fun: Some Negs live a vicarious existence, skipping from host to host with no attempts made to form lasting relationships. Earthbound, human-type Negs, especially of the addicted kind, most commonly fit this description. In this scenario, human addictive–type Negs seek enjoyment and sustenance by preying on vulnerable or like-minded humans.

Now that we have a sense of why Negs harass humans, let's look at how they do it. Negs are limited in the ways they can interfere with humans. The first limitation is that victims must be sensitive enough for attacks to be perceived. Non-sensitives are still vulnerable, but not in the same ways as sensitives; non-sensitives do not sense Neg interference in the same way as sensitives. Alcohol and drug use, of course, increases one's vulnerability to Negs. Negs need their influences to be sensed by victims in order to cause negative sensations and emotions in them, such as fear, pain, and anger.

Direct Attacks: Direct attack can happen when susceptible people come into close contact with other people carrying aggressive Negs within their space. This can also happen when a person enters a Neg-contaminated area, such as haunted buildings. If Negs sense vulnerability they will often act immediately.

Depending on the strength and experience of the Negs involved, this can cause a range of symptoms in the afflicted person, such as anxiety and fear; depression; head pain and pressure; distorted vision; difficulty breathing; cold, tingling, adrenaline-like waves; partial-to-full paralysis; muscular cramps; sharp pricks and jabs; plus unnatural thoughts and compulsions. Direct attacks normally only happen inside buildings. They are far more likely at night because Negs are always more active at night. Public places such as movie theaters and malls are also more likely to contain roaming Negs.

Direct attacks can be temporary affairs, especially if victims are only briefly exposed to Negs. But even short exposures can be exhausting; Negs can drain sensitives of vitality in minutes. Victims of a circumstantial direct attack will often be tagged and targeted for future Neg invasion. In a way, it could be said some Negs memorize the psychic scents of new victims so they can be tracked down later.

Long Distance Attacks: Using a method similar to live remote viewing (a modern term for an aspect of clairvoyant seeing at a distance) is one way Negs manage to overcome travel limitations (running water) to invade people from a distance. In this case, the Negs in question must either be highly experienced or hosted by someone with natural clairvoyant ability. However, the clairvoyant host (the human source of the attack) may not be aware they have these abilities nor that they are being used by Negs to attack others.

For example, a competent clairvoyant can connect with a person from a distance and view them in real time. To do this they need a strong connection, which can be provided by a photograph or personal item. If the clairvoyant has astral projection ability, he can use this vision to project to a target.

It is well known that spirits are capable of causing dormant psychic abilities to manifest in spirit mediums and channels. They do this by stimulating the energy body and activating these abilities directly. Negs are capable of doing the same thing. By stimulating the brow chakra of a human host, for example, what could aptly be called a real-time remote viewing doorway can be created between the host's Neg and its target. Through this doorway, Negs can then project directly to victims and carry out attacks. This is similar in principle to how humans induce out-of-body experiences and project themselves to chosen locations, by visualizing a target and willing themselves to shift there.

Energy Draining: Negs usually have low energy when they first reach a target site. They need time to build their strength to the point where they are capable of interfering with and/or attacking the target. Negs absorb energy at the target site, taking it from any available source. This is one reason why, when carrying out nocturnal attacks on sleeping victims, Negs seem to hurriedly feed the moment they arrive at the target. This is noticeable if one is awake at the start of such an attack. During an attack, energy is drained from victims by a kind of osmosis. Imagine an entity is a dry sponge and a human is a puddle of vital fluid. With contact, fluid/energy is absorbed, but exactly how energy is drained from a victim depends a lot on the type and experience of the Neg in question.

Entity Type, Intelligence, and Perceptions: Neg type, age, experience, and intelligence account for the variations in how Negs treat humans. These factors are responsible for variations in patterns of psychic attack and how Negs will react when counter-measures are applied. Some Negs have an "animalistic" intelligence and react on "instinct," but some are highly intelligent; the more intelligent Negs are, the more dangerous they are. However, because all Negs are bound by certain limitations, some semblance of a standard pattern will always emerge, and this is their greatest weakness. It's clear that Negs do not share the same emotions as humans. Higher emotions like love and compassion are alien to them. They do not have the capacity to comprehend these. My overall impressions of all Negs I have come into close contact with are that they have an insect-like intelligence and are incapable of higher emotions. All the Negs I have encountered so far have been interested in humans in much the same way as most humans look upon cattle, or upon wild game and/or playthings.

2

The Nature and Spread
of Neg Influences

To better understand the nature of Negs and how they interfere with humans, it helps to consider what I call the mind-split phenomenon. This is the experience of duality or bilocation that is often associated with an out-of-body experience (commonly called astral projection or OBE). Having an OBE is the nearest we can get to experiencing an environment similar to that in which Negs operate. The principles of the mind-split effect have far-reaching implications when it comes to understanding how Negs operate. It shows how they influence, attack, and even possess humans in the physical dimension. The mind-split shows how a single human mind replicates itself during an OBE; this highlights many principles as to how Negs operate.

The feeling of separating from the physical body during an OBE does not allow the underlying mind-split effect that is at work to be perceived. After a successful OBE, only one side of it is ever remembered: the astral experience side. After a failed OBE exit attempt, memories come solely from the physical body and/or its dream mind. But it is necessary to have memories from *both* sides of the OBE, the physical and astral aspects, before the mind-split can be comprehended for what it is.

The mind-split occurs at the beginning of an OBE, as well as at the start of normal sleep. The mind-split can also happen unnoticed during trance meditation (and it frequently does), when the physical body sleeps while its mind stays awake. During an OBE, your consciousness expands and projects a subtle energy copy, a perfect thinking reflection of itself, outside the bounds of your physical body as part of a unique natural process. This reflection can best be thought of as an independently thinking echo or replica of your consciousness. It reflects into a subtle energy vehicle I call the projected double (often called the astral body). This subtle body is internally generated within the human energy body (often called the etheric body) and then projected out. It is then maintained outside the bounds of the physical body via a subtle-energy linkage called the silver cord, which is usually invisible during an OBE.

Keep in mind this process never leaves the physical body empty. It is no more empty during an OBE than it is during its normal waking and sleeping states. The original copy of consciousness (of spirit, mind, and memory) always remains safely tucked away inside the tranced or sleeping physical body.

The projection of an echo of consciousness during OBE or sleep is part of the natural mind-split effect, which by nature usually happens unnoticed. The mind-split is not even apparent during a wake-induced OBE, when astral projectors remain aware the entire time, from exit to reentry. But the symptoms of dual existence caused by the mind-split are evident if you know what to look for. Most OBE case histories show symptoms of this duality to some extent. The mind-split has gone unnoticed for so long because of the subtle and enigmatic way in which it happens, and because the tendency of the physical brain is to store only *a single* memory for any given time period, even if more than one was generated.

When the projected double separates from its physical body, it takes with it a full copy of all memories up to the moment when the mind-split occurs. Many projectors hear a noticeable click at this time. Breaking away from its physical body/mind, the projected double thereafter records its OBE memories independently; but if the physical mind remains awake after the OBE exit, it will also continue recording memories independently. These are of an *apparently* unbroken existence within its physical body and of any dreams during this time.

In a nutshell: physical and projected aspects of a person's mind record two different memory sets, in two unbroken streams, from the moment of separation until they reintegrate at the end of the OBE when the physical body awakens.

This provides two different memory sets for a single time period: one set of physical body memories and one set of OBE memories. After reintegration, the strongest set of memories for the previous time period (usually the physical body's side) becomes the dominant memory set recorded by the physical brain. The physical body's memories have a stronger and more immediate impact upon the brain, with these being automatically recorded, as they are experienced. This makes the recall of OBE memories a difficult proposition.

During the reintegration of the physical body/mind with its projected double, if the downloading of the OBE memory-set into accessible levels of memory fails, there will be *no memory* to show an OBE ever took place. In this case, only memories of the physical side of the mind-split (often mixed with dream fragments) will be recalled. This is what normally happens after a *seemingly* failed projection attempt, where projection exit symptoms have been experienced (whole-body vibrations, pressure, rapid heartbeat, and continual falling sensation), but an OBE is not remembered afterwards. When OBE memories fail, they download into inaccessible levels of memory.

This model outlines only the lowest level of the mind-split phenomenon, between the physical body/mind and its projected double's mind, but further mind-splits occur above this event level. My experiments with this phenomenon show that at some time after the initial mind-split, the first level of the projected double will begin projecting (reflecting) further aspects of itself into higher dimensional levels.

If one ponders the replication of human consciousness involved in the mind-split effect, similarities can be found with human bio-incarnation, as well as with the way Negs influence, overshadow, and sometimes possess people. In a way, the spirits of all humans can be said to be possessing, or incarnating into, the bodies of hairless human apes. Expanding on this concept, my evidence suggests that Negs find loopholes in the natural bio-incarnation and/or OBE mind-split mechanisms and exploit these to their own ends. This can result in psychic attack, influence, or personality overshadowing. In a worst-case scenario, the original human spirit can even become paralyzed or pushed aside. This results in total psychic domination, and even worse, the virtual puppetry of full-blown possession, which is the darkest of spiritual maladies.

If, as my experience shows, a single Neg can influence and even possess many people simultaneously, then unknown aspects of the mind-split phenomena are likely involved with this process. To accomplish this, a Neg must have some way of sharing its singular self among many people. Logically, accomplishing this must involve some form of mind-split replication, whereby the original Neg inserts copies of itself into many people.

Two questions spring to mind at this point: Are there other dimensions crawling with seemingly unlimited numbers of Negs? Do they have some way of replicating?

One explanation I have been given by modern occultists is that a single powerful Neg sends out many lesser Negs, which it then directs. This is said to account for the behavioral similarities shown by multiple victims of mass influence or mass possession. But the controlling Neg would then need many identical lesser Negs to accomplish this. This seems unlikely unless it creates them, which is, of course, exactly what happens during mind-split replication.

The more traditional religious explanation for demonic possession is that a great number of demons can possess a single person. But this seems illogical because, in my experience, demons do not work well in groups, thank goodness. My experience is more in line with the opinion given by the old priest in the movie,

The Exorcist (allegedly based on a true-life story). When given a report by the younger priest on the number of demonic personalities he had identified within the victim, he says, "There is only one demon." In all the possession cases I have worked on, including my own, there has only been a single Neg involved. While multiple possession of a single person by many Negs is quite possible, most Negs will confuse the issue by hiding their true nature and identity and pretending to be many: "My name is legion."

Another explanation, in line with my experience, was given by a friend of mine, Romero Lourenço da Cunha, of Portugal, director of the European Hermetic Fraternity: "Demons are ubiquitous creatures that are capable of replicating themselves. A single, powerful demon is able to possess hundreds of people simultaneously. But there is no replication of the essence body of the original demon. A demonic replication is therefore a weaker, pseudo-living copy of the original creature."

The previous statements may hold a part of the answer. It can also be said that some Negs are created by the collective consciousness, by the evil deeds, thoughts, and nightmares of the darker side of humankind. But it is difficult to ascertain the truth here, so I must rely upon observation, experience, and reasoning, with carefully measured doses of intelligent speculation. It is invaluable to consider the evidence behind these issues with some understanding of the possibilities involved, especially when analyzing and countering often-perplexing Neg-related activities.

Neg replication is a difficult subject to consider because mundane human experience has so little to compare with it. The idea that all living beings exist apart as separate units of consciousness defies natural feelings and concepts of singularity. But there are significant precedences that contradict this. Living spiritual saints, masters, adepts are well known to manifest in many different places simultaneously through bilocation, and examples of bilocation can be found in most religion. Tibetan masters and Hindu yogis, even some Christian saints, are known for doing this. The power to accomplish this feat comes from having a greatly expanded consciousness. However, multiple copies of a single consciousness unit, be it yogi or demon, logically would still entail an extension of the mind-split effect that happens to everyone during sleep and OBE.

If you examine the history of witchcraft and demonology, or study accounts in the Bible, you can find many incidents of mass possessions. Families, convents, monasteries, towns, herds of animals—all reportedly have been mass possessed by demons. Often everyone affected will exhibit identical symptoms. But mass possession is disbelieved in the modern Western world. Anything resembling it is immediately attributed to mass hysteria or mass delusion. But this does not mean that it never happens.

The strongest types of Negs are demons, of which there are a great many varieties. True demons have a high but dark level of consciousness. They are ubiquitous and can be in many places at the same time, according to Kabalistic and occult knowledge. Demons are capable of replicating themselves, and spreading out among susceptible people, like pathogens. The number of copies a demon can make of itself and how many people it can spread its influence over depends on its level of consciousness. This also defines its rank in the demonic hierarchy. My research shows that a replicated demon has nowhere near the strength of its original; however, even replicated demons are dangerous and hence difficult to deal with.

The spread of a single demon among many people will cause similar symptoms to arise in all the people affected. These include health and behavioral problems, as well as supernatural manifestations, and strange urges and pressures. However, the strength of these symptoms will vary because they are affected by the personalities, strengths, and weaknesses of different victims. Fortunately, direct human contact with true demons is rare, especially contacts that result in full-blown possession. Problems involving replicated demons are far more common. In either case demons, originals or replicas, will often go to great lengths to conceal their presence, nature, and identity from humans.

Strangely, the spread and concentration of Negs in the modern world has a lot to do with plumbing. Cities and towns are heavily crisscrossed with underground plumbing, and pipes full of running water line every street. Apart from being a symbol of purity, running water has energy properties that are repulsive to all Neg types, including true demons of any rank. All Negs manifesting close enough to the physical dimension to affect it can be said to develop two-dimensional properties. They are not only connected to but also affected by conditions on the surface of the Earth. Experiences reported later in this book show the majority of Negs *cannot* cross running water *unaided*, including underground pipes, rivers and streams; even garden hoses.

Thus the spread of modern plumbing over the past couple of hundred years has severely *curtailed* the travel abilities of free-roaming Negs. This has forced them to find new ways to travel while they are manifesting close to the physical dimension. In my experience, they usually do this by hitching rides with susceptible people and animals, using them as shields to carry them over running-water barriers. Even so, Neg travel is still greatly limited.

Lower earthbound Neg types can become trapped in small areas, often inside buildings. This makes them more active than they might otherwise be, causing a significant *increase* in psychic invasions and Neg interference per capita.

For example, if a Neg wants to leave its current human host, it cannot simply wander off on its own searching for a new host. Underground running-water barriers (plumbing) prohibit this. So it must take what it can find from among the susceptible humans and animals its host encounters. This could make it necessary for a Neg to invade and attach to person after person to achieve its goals, or to travel to wherever it wants to go. And if a Neg's human host dies before it finds a suitable new host, it can become trapped inside a building by running-water barriers. This in turn can cause buildings to become haunted.

I have observed many groups of people suffering interference from a single Neg. Any out-of-control crowd is a good example of this. I have witnessed a case of multiple possession in which two men became simultaneously possessed by a single Neg. Therefore, it seems likely that stories and historical records of mass possessions may be credible.

I have interviewed people from other countries who claim to have witnessed larger mass possessions. One couple told me of a temple on the outskirts of their hometown in India where monks regularly held mass exorcisms. Groups of possessed people were brought in from outlying areas and exorcised en masse. Each group made similar repetitive sounds and actions, different from those made by other groups; this was because a different demon was said to possess each group.

On several occasions, I have traced widespread Neg problems back to a single source. Once, while helping a seven-year-old boy with serious Neg problems, I overheard him—shameless eaves-dropping really—talking to several friends from the same school and neighborhood. I could hardly believe my ears, but the con-versation was clearly about the same Neg I was struggling against at that time. They all knew the Neg, called it by name, and dis-cussed it freely among themselves, albeit in hushed voices so the adults could not overhear them. They were clearly in awe of and very much afraid of it and they spoke about who the Neg was cur-rently visiting and what it was doing to them.

I am comfortable with children, so I approached them and tried to join their conversation, but to no avail. I made it clear I knew all about the Neg (which was the truth), but still they played dumb. Even a bribe of cookies and juice would not loosen their lips. My intuition told me they were afraid to discuss this with an adult, as if they had been warned not to and feared the consequences.

It seems common for children to know more about paranor-mal matters than they will admit to adults, even if questioned carefully. They quickly learn not to tell the truth and risk ridicule, guilt, or punishment from worrying parents. Children are often forced into denying their own senses and pretending Neg prob-lems are not happening when they are. Blaming Neg-related problems on an overactive imagination is understandable from a parent's point of view, but this often convinces children that these are their personal problems, beyond the ken of adults. This drives them underground and forces many children to suffer in silence. Please do not make this mistake with your children; something can and should be done about children's Neg-related problems.

The evidence suggests that the majority of Negs use, and some even feed upon, the energies of living beings, human and animal, including children. Indeed, draining life energy and forming energy body attachments with living beings seem to be basic ingredients of most Neg-related activities. This seems instinctive behavior and thus has the potential to be used against them.

Drain and deny Negs replenishment of the energy they need to operate close to the physical dimension, and at least part of the battle is won. The intelligent use of running-water barriers, plus other active and passive countermeasures (see part III), plays an important part in weakening the hold of troublesome Negs. These countermeasures make life generally difficult for Negs and stop them spreading their influence. In most cases, this can be done without having to directly confront potentially dangerous Negs.

PART 11

The Phenomena: Signs That Your Life May Be Disturbed by Unseen Spirit Beings

An Overview of Part II

Part II begins by defining unseen influences and psychic attacks, and supports this with case histories. We then move on to the most common types of problems, such as how people become exposed and various problems that can result from this. Potentially hazardous places like cemeteries and haunted houses and risky practices like spirit channeling and Ouija boards are discussed.

Next come the underlying principles of psychic invasion and the spirit/human telepathic interface that must exist to allow psychic attacks, influences, and possessions to occur. I follow this with an explanation of how subconscious trauma memories (called core images) are at the root of all these problems.

From here we move to symptoms of supernatural activity that can indicate problems with a special focus on children's issues, and the different types and levels of possession and how they occur. Having once been possessed by a major demon myself, I discuss hands-on experience. Finally, we look at psychic influences and sudden compulsions that can cause suicides, murders, accidents, and crimes.

3

Unseen Influences

Psychic attacks are best defined as unseen supernatural influences that adversely effect people. Mild attacks can involve annoying pressure, anxiety, disturbed sleep, and bad dreams. More intense attacks can involve waves of mind-numbing terror, crippling physical pain, and overwhelming compulsions. Today, psychic attack is generally considered a kind of telepathic hypnotic interference in which one person accidentally influences or inflicts pressure on another. I wish it were this simple, but my experience indicates otherwise.

In its simplest form, a psychic attack is a temporary malady that generally causes no lasting damage. It is also usually unintentional. Most people would be distressed to learn they had accidentally inflicted harm on someone else, for example by brooding over a petty conflict. But there are exceptions. Psychic attacks supported by deliberate ill will, witchcraft, voodoo, or ritual magic are no laughing matter; they can be lethal.

In my experience, Negs are always involved somehow in the psychic attack equation. Every psychic attack is technically an attack by a Neg, but persons responsible for psychic attacks, the living human sources, are usually unaware that Negs are using them to attack others.

Here is the reasoning for this: If the living biological host of a Neg (the source) becomes angry at another person (the victim), this causes a strong psychic connection between them. The source's resident Negs will then do all they can to reach and punish the victim. This is a trade-off, a kind of unwritten law, that any entrenched Neg will assist its biological host in these matters. This has the effect of increasing the Neg's control over its living host, as well as giving resident Negs the opportunity to find potential new hosts, and/or to drain them of life energy. This last is a kind of opportunistic life-force feeding, common to all Negs. The more energy a Neg has to work with, the stronger and more proactive it will become.

Negs come in many different types, with various strengths and weaknesses, likes and dislikes, needs, desires and perversions, natural or learned. Some are predatory loners and opportunistic parasites. Higher emotions like love, mercy, and compassion are alien concepts to them. They have huge egos and one-track minds: they exist to feed, corrupt, use, and control.

Direct psychic attack is, unfortunately, only a part of the problem. Often starting in the human host's early childhood, the first psychic attacks usually ease off once the Neg involved has formed an attachment with its new victim. Typically, hypnotic and psychological conditioning devices are used to prepare each new biological host, so it's more useful and obedient to the will of the new resident Neg. This involves the implantation of psychological roots, through core images and energy body attachments. These devices eventually sprout unnatural fears, phobias, desires, and urges within otherwise healthy human minds.

As Neg influences develop, depending on the natural strengths of the biological hosts concerned, they can cause severe life problems. Varying levels of possession are also possible. While generally denied in the West, possession is widely acknowledged in many other areas of the world such as India, Asia, and Africa.

Full possession is rare, and for good reason. Negs need their biological hosts to provide life energy and to hold them close to the physical dimension. They also need their hosts as vehicles. Most Negs are incapable of interacting normally within human society; they lack higher emotions, basic human life skills and social graces, and thus cannot pass themselves off as normal human beings. They cannot work for a living, and maintaining normal human relationship is beyond them. Most Negs seem content to go along for the human ride and exert hefty influences on their unwitting hosts.

To illustrate the nature of these problems, the following are real-life case histories that show different types and levels of psychic attacks. Keep in mind that these are extraordinary examples. The majority of Neg-related problems are comparatively mild affairs.

Case History #1: Michael's Dinner Party

This case shows a direct psychic attack in its entirety. The source of the attack is clear, as is the start and end of the assault. This case also illustrates how running water forms an effective barrier against free-roaming or attacking Negs. No matter how one analyzes this, no other conclusion is possible: unseen supernatural forces were at work.

I [the author] arrived at Michael's dinner party just after sundown. Michael and his wife are new-age teachers with many years of experience, specializing in self-help, self-discovery, spiritual growth, and these sorts of things. Two other guests had already arrived—a couple from India who made their living in the hotel industry. We chatted about spirituality, metaphysics, and books, swapping stories and sipping wine while dinner simmered on the stove.

After dinner, we moved into the living room to continue our discussions. A pleasant three hours passed. Another couple, Maggie and Tom, showed up later for drinks. Maggie was a respected new-age teacher and healer. I smiled and greeted them warmly, but I was repulsed by this woman. I sensed an unusually strong Neg presence in both Maggie and Tom but it was particularly strong in Maggie.

Having a strong personality, Maggie quickly directed the conversation to her life and interests. Michael and I tried several times to steer it back to the original topics, but failed. Tom, a shift-worker, soon fell asleep on the sofa. About twenty minutes later, I began feeling symptoms of direct psychic attack. This started with cold shivers, pressure in my chest, and a painful cramp in my upper right back that forced me to stand to ease it. But there was no easing this cramp. The cramps soon spread through the right side of my back and shoulder. I fought to relax and hide my distress. No one else in the room seemed to be affected.

I tried hard to ignore what my senses told me was happening, but the muscles in my upper stomach, just under my ribs, started working against themselves. This caused a noticeable bulge in my flesh and a lot of pain. Afraid I was about to collapse, I hurriedly excused myself and hobbled out of the house, saying I would see myself out. If I could just make it to my car, I told myself, I would be okay.

In agony now, with two fists jammed into my stomach, I stumbled towards my car and fell onto the hood. All the pain vanished the instant I crossed the footpath bordering the property. Sagging against my car in wet-eyed relief, I breathed in the cool night air and thanked God for the sudden absence of pain.

Recovered, I went for a walk under the streetlights of the tree-lined avenue to settle myself and analyze what had happened. While it had all the hallmarks of a psychic attack, with Maggie being the most likely source, I started to doubt my own judgment. Maybe I was paranoid about the whole thing. After living with spinal injuries for many years, it was possible I had just pinched some nerves.

I returned to my car, touched my toes a few times, twisted, turned, and stretched. I had no pain or cramps. I sat in my car for a few minutes thinking about it. My stomach and back felt a little bruised, but there was nothing physically wrong with me. I could identify no physical cause for the violent cramp attack earlier.

I had not socialized for a long time and this evening had been a treat. I decided to go back inside and rejoin the party. I took one step back through the gate and collapsed to my knees. I rolled on the grass trying to free what I thought might be another pinched nerve, but to no avail. Struggling to my feet I retreated back through the gate and, once again, the pain stopped instantly. It was as if something unseen was waiting in the shadows just past the front gate.

I decided to experiment. Gingerly waking to the gate again, I stepped through and the pain returned suddenly. I stepped back and the pain stopped instantly. I repeated this a dozen times with the same result. There was definitely something lurking there with a precise *border*. It hurt me every time I passed through the gate.

I moved closer and slid one foot forward until it almost reached the gate. At an exact point, cramping sciatic nerve pain rushed up my right leg. This was fascinating. Logically, everything pointed to there being some kind of invisible barrier across the front of the gate. I was on one side and a powerful Neg was on the other, attacking me whenever I crossed the line.

It was not long before I realized what the barrier was: the main water supply pipe that runs along every street in suburbs, branching into each house. I located the water meter in the front yard. Looking at the asphalt path in front of the gate, I saw where the water mains had been unearthed in the past. A discolored indent lined the property a few inches in front of the gate. This was the line the Neg could not pass.

Continuing to experiment, I walked to the far-left side of the yard where the water main crossed the front of the driveway. The same thing happened again: instant pain if I crossed the line. I walked to the front yard of the next house to the left and repeated the experiment. Again the unseen thing attacked me. Moving further to the left, past the neighbor's water meter, where the water pipe flowed into that house, I repeated the experiment. Nothing happened, no pain. I walked into the neighbor's front yard and crossed their water supply pipe. This resulted in an instant attack.

I repeated the experiment in the neighbor's yard to the right of Michael's house and got exactly the same results. The attacking Neg was trapped behind the running-water barrier produced by the water mains and water supply pipes surrounding Michael's house. Satisfied, I returned to my car and drove home. I had no further problems with direct psychic attack, cramps, or pain in the weeks following.

That experience is a clear, uncomplicated example of direct psychic attack. Even though the source of the attack was clear (Maggie), the way the attack transpired showed the involvement of a decidedly aggressive Neg. It also shows how running water is an effective barrier to Negs. The how and why of this will become clear later in the book.

It was suggested to me that encountering the running water might have been coincidental with my passing outside the auric field of the person attacking me. However, if you look at what I did, this would mean this person had a rectangular aura, which is illogical. I have also developed and road-tested running-water countermeasures over many years, experimenting on myself and many others, including infants, during actual Neg attacks with consistent results. In my experience, the type of psychic attack one person can inflict upon another, with no Neg involvement, is limited. This is more like a personal energy conflict than an attack. This can cause pressure, anxiety, or annoyance, as one person tries to dominate the other, but it will not cause the same symptoms as strong Neg-related attacks.

Questions were also raised from this incident as to why I was singled out, and whether the source of the attack could have been anyone in that house, or from a free-roaming Neg resident in the house. If Maggie brought the Neg into the house with her, it would have had to cross running water on the way in (the water mains), which would seem to contradict my findings.

I have been sensitive to the presence of Negs ever since I exorcised myself from a possessing Neg. It could be said my natural shields were altered by that experience, and that my resulting increased sensitivity makes it easier for Negs to attack me. But this does not mean I endure this meekly, as much can be done about it. If you consider my line of work, which includes exorcism and metaphysical exploration, these attacks are understandable. I have experienced hundreds of Neg attacks over the years. While this can be unpleasant at times, it has also been the means through which I have been able to study Negs and experiment with countermeasures. Without this level of continuing experience, I would never have been able to write this book.

Hitchhiking rides with people is one of the few ways Negs can cross running water, so my intuition said Maggie was the source of the attack. However, Tom fell asleep, making him also suspect, as this would have made it easier for a Neg to leave him and attack me. I doubt the Neg was resident in the house prior to the attack. I had visited Michael's house many times, usually in the evening, and had sensed nothing untoward previously.

Case History #2 – Fred and Jesse

This case shows a similar type of psychic attack, but here a man and a child are attacked in the strongest possible way. This happened in the daytime, showing a Neg attack is not just a thing of the night. The man in the following case, while not a total atheist, did not believe in spirits and supernatural phenomena. He was a materialist with a mind not given to flights of fancy; however, his beliefs have changed considerably since this experience. Here is my account of the event:

It was mid-afternoon and I needed bread and milk. An old friend named Fred had dropped in for coffee and my young son, Jesse, then two, was taking a nap in his bed. Fred agreed to hold the fort while I went to the supermarket. I was only gone fifteen minutes, but all hell broke loose while I was away.

As I walked back to my front door, I heard Jesse crying and Fred calling hoarsely for help. I found them on their knees in the living room, Fred shaking like a leaf and unable to walk, Jesse crying hysterically, protectively clasped in Fred's arms. I could not believe that the hoarse, quivering voice I heard was that of my friend. I could barely make out what he was saying. "Robert . . . help . . . something's trying to get us!"

After I had left, something disturbed Jesse. He screamed and Fred checked on him. He found Jesse cowering in bed, pointing at the shadows in the far corner of the room. Fred's hair stood on end. He tried to pick up Jesse but an unseen force knocked him away. Everything went out of focus for him at this point. Whatever it was, it got hold of Fred and semi-paralyzed him. He had trouble getting to his feet as massive, bone-wracking shivers coursed through him. Not being one to give in, Fred staggered to Jesse and dragged him out of the room. They got halfway across the living room before he was again driven to his knees by the unseen force and was unable to walk or crawl any farther.

I sensed what had happened. I put Jesse outside the house, then went back to help Fred. He could not walk unaided, so I half-carried him through the back door. Fred straightened up the instant we passed the threshold.

When Fred was settled, thinking the attack was over, we went back in the house to get some cold beer to settle our nerves. Fred cursed and fell to his knees the instant he stepped over the threshold. Again, I half-dragged him back outside, and again he straightened up after crossing the threshold. While I was not directly affected by what was happening, all my alarms were going off.

I realized an underground water pipe crossed under the back of the house close to the wall. A garden hose was filling the swimming pool, so water was passing through it at the time. We experimented with crossing and recrossing the threshold several times, each time with the same result: a painful direct attack on Fred. He soon tired of this and refused to experiment further.

As I could come and go as I pleased, I got Fred a cold beer and a double whisky to settle his nerves, as he was badly shaken by the experience. We sat on the patio trying to work out what had happened. While I had my suspicions, I could not explain these to Fred in any way that would make sense to him. He left to go home shortly after this point.

However, Fred returned ashen-faced a few hours later. The attack started again soon after he left the house, in the form of waves of shivers and goose bumps as he drove. This upset him, but he tried to ignore it. Then, he experienced a strong compulsion to wrench the wheel into oncoming traffic. This got so bad he pulled off into a supermarket car park. He soon found himself shopping in what he described as a surreal, dreamlike mall.

He filled a trolley with things he did not want and could not afford, then tried to pay for them with a credit card he knew was expired. Suddenly realizing what he was doing, Fred made a hasty exit, leaving the unwanted shopping and perplexed checkout clerk behind. Returning to his car, Fred managed to drive home, but had to fight suicidal urges all the way.

After this, Fred suffered the classic symptoms of a major psychic attack. I helped as best I could with all I knew at that time. He held his own against what seemed a very nasty Neg bent on destroying him. While the stronger symptoms of direct attack eased after a few weeks, Fred's luck changed and his life went to pieces after this. He lost his job, his wife had an affair and threw him out, and eventually he moved away to start a new life. Over the next three years, he experienced frequent psychic attacks, nightmares, and night terrors.

All of his symptoms eventually eased, but only as Fred matured, changed his lifestyle, and grew stronger. One could say, looking back on all that happened, that this attack changed his life for the better. He now lives a moderate, healthy, more spiritual lifestyle. Fred was lucky to survive this level of attack but would rather have made these changes in a less painful way.

The experience with Fred was not entirely out of the blue. We had been having problems in our home for some time, and my family had just lived through several months of strong psychic attacks. Up until the time of Fred's attack, he had seemed immune and sensed nothing during his regular visits. Our household Neg problems did not decline after Fred's experience, so it seems he did not take our resident Negs away with him. However, he definitely picked up something nasty that day. Incidentally, this case shows why it's advisable to avoid haunted houses and people with a history of psychic attacks.

Case History #3 – David and Simon

Around 1980, I was involved in an extraordinary manifestation that was shared by eight people. The following case shows how psychic attack and possession can spread and affect more than one person at a time. It also shows how some popular countermeasures often do not help during serious Neg manifestations.

A group of friends and I were socializing, chatting, and generally enjoying one another's company. One of us, David, had been dabbling with the occult. Among other things, his house had been troubled by a poltergeist for several months, and he had been trying to contact this spirit. We had visited the week before and found there was something not right about his house. There were several cold spots we could not explain; items regularly went missing there; his couch had been found overturned several times; there had also been several small fires, and a wing of his house had burned down and been recently rebuilt. The new section was unnaturally cold.

David was intoxicated, gamely trying to play a guitar. From the awful sounds he produced, I doubted he had played one before. He was acting strangely, but we thought nothing of it because David was a fairly strange guy, even at the best of times. His brother Simon arrived and he was upset because his wife had just left him for another man. Simon was a professional jockey and did not smoke or drink alcohol. After some chitchat, Simon sat at the table and read the racing guide. It was a fairly average Sunday evening for us all.

David stopped torturing us and dropped the guitar, saying he felt dizzy. He was breathing rapidly and seemed more paranoid than usual. His eyes were glazed and he was sweaty and agitated. Suddenly, he moaned and started shaking, asking over and over for us to help him. Simon looked up and asked what was wrong, but we had no idea. David never took drugs, so we were not worried in that respect. Two of my friends tried to calm him down. David groaned and fell to the floor, convulsing and babbling in a strange, choking voice. He seemed to be talking in a foreign language. His brother Simon also fell to the floor, groaning, convulsing, and babbling.

We could not believe our eyes. I pinched myself to see if I was awake. After several minutes, both men settled into a kind of tranced, babbling, semi-convulsive state. Neither seemed aware of what was happening.

Three of my friends tried everything they could think of to help. Being keen born-again Christians, they prayed over the fallen men, hit them with bibles, splashed them with holy water, anointed them with oil, layered them with crosses and other paraphernalia they happened to have on hand, and prayed in tongues. None of this had any effect. There is no other way to describe it than to say the two brothers were possessed.

I sat back, watching everything, wracking my brain for some way to help. I could not do much to help physically as I was recovering from a minor diving accident I had the day before. (My right hand had been slashed by a stingray and I had several stitches.) I also had little experience with Neg-related problems at that time. I thought an altered state of consciousness might help. I had no idea how this would help, or even if I could achieve it under these conditions, but it was worth trying.

I told my friends what I was about to do, closed my eyes, and fell into a trance state. It normally took me half an hour to get settled into the full trance state, but it was as if something was waiting to help me do this. Within seconds, I felt the heavy wave of the full trance state, followed by a continual falling sensation. Just before I blacked out, white light poured into my mind's eye from above.

I came to slowly, pain shooting through my right hand. My bandage was bloody, as I had burst some stitches. Everyone in the house, including David and Simon, was kneeling in front of me, holding my hands and looking up at me with beatific smiles. I was confused and embarrassed by this. I have no memory of what happened after entering trance.

My friends said that shortly after closing my eyes, I sat up, raised my right hand, and appeared to bless the house in a strange, gentle voice. David and Simon broke out of their state immediately, dazed and confused. They said I spoke to them in a voice that was not mine. But strangely, no one remembered what was said, and it remains a mystery to this day.

After this extraordinary event, that house had a new soothing atmosphere. It was lovely to be in and nothing negative happened there for the next twelve months, after which my friends moved away.

Case History #4 - Interview with a Priest

The following case was related to me in detail by a dear friend who is a priest. This incident happened half a mile from where I was living at the time. It involved psychic attack and possession in a family, and was a scenario that did not have a happy ending.

Father James was called in by police to help with an unusual problem. He arrived at the location to find two nervous-looking police officers guarding the front door. They called to the owners inside but would not enter the house. Father James thought this strange, but soon understood when he found out what was inside. The first things Father James noticed were bottle-tops, cutlery, and other less-identifiable objects imbedded in the ceilings, doors, and walls. The small house looked like a war zone. There were a number of half-empty packing boxes, as if the family were in the middle of moving. A young man and woman with their two-year-old son were inside the house.

Father James introduced himself and joined John, Sylvia, and their son, Michael. He learned that their problems started the day Michael was born. Both John and Sylvia began having nightmares that same night. Soon, flashes and blobs of light were seen and frequent knocks and taps were heard throughout the house. Foul smells and icy cold patches wafted through the house. The baby slept badly and cried a lot. The situation steadily worsened, with objects being moved and going missing, and several unexplainable fires occurred. Soon, objects began floating about the house. Unhappy with the medical opinion given them (that it was mass hallucination), John began drinking and Sylvia took Valium.

Originally from New Zealand, the family had moved house several times in an attempt to escape the problem, but it always followed them. In desperation, they had moved to Australia some months earlier, and had moved twice since. They soon ran out of money and were now getting desperate. They were on the move so much they could not find employment. John was becoming an alcoholic, Sylvia was living on antidepressants and sedatives, and they hardly slept at night.

Father James was given a drink while they explained their situation. As he reached for it, the glass flew off the table and smashed against the wall. The next glass met the same fate. Although Father James was shocked, John and Sylvia said this happened all the time. Father James decided he was not thirsty.

Apparently, several priests of various faiths had already tried to help them in this house alone, but so far none had succeeded.

Father James took his ceremonial robes and other paraphernalia with him into the bathroom to change. He put the bag down and removed his jacket, but when he turned to get his robe the bag was missing. He found it in the kitchen at the front of the house. Again he went into the bathroom to change, but the same thing happened. This time his bag and robes were scattered through the garden. Father James recovered his things and repeated the process, this time keeping his foot firmly on the bag as he changed. Father James carried out the ceremony, but it seemed to have no effect.

Father James visited with me two years later and we discussed paranormal phenomena as he told me this story. It troubled him that the blessing and cleansing rituals he performed seemed to have made matters worse for the family. He had not been asked to return to that house. Although Father James had not been invited back, he kept tabs on the situation through his police contacts. John hanged himself a few months after Father James' visit; shortly after this, Sylvia had a breakdown and was committed to a mental hospital; having no immediate family, Michael was made a ward of the state.

Paranormal or Mental?

Paranormal phenomena cannot be explained away, or even explained at all, by modern science. Many say these things simply cannot occur. Consequently, all Neg incidents are considered to be mental problems because science cannot conceive of them being anything else. Because of this widespread denial, Neg problems spread unchecked.

Many psychological problems are caused or exacerbated by Neg influences. A lot of the darker things that plague humankind are Neg-related. In my opinion, many serial rapists, murderers, and other such human monsters are possessed. An autopsy might find such persons have brain disorders, brain tumors, or biochemical imbalances, but which came first, the chicken or the egg, the physical symptoms or the Neg possession?

The four real-life case stories presented here highlight several important factors about Negs and how they operate. The first two show that free-roaming Negs cannot easily cross running water, not while they are manifesting close enough to the physical universe to affect humans. They can, however, use living beings (human or animal) as shields to carry them across the energies running waters generate. But this still makes running water a powerful defense against direct Neg attack.

The current general view of spirits and ghosts is that they are like invisible birds that can fly and move freely in all directions, unimpeded by anything in the physical universe. This is understandable, given our limited mortal conception of spirit existence, but my experience shows this view to be inaccurate. Apart from water being a powerful symbol of purity, the energies generated by running water have a strong effect on many types of spirits, particularly on Negs.

The second case history involving Fred and Jesse also shows how running water instantly breaks an attack. However, this also shows that running water alone does not form a perfect defense. The attacking Neg obviously managed to attach to Fred because it followed and continued tormenting him for a long time after the initial attack. It is possible that if Fred had crossed running water sooner after the attack started, he would have completely broken the attack before the Neg could attach itself to him. Years of experiments with many other people suffering major Neg attacks have proven this to be more than likely.

The third case of David and Simon shows how some Negs can attack, influence, and even possess more than one person simultaneously. This highlights the ubiquitous nature of powerful Negs, demons in particular.

The fourth case history is a horror story. It shows a worst-case scenario, in which a powerful Neg (probably a demon) succeeded in attaching to and destroying an entire family. The reasons for this attack are clouded, but it obviously involved the baby because the trouble started soon after his birth. This case highlights the need for not only an understanding of Negs and how they operate, but knowledge of practical countermeasures. Neg problems can be minimized in this way, before they become firmly entrenched and produce havoc.

Later in the book, Neg-related problems will be analyzed in more detail before I offer advice and countermeasures. A big part of my approach to psychic self-defense is education. If one learns to avoid certain things and to take certain precautions, and to recognize the signs and symptoms of potential Neg-related problems, most can be avoided entirely.

4

Exposure and Contamination

How people become exposed to and contaminated by Negs is a complex matter. There are as many possible explanations as there are different types of peoples, cultures, lifestyles, and Negs. My explanations here are general, rule-of-thumb indications based on experience and reasoning.

People can become exposed to, and contaminated by, Negs in a variety of ways, but this does not always automatically occur, even when exposure risks are high. This is due to individual susceptibility, which varies from person to person. Some people have strong natural defenses and can withstand anything without so much as goose bumps, while others need only momentary exposure to be affected in some way. When Neg contamination occurs, it's generally accidental or brought about through circumstance, although there are exceptions to this. Lifestyle, mental and physical health, beliefs, strength of mind, and the company one keeps—these are probably the most important factors, while common sense, moderation, inner balance, and tolerance will help one avoid Negs.

Innocence and Immunity to Negs

While I wish otherwise, age and innocence offer no protection against Negs. Youth, innocence, and purity are actually strong Neg attractors. While all babies are born pure, one must consider the environment they are born into. Babies have little self-control and mental strength, and only partially formed personalities and intellects. Thus, many babies and children suffer greatly at the hands of supernatural influences. They cannot defend themselves and often cannot even complain. I have seen babies as young as nine months old suffering massive psychic assaults. I have also dissolved these attacks (when allowed to intervene) and have on many occasions handed happy babies back to worried mothers a short time later.

Some people like to believe all children have guardian angels standing watch over them at all times, especially while sleeping. But thousands of children are harmed and killed every day through accidents, diseases, famines, and wars. Even so, this belief in protection is, on the part of worried parents, understandable, especially when considering unseen influences. Many people believe that if they lead good lives they will never be troubled by the negatives in life. They believe in the adage "like attracts like" and that if they are good they will only attract good things. While this is laudable and partly true, it does not provide complete Neg immunity, but neither does this attract Neg-related problems. Circumstances and other factors are involved in one's potential for Neg exposure and contamination.

Factors Involved in Natural Neg Susceptibility

Psychic sensitivity is an important factor concerning Neg problems. People with some degree of psychic sensitivity are more susceptible to psychic influences than are people who lack this sensitivity. However, psychic insensitivity does not offer total Neg immunity. It lessens one's chances of attracting Negs, but it also *masks* the symptoms of Neg interference. Sensitives will feel the symptoms of psychic attacks, whereas insensitives will not. The end result is the same, but insensitives will not be disturbed by the symptoms of psychic attacks.

For example, telepathically or hypnotically induced Neg urges are felt more keenly by sensitives than insensitives. A Neg may telepathically broadcast a negative emotional urge, like anger, to cause a person to lose control and fight with a loved one. Sensitives may feel powerful compulsions, compared with insensitives who may feel only minor urges. The ramifications of this are obvious. Sensitives are easier to influence than are insensitives, and for this reason, Negs are more attracted to sensitives.

The matter of sensitivity is similar to hypnotic susceptibility. In a public demonstration of hypnosis, the stage personality will select only a few susceptible individuals from the audience, and they will often bring exceptional hypnotic subjects to liven up the stage show. Like Negs, the stage personality is more interested in susceptible than non-susceptible persons because they are easier to influence and control.

Children and Negative Influences

Children are generally more sensitive than adults. Sensitivity is innate to childhood, as is the emotional, telepathic, and psychic bonding between parents and siblings that comes with it. Children believe in Santa Claus, the Easter Bunny, the Tooth Fairy, and Peter Pan. All of these fit the bill as supernatural beings, albeit of the nicer variety. As we know, children also believe in fairies and magic, and some children have invisible playmates.

Parents foster many of these beliefs because they are a beautiful part of childhood. They do no harm, but they do support open belief in unseen beings and supernatural forces. When children get scared at night, these beliefs can foster sinister experiences. The bogeyman and monsters under the bed are examples of how seemingly harmless beliefs can have negative aspects. However, discouraging children's beliefs in Santa Claus and the Easter Bunny will not help immunize them against Negs.

As children are naturally sensitive, they are naturally more susceptible to psychic influences and attacks. Many children are naturally psychic to the point where they have visions and see auras around people. Children like this show strong natural psychic abilities and are, therefore, more at risk than other children; such children should be guarded accordingly.

For these reasons, children suffer more than adults at the hands of Negs. They sense and feel more keenly, are more gullible and easier to influence, and are highly susceptible to Neg influences. At night, children feel Neg presences intensely. Children are easily frightened and this is used against them. During Neg attacks, children can be brought to the point of mind-numbing terror. When this point is reached, their natural defenses fall, and they lay open to invasion, to telepathic and hypnotic manipulation, and ultimately to long-term psychological conditioning.

Adults and Negative Influences

Belief plays a large part in psychic sensitivity, especially with adults. If people are open-minded, they are more sensitive than close-minded materialists. Beliefs create conceptual filters within the mind. These filters shape what can be perceived by a mind. Strong disbelief creates strong barriers and, in a way, can protect people from sensing Neg presences and interferences. This will not stop them from happening, but it will buffer them from being perceived.

This seems part of the reason why so many people do not acknowledge the existence of unseen beings and forces. Whether it's subconscious racial memory or intuition, this attitude creates useful mental blocks and conceptual barriers that offer some level of protection. Disbelief and insensitivity will not entirely immunize one against Negs, but they significantly reduce one's susceptibility to them.

Exposure to Negs through Circumstances

Certain circumstances can increase the chances of exposure to Negs, such as association, sexual contact, dangerous practices, occult dabbling, black rites, exposure to haunted places, negative energy links, contact with secondhand items, body parts, and fluids. Neg exposure is often a matter of bad luck, but much can be done to minimize risks. More than anything, this is a common sense matter. Let's examine these in detail.

Association: Care in the company one keeps is paramount to living a Neg-free existence. This advice applies to babies and children as well as adults. As any parent knows, associating with people of low morality and conscience, or with those living in unhealthy environments, can have adverse effects on children. Ask mothers how they feel when persons they instinctively dislike want to hold their babies; you will often find they are filled with trepidation. A mother's intuition should always be deferred to in such matters and excuses made to disallow contact. This simple act, while seeming to be mildly antisocial on the surface, will significantly reduce the chances of babies experiencing Neg-related problems.

Most people follow some standard of lifestyle and conduct which influences their choices of friends and associates. It is wise to consider not only the integrity and personality of others, but also the company they presently keep and have kept in the past. This might seem antisocial, but it significantly affects your Neg exposure levels. Even so, this can be a difficult ideal to achieve. While everyone can pick their own friends and associates, they cannot pick their own family and family friends.

If one associates with people with Neg problems, or with people whose personality or lifestyle may attract Negs, the chances of picking up Neg-related problems is greatly increased. The more time one spends with such persons, the higher the risks of Neg exposure and contamination. While it's difficult to tell if Negs are attached to a person, risks are increased if one associates with persons of low morals or with those who come from unwholesome, unsavory, or negative environments.

This is especially so with children and young people because they are so easily influenced and led astray. Their school environment, plus the friends they associate with after school, can affect their potential for exposure to Neg forces. While it's sometimes impossible to do much about this, being forewarned is being forearmed, and young people can be educated about the risks involved, and this can influence what company they choose to keep.

Sexual Contact: Sexual contact with a new partner is probably the most dangerous time for anyone in relation to picking up Neg attachments. During sex, a strong energy bond temporarily forms between partners. This allows Neg influences to spread. Through this link, a Neg resident in one person can easily sink attachments into the other person. The average person will not be aware of this happening.

The risks of picking up a significant Neg attachment are greatly increased if sex is forced. While the emotional connection here is quite different from normal sex, it still exists. Forced sex, rape, or sexual assault of any kind, by any gender combination, can cause significant Neg attachments. All sexual assaults that produce psychological trauma will generate a strong potential for core images. Core images are trauma memories. These provide openings into the minds of victims, which Negs use to connect themselves and exert their influence.

As with any violent or evil act, the energies released during sexual assault can attract Negs. Even if no significant Neg attachments are made at the time of assaults, these negative energies can generate conditions that attract Negs like moths to a flame. Long-term Neg-related problems can occur under such circumstances, and these problems may or may not involve actual psychic attacks; it depends greatly upon the psychic susceptibility of the victim.

Victims of sexual assault can become attractors to further sexual violence in the future if they have become Neg-contaminated. It's often said that hardened sex offenders can pick out easy targets (victims with a history of sexual abuse) from a crowd with uncanny accuracy. All psychology aside, the reasons for this may have a lot to do with Neg influences on both sides. Victims' Neg influences, unbeknownst to them, broadcast "Victim Available!" signals (a subtle attractive force), while sexual predators broadcast a "Seeking Victim!" signal (also a subtle attractive force). The result is that victims and predators alike are unconsciously attracted to each other.

Dangerous Practices: Many of today's Spiritualist or new-age group development practices are unwise. They offer little practical defense against potential Neg-related problems. It's all too easy to pick up Neg influences. Over the years, I have spent many hundreds of hours in development circles and séance rooms, and have experienced a great variety of Neg phenomena. Typically, the protection offered against Negs is usually ineffective while the practices engaged in are often risky.

Keep firmly in mind that if one joins any type of psychic or spiritual development group, or a spiritual meditation group, one should never rely on one's teachers for one's own safety. Protection is a personal responsibility. Very few teachers can offer any help if anything goes seriously wrong. This is no slight on teachers, who are generally well meaning and would help if they could; it is merely a fact of psychic life.

Group prayers offer some defense against Negs, but only if people understand and believe in the prayers. Understanding and belief are required for prayers to work effectively, and some knowledge and skill are required to create effective visualized barriers and to keep them in place. This is beyond the abilities of most novices, but until this experience is gained, only imaginary barriers will be created with little defensive worth.

The trouble is that, over the last twenty-five years, I have noticed a disturbing trend towards oversimplifying group protection mechanisms. The principles of group protection generally used today grew out of early Christian and Spiritualist practices. In many cases, the old ways have been modernized to the point where they become useless.

I have attended many Spiritualist churches and development circles where the old ways are adhered to and good defenses created, such that Neg-related problems are rare. This protection involves a seemingly elaborate process of group prayer, invocation, and visualization, often taking five minutes or more to accomplish. Today, this is often simplified to a short prayer (usually spoken by the group leader only) and a group visualization of a circle of white light around the group.

One can imagine as many angels and circles of white light surrounding a group as one likes, but these will offer little real protection if poorly done. One can pray for protection and qualify this prayer however one likes, saying that only such and such spirits may approach, but this will not stop wandering Negs from entering the circle and interfering with group members, if group and individual defenses are poor. One must also consider resident and hitchhiking Negs that may have been carried inside a protective circle by group members. Most Negs are difficult to detect, no matter how sensitive one is. Negs hide inside people and use them as a shield to prevent detection by sensitives.

The practice of openly inviting spirit beings to enter and control one's body/mind is lunacy. Unfortunately, most group members do this passionately. Many would be happy for "any" spirit to do this, just so long as "something" actually happens. Many times I have seen people get into strife because of this unwise approach, yet a great temptation leads to this unwise practice—to have some wise spirit being communicated through such people. This elevates individuals to positions of respect and admiration among their peers. While such people generally have good intentions, often of spiritually aiding humanity, the motivations of the Negs are another matter.

The fact is that one does not need spirits for psychic and spiritual advancement. It's far preferable to get in touch with one's own inner self, to develop contact with one's higher self, rather than to seek the help of *unknown* spirit beings. One should not look outside oneself for spiritual knowledge and development. As psychic development is a side effect of spiritual development, one best not sought for its own sake, it's unwise to skip the long-term application of self-discipline necessary for true spiritual and psychic development to unfold.

Psychic abilities hold glamor, such that if sought for their own sake, they can greatly distract one from spiritual progress. Instead of stripping away inner barriers between one's inner and higher self, new barriers and distractions are created and existing ones reinforced.

It is fairly common for group members to pick up Neg influences, and even to become overshadowed during sessions. This is usually only temporary, but can occasionally have more lasting effects. Overshadowing is a mild form of possession by a spirit entity, similar to what happens to trance channels when spirits communicate through them (a process called trance mediumship). Channeling, as many know, is a modern term loosely used to describe a variety of psychic and mediumistic abilities including psychic sensing, trance speech, clairvoyance, clairaudience, transfiguration, and spirit writing (automatic writing).

Not all Neg-related problems that arise through group development practices can be overcome with a few quick healing prayers. This is partly due to permission issues involved in openly inviting spirits to enter and take control of students, and partly because very few people can actually do anything about Neg problems when they occur. No matter what anyone might say to the contrary, removing an overshadowing or possessing spirit is no easy task.

In most cases when Neg problems occur, troubled students are instructed to visualize shields, barriers, and other such defenses. Using these to solve Neg problems is difficult because constructing an effective personal shield takes skill, time, and effort. Visualized countermeasures are often fiercely defended by users as being perfectly effective, if done correctly. But this is of little help to Neg-troubled students. They are usually told to surround themselves in white light and/or to send the problematic spirit to the light. If a Neg does not leave, what does one do next to get rid of it? Added to this, it's particularly difficult to do anything by way of self-defense visualization when one is trembling with fear.

The typical kinds of problems that can arise in development groups were made evident to me many years ago while in my late teens. My mother was attending a new development group run by a man of reputed experience and ability. During a session, my mother was overshadowed by a spirit said to be that of a convoy sailor killed during World War Two. After the session, the group leader said he would take the spirit with him and guide it to the light. Unfortunately, this gesture did not remove the spirit and the overshadowing continued.

My mother's main symptoms were sensing the odor of damp wool, feeling cold, and shivering. I remember my mother walking the hallways of our home late at night, shivering and praying. All of us could smell the damp wool and feel the uneasy atmosphere around her at such times. This condition came and went intermittently over a week, then suddenly stopped.

Here is another case. A young woman named Trish, a novice to this work, was attending her fourth group meditation meeting. She was forcefully overshadowed by a spirit. At the start of the session, the group leader said a prayer for protection and guidance, and then the group was asked to visualize a protective circle of white light around it. Halfway through the meditation session, Trish became paralyzed and experienced a continual falling sensation, head pressure, rapid heartbeat, cold shivers, disassociation, and waves of tingling energy pulsing up through her spine. These are typical symptoms of when a spirit enters and overshadows a person.

The group leader noticed that Trish was having a hard experience and tried to help her by instructing the group to concentrate on Trish and to send her energy. After Trish had recovered, the group leader said she had seen the spirit of a lost young girl with Trish and that Trish had been instrumental in rescuing her. While Trish had held the little girl spirit inside herself, the group had sent it to the light. Based on this experience, the group leader decided to let the group do rescue work (rescuing lost spirits) using Trish as the channel.

This experience shook Trish and she contacted me for advice. I was horrified, to say the least, because this is as risky as it gets. Trish was lucky to escape that first experience with no lasting problems; on my advice, she did not continue with that group. For what Trish wanted to learn (basic meditation and energy work), I advised her to take up Zen, tai chi, or chi kung.

Occult Dabbling: Another common source of Neg trouble comes from occult dabbling. This attracts many inquisitive people who often are chasing only thrills and entertainment. The freaky can be fascinating. You can buy all kinds of gadgets and instructional books to show how to make contact with spirits, cast spells, and do other interesting things. But what the suppliers do not explain are the risks, so it's wise not to play with forces you don't understand.

Probably half the Neg problems I have encountered over the years resulted from some type of occult dabbling. The Ouija board is the most common spirit communication device used today. Many children get hold of these, or make their own, and play games involving open spirit invocation with no controls or protections whatsoever.

Many who dabble at spirit communication, such as with a Ouija board, give permission to any and all available spirits to communicate with them. No matter how this is worded when spoken aloud, in essence this is an occult invocation. By and large, no protection or precautions are taken because most people think this unnecessary. Many people naively believe spirit contact is not dangerous, so they do nothing to ensure their safety.

When chided about the unsafe nature of these practices, more than one person has said to me that they do not care what comes through, as long as something comes along to entertain them. Most people are under the naive impression that if a bad spirit comes through they can just tell it to go away and it will. Neg influence and possession are widely disbelieved in, so no risks are believed to be involved. But getting rid of a bad spirit that may come into you during a Ouija session is no easy task, and most definitely it is not easy for a novice. Here's an example that makes the point:

I talked to four children, aged eight to eleven, who had been dabbling with a homemade Ouija board. They had made this secretly and gathered in a locked room while their parents were busy. An invocation from the popular TV show *Charmed* was used. It was all very hush-hush and thrilling for the children, but the first words to come through were "Kill Dolly," who was their poodle.

According to the children, several spirits communicated with them. Some were "nice" and some were "nasty." Nice comments were interspersed with swearing, cursing, and threats. Nightmares resulted from this game as the children worried about what had happened and fretted about the guilt of hiding this from parents. Fortunately, no lasting harm resulted to them from this disturbing game, but harmful potential was present.

A golden rule for avoiding Neg problems is this: never dabble with any kind of spirit communication, be it a game or otherwise, and never stay in a house where this is being done. Also, avoid anyone who does this on a regular basis. It can be dangerous to associate with such persons as their Neg exposure levels are likely to be higher than average.

Here is another case. Elaine had two children, a girl, three, and a boy, seven. Elaine had a long history of bad associations with disreputable people. A problem occurred one night while she played the Ouija board with friends who were drunk and/or high on drugs.

The first sign of trouble was when Elaine's daughter walked into the room, had a mild trembling seizure, and began talking in an adult male voice. Everyone thought this was fascinating. (This three-year-old had a speech impediment and normally spoke unclearly.) Elaine fell into a trance herself and began channeling a spirit. This spirit was reputedly a woman of royalty, and Elaine's voice and mannerisms changed dramatically. Again, everyone thought this was fascinating and fun. Next, flashing lights appeared and strange noises were heard, and these grew worse until everyone present was uneasy.

When I arrived at the house, late one afternoon, Elaine and two other women were sitting at the dining table drinking wine. I introduced myself and was told the story. Hiding my shock, I began to make observations. Elaine went in and out of trance and occasionally changed into the royal lady spirit. When she did, her voice, facial aspects, and mannerisms changed dramatically. A spirit was definitely involved.

Elaine's two children worried me, though I could do little for them because their mother loved all the attention. She had called on me hoping I could get her some official attention, publicity, and money. She was under the impression I worked for the university as a parapsychologist. I have no idea where she got this idea. Elaine's daughter, Mary, was sitting listlessly next to her, eyes glazed. I knew she was suffering an overshadowing or worse. This little girl seemed to be the epicenter of the problem. Somehow a door had been opened and she had been the key.

Mary's seven-year-old brother, David, sat several feet away at the breakfast bar. He was also in trouble. I listened and watched him closely. He had dark circles under his eyes and had obviously been sleeping badly. He quietly repeated the multiplication table while rocking back and forth, hugging himself. I could tell he was under strong Neg attack, and he seemed to be hearing voices. The look of helplessness in that child's eyes was something I have seen many times. I walked over and patted him on the shoulder. I asked him if saying his tables helped stop the voices. This shocked him and he stopped. I promised to help, but said I had to help his sister first.

My higher self (or whatever we call it) was already manifesting in me and the room began taking on a surreal quality. I told Elaine I was going to sit for a moment, and that she should bring Mary to me when requested. I explained that Mary might resist, but that this was normal and everything would be okay soon. Although Elaine was reveling in the attention, she was also frightened by my focus on her children.

I slid into trance and the presence of my higher self suffused me. Silence grew in the house. I gestured to Elaine to bring Mary, and she picked her up and got halfway to me before Mary screamed and fought violently. When she was within reach, I immobilized her in my arms, even though she struggled violently. The energy welled up through me as I began the healing. As it flowed through my hands, Mary fell asleep. A few minutes later, I handed a sleepy-looking angel back to her mother, who carried her off to bed.

Next, I asked David to come to me. He jumped onto my lap, but fell asleep a few moments later as I began the healing on him. After I finished, his mother put him to bed. Both children slept all night and most of the next day, a thing they had not done for a long time. I tried to give Elaine healing as well, but could not connect with her. Elaine said she felt better, but I sensed her clinging to the spirit. No matter what I said, I could not penetrate this connection and her need for attention.

I received a phone call from Elaine a few days later. David and Mary were both doing well. Elaine invited me to a séance she was holding at her house late the next night. She hoped I would come in case there were any more problems, but I respectfully declined.

Black Rites: Probably the most intensely Neg-plagued people I have come across have at some time been involved with Satanic rites or black magic practices. I have tried to help many such people over the years, but this circumstance comes with its own problems. In some cases, victims have attended a Black Mass or taken the Black Eucharist. This is a bit like catching a spiritual disease. Sometimes only one exposure is needed to cause serious long-term Neg contamination. In a way, this can have the opposite effect of Christian baptism in that, through these dark rituals, one dedicates one's life to the forces of darkness.

Most people suffering these types of Neg problems hear voices and suffer regular psychic attacks. They will often move house frequently in an attempt to leave the Negs behind. But they always catch up. Such people have caused serious damage to themselves. Permission is the key issue here in that permission has been given to the Negs to interfere. This is regardless of whether the persons understood the words they were saying at the time. In a way, it could be said a pact has been made with the Devil; breaking such a pact is not easy. To young people seeking thrills, attending black rites might sound like fun, but trust me, this is like playing Russian roulette with only one empty chamber in the revolver.

While much can be done, the cure for Neg interference from participation in black rites is often difficult. Serious physical and spiritual lifestyle changes must be made. You can no longer live as normal people do. You must maintain a wholesome spiritual life of moderation and self-discipline to minimize Neg influences. These changes are not easy for some people. So, in many cases, people just put up with Neg problems and call on someone like myself to help when things get bad. While it's possible to deter Negs using various countermeasures, they cannot be kept away unless wholesome spiritual lifestyle changes are implemented by the people affected.

The following case is instructive in this regard. Several years ago, I was asked to help a friend of a friend with Neg problems. Bill was thirty-five and happily married with four children, but he had experienced problems since he was seventeen when he had attended several meetings with a Satanic cult. During these meetings he had been "baptized" and had taken the Black Eucharist. Bill started to worry about what he was getting into and left the group.

Bill's problems began soon after leaving the cult. Dark nightmares and monstrous visions came and went, as did a wide range of supernatural phenomena, including poltergeist activity and voices. Bill was under continual psychic attack for several months, and while this died down eventually, he was never entirely free of it and it would flare up regularly. Most troubling of all were the voices. Their intensity and clarity varied with other intermittent manifestations, but they never went away. At the least, Bill heard a soft muttering and chuckling, but at their worst, the harsh voices cursed him continually.

Despite all this, Bill was managing well. He had a strong mind and kept himself busy. However, the phenomena around him had grown to the point where they were disturbing his family.

I offered to help and Bill agreed to undergo deep healing, my term for contact healing done from an altered state of consciousness. We retired to the main bedroom, locked the door, and drew the blinds, then sat facing each other on chairs in the dim light. At my direction, Bill closed his eyes and relaxed as I settled myself into trance.

A cold draft wafted over us and taps and knocks began in the room. Opening my eyes but still in trance, I saw flashes of light everywhere. Bill spasmed and went rigid in his chair. His face disappeared behind a murky-green mist and another face appeared over it, as Bill transfigured before my eyes.

The thing before me had a face like an evil witch, with hooked nose, blackened teeth, hairy warts on leathery, wattled skin, red eyes, and an untidy mane of hair. It cackled with glee, raised claw-like green hands, and leapt at me. We fell to the floor with its "hands" (using Bill's hands) fastened around my throat. Bill's body was small and wiry, half my size, but he had gained enormous strength. I could not breathe and could not tear its hands away from my throat.

Thinking quickly and using every ounce of self-control I could muster, I half stood and fell back onto the double bed, dragging it/him with me. Using my superior weight, I wrestled it/him on top of me and then threw myself off the bed so I landed on the hard floor with it/him pinned directly under me. The breath whooshed out of it/him and his hands fell from my throat. Before the witch could recover, I put Bill in a headlock and wrapped my legs around his waist, pinning his arms. Leaning back against the wall, I took a few deep breaths and forced myself back into trance again.

As during other spiritual emergencies I have lived through, I was pulled into trance very quickly with a heavy falling sensation. Connecting with my higher self, I gave Bill a deep healing. As the energy coursed through me, Bill went limp in my arms. I finished the healing, which only took a minute, and then put a sleeping Bill to bed. He slept for twenty-four hours and did not remember anything that had happened after entering the room with me.

As this incident happened several years ago, I can provide hindsight today. Bill's voices and most of the phenomena stopped completely for over a year. Some of Bill's problems returned over the next few years, but these were mild. Their return happened because Bill refused to make significant lifestyle changes. He still used alcohol and recreational drugs daily, had no time free for church or meditation, and kept rough company.

Neg-related problems are far more likely, and usually more severe, if people follow hedonistic and/or unspiritual lives. Regular, and especially heavy, drug and alcohol use, plus other unwholesome activities, generate negative energy. This accumulates in the nonphysical atmosphere around people, and over time it erodes their natural shields. While these things in themselves will not actually cause Neg-related problems, they do increase the risks of exposure and contamination. This is like how poor diet and lack of exercise weaken the immune system and increase the chances of the physical body catching a disease when it is exposed to one.

Neg-related problems can sometimes be a wake-up call for people to make lifestyle changes, or to live more wholesome, spiritual lives. If ignored, Neg problems will usually worsen progressively, especially if they are severe to begin with. If Bill had listened to me and modified his lifestyle, I am sure his Neg problems would have disappeared entirely. But we are all creatures of habit, and lifestyle changes are difficult.

Most people I am called on to help expect me to put on a magic show, to wave my wand, and make the Negs go away. I wish it were this simple. While much can be done, metaphysically speaking, some effort is generally required on the part of victims to change their life conditions to the level where Negs are repelled and/or disempowered.

Haunted Places, Ghosts, and Echoes of the Past: Places can become contaminated by Negs—not just houses, objects, and people, but open areas of land. There are many reasons. Currents of subtle energies, both positive and negative, flow through and over our planet. Areas where strong flows of negative energy exist can contain doorways into negative realms. Most areas of strong Neg energy are unsuspected by people and usually nothing bad will happen unless someone builds a house over one. People usually sense such negative areas instinctively. For example, if people are hiking and come across one, it's doubtful they will camp or spend much time there. Intuition prompts them to move on because it does not feel right there.

Violent and evil acts performed in a locale can open doorways into negative dimensional realms, especially if these occur in areas with a strong negative energy flow. Sometimes these doorways can stay active long after the events that generated them are forgotten, leaving open gateways into negative realms for others.

Whether a doorway exists naturally or has been created through black magic or evil acts, it will rarely become active enough to produce strong paranormal phenomena, unless living beings, especially humans, spend time there. When humans are present, Negs are provided with the energy necessary for manifestation and the reasons for manifesting. This is especially so when sensitive, susceptible people are present. This is why children, especially prepubescent children, are frequently associated with paranormal manifestations. Children radiate lots of energy, especially if they are naturally mediumistic. This provides Negs with the energy necessary for manifestation.

Badly haunted houses are rare because the right combination of negative energies, doorways into negative realms, plus the presence of susceptible, mediumistic human beings, is necessary. Ghostly apparitions usually only appear when conditions are right and when enough energy is present to allow their manifestation. Psychics will often pick up clues about the origins of hauntings. These are often "echoes" of the past from terrible events that caused humans great despair at that site. Echoes of these persons or events will sometimes be seen as ghosts. Ghosts can manifest strongly enough, given the right energy and light conditions, to become visible, so that at times a strong apparition can be recorded on film.

Echoes of the past are always vague and confused. This is because as ghosts, they are not real beings. Not much sense is ever had from them; they are capable of nothing more than vague dialogue concerning what happened around the time of their death. They are much like dream characters; they are one-dimensional thought-forms that cannot engage in meaningful communications.

Buildings containing doorways into negative realms are usually deemed haunted. These are places where frequent paranormal manifestations occur. Some of the worst places for this are old jails, mental hospitals, and asylums; places where large numbers of people have suffered and/or died will usually carry multiple doorways. An uneasy atmosphere will usually be felt there by sensitives in such places, especially at night, and ghosts will frequently be seen or felt by sensitives. The greater the suffering and the longer it lasted, the stronger will be the doorways, and the stronger will be the Negs involved.

It often seems as if the ghosts of haunted houses do not like company and are trying to drive humans away. But in my experience, if Negs are involved (former human or otherwise), they will torment and attack humans as a matter of course. Such spirits are not trying to drive humans away for no reason; they are simply acting according to their nature.

Cemeteries and ancient burial grounds can also be classed as haunted. These usually contain many ghosts and astral shells. Old burial grounds are also often protected by powerful shamanic curses, invoking harm upon anyone who dares to desecrate them, and some curses can last thousands of years.

People often cling to their physical bodies for several days or more after their deaths. This causes ghosts to accumulate in cemeteries where their bodies are buried. Negs are attracted to cemeteries, partly because of the grief and other strong emotions expressed by mourners and partly because of the concentration of ghosts found there, which generates an attractive atmosphere for more Negs.

Negs that were attached to people when they died and were buried also tend to accumulate in cemeteries. In modern cemeteries, running water adds to this equation, in that water mains surrounding cemeteries form barriers that tend to trap many lower Neg types, including earthbound spirits (ghosts), within the cemetery boundaries. This results in the ghostly accumulations common to cemetery grounds.

Day visitors to cemeteries are more exposed to Negs than usual, simply because of the increased number of ghosts and Negs found there. This is especially so for sensitives if they are experiencing strong emotions of grief. However, in full daylight the risks are minimal. Night visitors, however, are far more at risk because ghosts and Negs are generally more active at night.

During the daytime, Negs and ghosts have far weaker abilities for manifestation and influence, especially outdoors. There is some truth to the old legend that vampires and other such nocturnal monsters cannot cross running water and are destroyed by sunlight. Most Negs, including ghosts, avoid daylight and seem driven to hide from the Sun by moving below ground or inside buildings. It can be said that the subtle energies of which Negs and ghosts are composed are damaged by sunlight.

Most Negs and ghosts will eventually realize they are trapped within cemetery boundaries, but without knowing why. Thus Negs and ghosts found in cemeteries are more likely to actively try to enter visitors so they will be carried outside the bounds with them when they leave. A Neg trapped in a cemetery with no attachment to a living human host will make every effort to attach itself to any susceptible person it encounters.

Spending time in haunted buildings and cemeteries, especially at night when Negs are most active, is one of the easiest ways to pick up Neg-related problems. Here are two typical examples, the first given in the words of Barry, the man concerned here:

> When I was about seven years old (I'm 36 now), we moved house. From the start, I was tormented almost nightly by unseen beings. This lasted for about a year. It began with me hearing evil voices and laughter and seeing things like doors and curtains opening on their own. These incidents terrified me. I would be paralyzed with fear until I could find the strength to scream out in terror and run to my mother's room.
>
> At first, she believed I was having nightmares due to emotional trauma because of her recent divorce. The incidents grew more frequent, and she began to worry. I was sent to a string of child psychologists, but nobody had any answers. Nothing helped, and the attacks continued.
>
> One time, I awoke in the middle of the night out of a deep sleep. (I slept with my light on due to fear.) I woke facing the wall and saw a shadow of a boy my age walk past my bed. I was frozen in fear, which became worse when I realized the light fixture was attached to the wall I was facing, so the shadow could not have been cast from behind me. The shadow then grossly distorted before vanishing.
>
> Another time, I was reading in the afternoon. I had a washcloth, which I used to cool my eyes because of allergies, draped over the foot of my bed. The room was well lit and I was wide awake. Suddenly, the washcloth straightened out and rose three feet into the air. It hovered there, motionless. I was frozen in fear. I finally managed to cry out for help and heard my stepfather coming. As he approached, the washcloth slowly descended and

landed on the bed just as he opened the door. I told him what happened; he said I was dreaming, but I knew I was completely awake the entire time.

On a third occasion, I was in the bathroom getting ready for school, when suddenly I heard a loud growl behind me from inside the shower recess. I told myself it was just my imagination and tried to ignore it. But it grew louder until it became a roar. Then, the shower curtain flew out and wrapped itself around me. Terrified, I broke free of it and ran out of the bathroom, headfirst into my stepfather. He told me not to bother my mother again, as she was at her wits' end with all of my imaginary problems.

We moved house a week after that incident, and the problems stopped as suddenly as they began. To me, that house was haunted, but I was the only one who ever saw or heard anything freaky.

Here is a story about Elizabeth, forty, who was a businesswoman from a nearby town; she was divorced with no children. She presented me with a negative entity problem. Elizabeth was not religious and had no interest in spiritual matters, and nothing paranormal had ever happened to her before the start of her current problem.

In 1989, a few months before we met, Elizabeth had visited an old museum in the city. It had been used as a women's prison and mental asylum one hundred years earlier. It had a terrible history and was well known as a haunted place. A local entrepreneur ran organized trips there after dark and called them Haunted Tours. Elizabeth had been talked into taking a tour by a group of friends. A bad mistake, as it turned out.

During a tour of the old cells, they all felt a disturbing atmosphere. This was soon followed by cold chills and a strange smell that came and went, a cross between rotting meat and cat urine. Within minutes, the women had goose bumps and felt ill. Then, Elizabeth felt a cold hand touch her shoulder from behind. This made her jump and she quickly left the building.

Everyone but Elizabeth was okay, once outside, but she could not get rid of the smell and still had goose bumps and tingling chills. Over the next few days, these problems grew worse. Soon she began hearing a voice; this was an objective voice, like a real person talking in her ear. This terrified her at first, and she thought she was going mad. Although this is a classic symptom of schizophrenia, hearing a voice was her only symptom.

The voice told Elizabeth it was her spirit guide and that they had great work to do together. It said she must begin developing herself, preparing for the coming Earth changes, when she would be a leader and teacher. These are typical of the mission-bestowing messages Negs often use to gain favor with humans.

Elizabeth was not interested and just wanted to get on with her life. She ignored the voice as much as she could, hoping it would go away. But it soon began to punish her for her lack of interest. This took the form of what Elizabeth called "goosing," which she described as mild but startling electric shocks from her head to toes. This happened frequently day and night, depriving her of sleep; soon Elizabeth began having nightmares and heard strange noises around her house. The spirit kept restating its original words, saying it knew best.

Elizabeth sought the help of a new-age group in her town. After hearing her story, the group leader encouraged her to make friends and work with the spirit. She also invited Elizabeth to join the group, but Elizabeth was not impressed and wanted nothing to do with all this.

I agreed to help her, but explained this would involve some experimentation. It was fascinating to work with someone experiencing an objective voice. I had heard such a voice myself on several occasions prior to this. Elizabeth said she felt a light tingling, starting in her feet and spreading rapidly up her legs and torso a moment before each voice episode. (This was similar to my own experiences with objective voice.)

I communicated with the entity through Elizabeth. It was not evil, but it was not exactly good either. It was vague, deceptive, and frequently contradicted itself. It flatly refused to leave, repeatedly stating that they should get on with their development work in preparation for the coming Earth changes, which it said would start in 1995.

I do not know if anything I did helped. I could not remove the offending entity, but after a few weeks, Elizabeth's problems were reduced to more tolerable levels, and she went on her way. She heard the voice less frequently, the goosing and other phenomena stopped, and she slept better. I moved out of town soon after this and we lost touch, but a few years later, I heard Elizabeth had joined the new-age group in her town and was channeling the same spirit.

Negative Energy Links: Neg-contaminated objects can cause problems for susceptible people. Objects can provide links with Negs associated with the object's previous owners. These links can also attract Negs to where a contaminated item currently resides, giving Negs a foothold into new areas. Psychic attacks, Neg influences, and hauntings can result from having contaminated objects in one's possession.

The principles involved with this are similar to the principles of psychometry. Psychometry (psychic sensing of the energies of objects) is a popular method of using extrasensory perception (ESP). Persons using psychometry give readings for people by holding personal items and psychically sensing ("reading") them. A sensitive can also do this with a flower, reading impressions left in a flower by the person who held it.

Secondhand Items: Secondhand furniture and clothing, ornaments, and bric-a-brac can contain residual impressions (vibrations if you like) of previous owners. Personal items, especially hard objects worn on the body such as jewelry and watches, absorb the vibrations of their owners. The longer an item is worn, and the more the owner values it, the stronger these vibrations will become. Letters, books, photographs, and other such personal items can also provide strong links.

Sensitives will often feel the vibrations of previous owners when they touch secondhand items. In its most basic form, this type of sensitivity will cause an intuitive response, affecting whether or not the sensitive likes or dislikes such objects. It's always best to trust one's instincts when considering secondhand objects; and typically women are far more sensitive in this respect than men.

Body Parts and Fluids: Body parts, such as hair, nail clippings, and blood and other bodily fluids, contain the strongest of all personal vibration links. Through these, Negs can easily track and locate people. For this reason, care should always be taken to dispose of these things carefully. It's also wise to think twice before giving a lock of hair to anyone you do not trust.

It's fairly well known that voodoo dolls and other such items used for magical practices must contain a part of the person they represent, i.e., fingernail clippings, hair, and blood. This is common to all forms of magic, black and white. While deliberate magical attacks are rare, they are always dangerous. If body parts or personal items are acquired by a skilled practitioner, a magical attack can be lethal. Menstrual blood and semen are the most prized substances for deliberate magical attacks.

Accidental psychic attacks will always be stronger if the attacker has in his possession a personal item of the intended victim, such as a lock of hair, nail clippings, a photograph, letter or piece of jewelry, or clothing. Any of these can provide strong enough links that could enable psychic attacks to occur, even if the attacker has no knowledge of magic, or deliberate intent to use it.

The most usual scenario, in which an accidental attack involves a personal item, is when a jilted lover broods over a letter or photograph of his/her former lover, maybe while holding or wearing something like a jacket or lock of hair belonging to them. This level of despair and brooding can be enough to precipitate a strong psychic attack on the person. Any Negs attached to the jilted lover could use this link to locate and attack the target.

In this chapter, we have looked at the various ways Neg exposure and contamination can occur, including the risks involved with keeping bad company and living unwholesome, unspiritual lifestyles; how drug and alcohol abuse increase the risk; how circumstance, beliefs, and psychic sensitivity affect individual susceptibility; how children are more vulnerable than is commonly believed; how sexual contact and assault can pass on or generate

Neg-related problems; how dangerous practices like occult dabbling and black rites can cause serious long-term problems; how group protection methods often fall down in practice; how haunted houses and cemeteries have concentrations of Negs and ghosts, and why these places should be avoided at night; and how secondhand items and body parts can provide links with Negs.

Taking all these into consideration, it is clear that common sense and prudence can help you avoid the most common sources of Neg-related problems to a great extent. The next chapter expands on this by describing the most common types of psychic attacks.

5

Types of Psychic Attacks

There are many ways psychic attacks can occur, and there are as many potential causes and sources. This chapter defines and discusses the most common types.

Psychic Influences: A negative psychic influence can be defined as a negative thought, urge, or compulsion that is inconsistent with the true nature of a person. This is caused by a telepathic, hypnotic, or emotional broadcast originating from a mind other than the mind of the person experiencing it.

A low order of psychic influence, for example, can be experienced by talking to any good salesperson. However, anyone who is passionate, selling goods or ideas, will exert some level of psychic pressure on an audience. The more skill and natural ability salespersons have, the stronger will be the psychic pressure they broadcast, and the weaker the defenses of people experiencing this pressure, the more they will be influenced by it.

Psychic influences among humans are a natural part of life. For example, a man pursuing a woman may exert a strong psychic influence to convince her to agree to his advances. This influence may affect her day and night, but it will always be stronger in his presence. But there is no malice, psychic attack, or damage in this case, just psychic coercion. This same type of situation can also arise in commerce, where one person persuades another to make a trade or deal. Each time a person succumbs to a psychic influence, its source gains power. The reverse applies, and each time a psychic influence is resisted its source loses power.

Psychic Attack: Psychic attacks involve related but stronger influences than these and involve more energy and direct pressure. The energy involved can generate various types of paranormal phenomena; the degree of phenomena experienced is stronger if victims are mediumistic, thereby providing a source of energy to power the phenomena.

Typically, people under attack will first experience nightmares and other such nocturnal sleep disturbances, plus anxiety attacks and symptoms of stress. They can also experience a variety of unusual ailments such as dietary intolerances, sudden illnesses and infections, stomach and bowel disorders, muscular cramps, pricking and jabbing pains (especially in the feet), plus misfortune and bad luck in just about everything. Typically, the lives of people under strong psychic attacks start to fragment and come undone.

Psychic attacks always include some form of influence. Peculiar, unhealthy, or socially detrimental urges are common. Preexisting weaknesses will be exploited and magnified, often to obsessional levels. For example, if one has a mild drinking problem, this can escalate to an obsessional urge to drink continually under a psychic attack's influence.

Psychic Attacks by Living Humans: The simplest of psychic attacks are caused by the intrusive emotional energies exerted by strong personalities. This type of pressure is evident to sensitives when they argue with a person of strong personality. The pressure is usually first sensed in the solar plexus accompanied by mild confusion, a difficulty in organizing one's thoughts. This can escalate into other symptoms, such as loss of attention, sudden tiredness, sweating, head pressure, headache, chest pressure, difficulty breathing, disassociation from reality, nausea, and vertigo.

In its worst form, this can progress to cause stomach cramps, vomiting, diarrhea, fainting, and physical paralysis similar to that caused by extreme fear; one can even be forced out of body.

The more severe symptoms are caused by Negs working from inside the human psychic aggressor. In a way, it can be said Negs reach out from inside their living hosts to pressure and control others. Some Negs live vicarious pseudo-existences through their living hosts. While varying in intelligence, strength, and experience, Negs generally have huge egos and are petty and vindictive. They like attention and delight in controlling, manipulating, and tormenting others.

People with strong Negs inside them are generally single-minded, moody, and easily offended. They are always trying to further their control over others. When these people are angry or in a bad mood, sensitives will detect a tangible negative aura and psychic pressure surrounding them; this is especially noticeable at close range and decreases with distance.

Unintentional Attacks by Living Humans: Conditions that can cause unintentional psychic attacks arise when one person (the psychic aggressor or source) becomes annoyed with another person (the target or victim). If the aggressor broods or obsesses over this annoyance, a psychic attack can result. While this can happen at any time, it will usually begin during the evening while the psychic aggressor is sitting quietly obsessing over the annoyance. The aggressor may appear to be quietly watching TV, but in the back of his mind he is seething over the annoyance.

Most people when they watch TV relax and shift into a light semi-trance state. If a psychic aggressor is obsessing about something at this time, this state can allow his resident Negs to connect with and attack the target victim. This can become worse if the aggressor continues obsessing while he is falling asleep. Once asleep, more energy is available to empower resident Negs to carry out psychic attacks.

The amount of energy available to resident Negs is a limiting factor. There is far less energy available to Negs while their living hosts are awake and using all their available energy to function, think, walk, talk, or work. But this changes when such persons relax and/or fall asleep. This is one of the reasons why most psychic attacks begin sometime after dark, especially after bedtime. When targets relax and/or try to fall asleep, they also become more sensitive and thus more susceptible to psychic attacks; this is especially so if they are mediumistic.

The strength of a psychic attack depends greatly on the power, intelligence, and experience of the Negs involved. The personality pressure that psychic aggressors can bring to bear on others is a good indicator of the strength of the Negs resident within them. While this type of psychic attack is not carried out intentionally, some people instinctively know that by brooding over their enemy's transgressions they are doing them harm. Even though they may not believe in the paranormal, in the back of their minds such people intuitively know the truth of what's going on. Ignorance of the laws involved in these matters, however, is no excuse.

Deliberate Attacks by Living Humans: Deliberate psychic attacks precipitated by living humans are uncommon, but they do happen, and usually black magic, witchcraft, or voodoo are involved. All practitioners of magic, black or white, are capable of deliberate attack, and while the rituals, devices, and intentions are different, the principles of black and white magic are the same.

Dire warnings are generally given to students of white magic about the consequences of using their craft to harm others or for self-gain. The warnings stress that whatever is sent out will come back, doubled. This means if one person causes another to have a car accident, the perpetrator will have two accidents, or an accident worse than the one "sent." Advanced practitioners of magic, however, have ways around this law. They use students to perform the rituals that would trigger a backlash. Novice students thus accrue the negative consequences of their master's deplorable actions. Not surprisingly, advanced practitioners of black magic often go through many students.

A few years ago, a woman I knew who was a novice white witch, placed a curse on a man who had wronged her. She used a wax effigy with some of this man's hair for the ritual. She was open about it and even told the man in question what she was doing. A few weeks later he fell and broke his leg. The backlash happened a couple of months later, when the woman in question fell out of a tree and broke her leg. Her leg did not heal properly and several weeks later had to be broken again and reset. The end result was this woman had two broken legs and suffered for the best part of a year, while her victim broke his leg once and recovered in a couple of months.

A few months ago, I met this woman again. She was complaining about a man who had wronged her and saying that she was planning to curse him. I reminded her of what happened last time and how it would likely happen again. But she was so angry she did not care. She was prepared to have two broken legs just so this man would suffer. To me, this is not only unethical, verging on evil, but it goes against common sense.

Many decent, highly spiritual practitioners of white magic may recoil at the thought of this and believe incidences like this rare. Keep in mind that instructional books on magic are freely available in bookstores; luckily, the majority of people do not have the training and skill to follow the instructions even if they have the books. Yet some people make up for this lack with natural talent and instinctively know how to do this, and often they have no qualms about doing such rituals.

The consequences of deliberately attacking another person can be enormous. As mentioned, negative energy always recoils back upon the perpetrator. Such disreputable behavior also attracts negative entities; working with Negs in this way, even if Neg involvement is unknown, can form strong bonds, and Negs *always* demand something in return for their help.

Attacks Precipitated by Neg Spirits: Whether it's intended by living humans or otherwise, Negs are always involved in a psychic attack. But Negs do not need living humans to direct them, unconsciously or otherwise, to carry out psychic attacks. They are capable of doing this unaided. Some Negs are intelligent, thinking beings, while others are like animals, acting on instinct. Most are opportunistic loners by nature; some are dangerous to humans, and some are not.

A primary motivation for Negs is to feed off the energies of living beings to support their needs. The fact that most Negs also attack and torment victims often is a secondary consideration. Fear and suffering caused are often incidental to Neg energy feeding, but they are also a means to an end. Negs will often torment humans because this is the easiest way to break through their natural defenses. Our fears are our greatest weaknesses, and Negs will always exploit these to their own ends.

Random Psychic Attacks: Random attacks occur when circumstances bring susceptible persons into contact with Neg-carrying hosts and/or with free-roaming Negs. These types of attacks often have no apparent reason. They are usually of short duration, unless the Negs concerned are in the habit of forming long-term attachments with humans. Not all Negs desire these; many free-roaming Negs can be likened to insects or wild animals that only feed when the need arises.

Long-Term Attacks: Long-term attacks can occur when Negs attach to humans and then attack them regularly. A lengthy attack, lasting for weeks, months, or years, will often involve an intelligently orchestrated campaign. The underlying intention is to slowly break down a person's natural psychic defenses, to strengthen a Neg's energy body attachments, and to improve its psychological controls. Attacks may repeat at regular intervals, often at particular times of the year or when suitable circumstances arise.

Single or Group Attacks: Psychic attacks can affect one person or many. Often a person under psychic attack is the only one in a family or group to experience any symptoms, while people around them may not sense anything, but some psychic attacks have a wide focus that can affect groups, even families. The more sensitive members of such groups will, of course, sense the symptoms more keenly than insensitives.

Attacks that Follow Family Lines: Some Negs follow a family line down through generations. Their long-term interference can thus be deemed hereditary. This is not unusual, as Negs will attach to each new generation of children. This provides hereditary Negs with a constantly renewable energy source. Some Negs will even replicate themselves and spread their influence through a family tree. Hereditary attachments can result from curses cast on a family line, as a powerful curse can last many centuries.

Attacks on Children: Psychic attacks on children are extremely common. Most children will, at one time or another, experience some form of Neg-related psychic attack. Unfortunately, babies are unable to tell what is happening while older children are generally disbelieved when they report psychic phenomena. Imagination and bad dreams often account for a high incidence of nightmares, night terrors, and other such nocturnal childhood problems, but not all of these maladies have such simple causes.

Children are prime resources for Negs because they are young, have unformed personalities, and malleable minds that are easily cracked open, attached to, conditioned, and influenced. They also have an abundance of life energy. Taking all this into account, it's not surprising most Negs make a beeline for children whenever they are available, especially if they are sensitive, mediumistic children.

Negs are opportunists. During psychic attacks on adults, their focus will often shift to include any children present. Apart from being easy, energy-rich targets, children are often used as part of a campaign against adult targets. Children are used to destabilize and weaken adults, to spread disharmony and negative atmospheres throughout a family. Negs thrive under such conditions.

Attacks on Pregnant Women: Pregnant women sometimes experience psychic attacks. Certain types of Negs seem attracted to pregnant women, and they may seek to attach to the mother to bring the unborn child within reach. The type of psychic attack used is similar to the night terror attacks (also called sleep terrors) often used on children. Pregnant women under such attacks will usually experience a number of waking paralysis episodes (also called sleep paralysis), often accompanied by feelings of dread and terrifying visions.

For example, both my mother and sister experienced similar psychic attack symptoms during their first pregnancies. While pregnant with her first child, my mother had bouts of waking paralysis, feelings of dread, and an image of a tall man in dark clothing approaching and molesting her paralyzed body. My sister had an identical experience during her first pregnancy. My mother recognized the signs and kept watch over my sister day and night for several days. I was present during one such attack.

My sister twitched and whimpered in obvious distress, but could not be woken. All we could do was pray and comfort her until it was over.

Over the years, I have spoken to a number of women who have had similar experiences. This type of attack seems more common during first pregnancies, and only affects a small percentage of women. It's reasonable to suggest that because of the similarities between pregnancy attacks and night terror attacks in children, there may be a relationship, such as the types of Negs attracted to pregnant women may also be attracted to children.

Ill Health Attacks: Ill health can also attract a Neg's attention and result in psychic attacks. When people are ill, their natural defenses are low as the physical body diverts its energy into healing itself. During a serious illness and its convalescence period, energies can become so depleted that natural psychic defenses become nonexistent. It's common for seriously ill people to reach a point where they begin seeing people and beings that others cannot see. This shows a weakening in the veil between the physical and subtle dimensions, but such weakness can expose sick people to unseen beings and their influences.

It is wise to have in place some of the passive countermeasures given later in this book as a defense against ill health attacks. Ideally, a sick room should have plenty of natural light and be well ventilated with fresh air; it should be a cheerful room with plants, fresh flowers, bright colors, and cheerful music. If a strong, positive atmosphere is generated, Negs will be less attracted to the room and its occupants.

Panic and Anxiety Attacks: Panic and anxiety attacks are complex psychological disorders that can ruin lives. In my experience, these can result from psychic attacks and Neg influences; this is especially so where symptoms are nocturnal only or where the onset is at random and for no discernible reasons. I have had success helping people with these conditions by applying the countermeasures given in this book.

Side-Effects of a Neg Invasion: Once a psychic attack has occurred, victims are often left with an enduring weakness. Because of this, more such attacks are possible in the future.

Subtle changes occur in the mind and energy body of a victim after the first successful psychic attack. This is especially so in cases in which a victim's inner defenses have been seriously breached. People with a history of psychic attacks and Neg influences often realize they were changed by early attacks. Subsequent attacks always have similarities with earlier ones; the same weaknesses are exploited time and again. People have often remarked to me that it seemed as if earlier attackers left "notes" tagged to them, listing weaknesses and giving directions on how best to get at them. Many believe their aura was damaged and holes made in it, weakening their natural defenses. These weaknesses seem visible and available to all new attacking Negs. It would be logical for new attacking Negs to use what is readily available, resulting in similar patterns arising during all subsequent psychic attacks.

In this chapter, we have taken the first steps towards understanding psychic attacks and the wide range of phenomena that can be involved. The differences between psychic influences and psychic attacks are also becoming clear, as are the roles Negs play in these. We have also seen how common mind-to-mind human psychic influences are quite different from influences and attacks involving Negs.

In the next chapter, we will delve further into the principles and mechanisms involved with psychic influences and attacks and see how these relate to possession. We will explore the telepathic interface that allows Negs to interfere with humans in the first place. For psychic influence, attack, or possession to occur, there must be common mental ground between humans and Negs. As the only thing humans have in common with Negs is the mind, this interface must exist within the human mind. We also will look at energy body attachments and see how Neg attacks follow predictable patterns.

6

The Underlying Principles
of Psychic Interference

Exploring Neg-related activities is no easy task. There are many variables to consider and significant parts of the phenomena will always remain hidden to us. This chapter reveals some of the underlying principles at the root of all Neg-related problems, based on long-term study of psychic influences and attacks. It is obvious that Negs have strong telepathic abilities, but the way Negs influence, attack, gain control of, and sometimes possess, some people indicates there is more to this equation than simple telepathy. Negs also affect the physical body, causing a variety of physical symptoms and disorders, so the human energy body (also called the etheric body) is very likely involved as well.

Telepathy is the ability to send or receive information from one mind to another. All humans have innate psychic and telepathic abilities, but these are not normally recognized because the average person cannot intentionally use them. Some minds can sense and influence other minds, as well as sense and influence emotions. The human mind can also be affected by minds from other dimensions, by spirits. All spirits, including Negs, are nonphysical mental beings with telepathic abilities of varying strengths. Spirits stimulate telepathic receptivity in sensitive humans, such as through various forms of channeling or mediumship.

We know where the physical brain is, but locating the elusive nonphysical essence of the mind is not so easy. Likewise, intellectually grasping anything beyond the physical dimension is difficult without previous personal experience to support the task. For example, you cannot point and say *"that* is the astral dimension" or *"this* is my mind" or *"that* is the spirit world,*"* even though much evidence supports their existence. Unseen dimensional levels (and their inhabitants) are known to affect the physical dimension (and its inhabitants). A mind-to-mind interface must exist between the physical and nonphysical planes to allow this.

The energy or etheric body is a reflection of the physical body in a subtle form. It contains the brain (and its memories) in a nonphysical form. Logically, these subtle aspects of the brain and mind form a part of the human/spirit interface because they extend into nonphysical dimensions; this is especially so during sleep. Telepathic and psychic sensitivity increase during sleep, as does hypnotic suggestibility. This makes sleep the prime time for Negs to interfere with humans, to insert core images, to form attachments, and to insert posthypnotic suggestions.

Core Images—Key Doorway for Negs

Core image is a descriptive term for an abnormal area of conscious or subconscious memory. These are enduring psychic disturbances that can be generated by unpleasant or traumatic experiences. These exist as mental images, as little knots of painful memories and unresolved issues. The human mind generates natural shields to protect itself from intrusive subtle energies and psychic influences. Core images generate and accumulate negative energies, which can cause holes to appear in these shields. Negs make use of these holes to gain access to the human mind. In a way, the shadowy holes that core images cast provide

Negs a way into the human mind and a place in which to hide unnoticed.

Core image treatment (see part III) is in some ways intimately related to all modern psychological and self-help therapies. These involve various ways of probing and resolving negative experiences (core images) and changing how these affect the mind and body in positive ways. But core-image work goes beyond these traditional forms of psychology by tackling problematic mental imagery directly.

There are many different types of core images and there are many ways they can be generated, but all share similar properties. Most bad memories drift away and get lost to memory, outwardly troubling people less and less the more they are forgotten. But if Negs latch onto them (much like bacteria entering an open wound), they can fester and cause serious problems. Let's consider some of the types of core images.

Natural Core Images: Natural core images result from real-life traumas, bad experiences, and painful, unresolved issues. The more painful or traumatic the incident, the larger and more powerful can be the core image it is capable of generating. However, the definition of any bad experience is relative to one's perspective on it at the time. For an adult, these bad experiences may stem from car wrecks, broken romances, or losing loved ones; for children, from losing much-loved pets or toys, from being scared by an animal or creepy movie.

The number of core images accumulated during a life, and how strong these are, is directly related to how sensitive a person is. Sensitive adults and children can easily be traumatized by seemingly trivial experiences. This type of sensitivity plays a significant role in the mysterious equation of who is and who is not susceptible to serious Neg-related problems.

During childhood, most of us accumulate many natural core images. Most of these are trivial matters that quickly fade from conscious memory. As adults, we begin accumulating a new set of core images, from social dramas, misfortunes, and life's ups and downs. The power a natural core image can generate stems from its inner significance to the person experiencing it.

When a Neg first approaches, it uses whatever existing core images it can find to gain access to a human mind. It will choose the strongest natural core image available, especially if this is the first time that person is being approached by any Neg. It will choose the largest hole it can find in that person's natural psychic shielding. But this only gives it a tenuous, temporary connection with its victim's mind. It needs more than this to secure its position.

Implanted Core Images: Implanted core images are telepathically created and implanted within the subconscious mind. Negs implant multiple core images to secure their positions. Negs insert these during sleep, by telepathically manipulating dreams and implanting post-hypnotic suggestions. Many bad dreams and nightmares stem from core images being implanted, reinforced, or used during sleep. Multiple implanted core images form networks of shadows within the mind, like a spreading infection. The larger these networks grow, the more influential Negs become.

Spontaneous Core Images: Mind's-eye imagery can be spontaneously produced in response to Neg activities that involve core images. This type of imagery is always unusual and often disturbing. However, this is usually only noticeable in people who have some level of clairvoyance (mind's-eye vision ability). This type of imagery will also sometimes be seen by non-clairvoyants during pre-sleep or meditation or remembered through dreams. If traced back through core-image treatment methods, the root core images behind this type of mental imagery will often be discovered.

Discovering Core Images

I discovered implanted core images by accident while pondering the Neg/human mental interface. I had long suspected that trauma memories were involved, and I was searching for more effective ways of tackling these. I needed to know how Negs used these to exert influences and carry out psychic attacks. I had several real-life problems that I suspected involved trauma memories. I reasoned that if I could find a way to deal with these I would be able to teach others how to do it.

I became suspicious after I had a series of very disturbing dreams over a three-week period. All shared a similar theme. These were not normal bad dreams and had no identifiable cause. Each woke me, leaving me stressed and sweating, my heart pounding. Once awake, I obsessed over these dreams and could not get them out of my mind. Their images were so disturbing that I had frequent flashbacks in the following days. I would experience heart-pounding stress even as I fantasized changing the events they portrayed.

The setting for these dreams was the rail depot of a transport company I worked for in my youth. I did have a traumatic experience near there, but that event had nothing to do with the mental imagery I was experiencing. In hindsight, I now know that the natural core images generated within me by the real-life event were used to implant the disturbing mental imagery that was troubling me. Implanted core images were grafted onto a natural core image.

The first dream scenario involved me making a foolish mistake, getting covered with acid as a result, and dying horribly. The next scenario involved a similar foolish mistake by myself, but this time many innocent people were covered in acid and died horribly, which induced great feelings of guilt in me. These were ridiculous mistakes that I would never have made in real life.

Suspicious, I worked on these core images during trance meditation to see what I could discover from them. I relived each of these in my mind's eye and again found myself experiencing the same symptoms of stress. I chose the first dream and examined it closely. I relived it again and again and studied the effects it was having on me. Then, I had an idea and used my Body-Awareness Hands[1] on it.

I grabbed hold of the scene and pushed it away from me, as if it were a still picture, until it became a glowing, indistinct, pale rectangle, about postcard size, that I could see in my mind's-eye. I then tried to turn it over, to see if anything was behind it. I felt strong resistance from it and it would not turn over.

I am very good at body-awareness actions and this resistance surprised me. I felt enormous mental pressure building within me as I wrestled with it. It was like trying to turn over a huge concrete slab. Gritting my mental teeth, I applied more and more pressure until I felt it start to move. Giving it everything I had, I felt a distinct ripping sensation inside my mind as I forced it all the way over. In my mind's eye, the clear image I saw beneath the turned core image stunned me. It looked like a large tree stump with a jumble of gnarled black roots half torn from the ground. The exposed roots were torn, but the rest were intact. I saw black, ropy lines of force extending from this structure and curving back towards me.

Continuing with my experiment, I adapted a technique from Dion Fortune's *Psychic Self-Defense* called the Ritual of Severance. This ritual (normally done during an OBE) involves using an imaginary sword and flaming torch to cut and burn away Neg attachments. I imagined my awareness hands were holding a sword and a flaming torch. In my mind's eye, I attacked these roots enthusiastically with the sword and then incinerated them with the torch. I then called up the original core image and relived it again in my mind's eye, but now it caused no disturbing symptoms of stress. When I repeated the previous process, it turned over easily and beneath it I saw nothing. After this, I treated the next suspicious core image, beneath which I also found a similar root-like structure, in the same way.

Spurred on by my success, in the weeks to come I dragged up every bad memory I could recall, including early childhood memories, and treated these in the same fashion. Some potential core images turned easily in my body-awareness hands and had nothing underneath. Others were difficult to turn and had a variety of peculiar structures beneath them, including the occasional Neg. Some core images had roots and ropy-black lines of force; some had what looked like pipes, wires, and circuit boards; and some had abstract symbols and unidentifiable structures. Because of the great variety of mind's-eye imagery produced, I concluded these were being created by my subconscious mind as it attempted to visually depict the negative energy structures I was disturbing.

The first time I encountered a Neg while turning over a core image, I nearly leaped out of my skin. I am not afraid of Negs, but it was a shock. While turning over a core image, I felt something move under my body-awareness hands. As I turned it all the way over, an astral snake appeared between my body-awareness hands, thrashing violently. It was not happy, especially when I started attacking it with my sword and torch. It thrashed and reared for about twenty seconds before it escaped to God-knows-where. Astral snakes are a fairly common Neg type; they look like large, black snakes with spiny fringes along their backs, although their size and length seem unimportant. This one looked to be about four feet long and as thick as a man's wrist.

I have been hooked on core-image work ever since I discovered it. This is, by far, the most effective way of dealing with core images and Neg attachments (and resolving the problems they cause) that I have found. The end result of the session with the astral snake was that a peanut-sized granuloma (a gristly tumor) on the back of my neck disappeared overnight, as did some health problems that had been troubling me for years.

I continued experimenting with this core-image removal method, pondering the how and why of it all. Then, I had an experience that taught me more about the nature of Negs and implanted core imagery. This was an OBE mind-split.

I was trance meditating at my desk one afternoon, thinking deeply about the nature of core images. A spontaneous OBE began, and I felt all the usual OBE exit sensations: rapid heartbeat, vibrations, and tingling energy surges. Yet my consciousness remained centered in my physical/energy body. This was not unusual for me, so I continued with my meditation, knowing an OBE was in progress.

I soon developed real-time astral sight (I began seeing into the real-time astral dimension around me) and saw a shadowy version of my room through my closed eyelids. Then, a hand appeared in front of my face, coming from my left. It seemed to be waving at me, as if trying to get my attention. I looked to my left slightly with astral sight and a head came into view. It was myself, or rather it was my astral double (the aspect of me having the OBE). My vision of "him" was crystal clear and in full color. I observed him with peripheral vision and noticed he was also looking straight ahead. By not looking directly at each other we were both deliberately avoiding any connection between us that might cause astral feedback.[2]

I saw my projected double pulling something from my physical body. He lifted it and showed me what looked like a length of black rope. He pulled on it and a horrifically clear 3-D vision appeared before my eyes. I saw a close underwater view of my two young sons drowning in a swimming pool. Each had a foot tied to a heavy weight lying on the bottom of the pool. They were reaching out to me and pleading for help. The vision continued for about half a minute and I watched them struggle and die.

I have considerable self-control, but heart-pounding stress symptoms arose and sweat ran down my face. I had no memory of this vision or of ever having a nightmare remotely like it. But it came with a hauntingly familiar feeling, like something important I had forgotten.

This scene faded away and I saw my projected double's hands move again, pulling on another black rope, producing another equally scary vision about my two young sons. This time they were inside an industrial oven being roasted to death—a disturbing thing to watch. I had no memory of ever having had such a nightmare, but again it felt hauntingly familiar.

From this experience, I concluded that these were core images that had been implanted into my subconscious memory without my knowledge, probably during sleep. These powerful core images were obviously related, as their central theme suggested. Somehow my projected double (my astral counterpart) had stumbled upon a way of showing these to me (his physical counterpart). I ended the session and felt my astral double reintegrate with me with a tingling, surging, upward, whole-body rush.

Unfortunately, I did not recover my projected double's memories from this experience. But this was not surprising, given the strength of my physical body's memories of that same time period. As mentioned earlier, the physical brain will only store one memory for a single time period, and this is always the strongest memory. I treated these core images later during another session, and found Negs hiding beneath each of them. In this case it was astral spiders.

Energy Body Attachment Points

Energy body attachment points relate to particular areas within the mind. In a way, it can be said that Negs reach through core images and sink energy connections into the substance of the energy body, using the mind/body connection. This in turn affects the particular part of the physical body that relates to the energy body at the point of insertion.

The most noticeable physical manifestations of energy body attachments can be skin blemishes. Anything from dry or rough patches of skin to various moles, cysts, nevi, tumors, granulomas, etc., can result. The skin of the physical body reacts when its energy body is penetrated by Neg attachments. The end of an attachment may involve an organ inside the physical body, but it has to pass through the outer layer of the energy body in order to do this. This outer layer of course is represented by the skin, which is the largest organ of the physical body.

Different Negs have different methods and patterns of energy body attachment. The principles of how energy body attachments affect the physical body are similar to how acupuncture works: small needles are inserted to affect subtle energy flow through the energy body, which in turn affects how the physical body functions.

Elements of a Psychic Attack

All Neg influences and psychic attacks involve core images and/or energy body attachments somewhere in the equation. The main thrust of many Neg attacks seems to be to use whatever core images are available to attack and weaken the victim and eventually to attach to the energy body. During direct psychic attacks, Negs are not usually attached to a person's energy body, and my experiments with active countermeasures support this view. Therefore, the fact that a person is being attacked generally indicates that energy body attachment has not yet taken place. The exception to this is when Neg attacks result from positive lifestyle changes. In this case, damaged and broken Neg control devices (core images and energy body attachments) are being reinforced or reinserted, necessitating a new campaign of psychic attacks.

Neg-induced telepathic influences are always used during psychic attacks, to alter normal thought patterns in negative ways. Emotions are powerful stimulants, and how we feel inside has a lot to do with our external behavior. Emotions affect how we react to our environment as well as how we interact with others. For example, if one is angry, one may find loving kindness and helpful advice irritating and meaningless. Energy body manipulation, combined with telepathically induced mood alteration, forms a strong control device. This can induce pleasurable endorphin releases, bursts of vitality, and sudden elation. This can also induce tiredness, depression, and anxiety. By applying these devices over time, inflicting reward and punishment, Negs psychologically condition people to respond to Neg-induced thoughts and urges.

Through these methods, natural weaknesses are exploited and steered in directions Negs prefer. When people obey Neg compulsions, they are immediately rewarded with pleasurable endorphin releases, cessation of pressures, and short-lived feelings of euphoria. If Neg compulsions are resisted, punishment usually involves psychic pressure and induced anxiety, that is, very strong urges to submit to compulsions. Punishment generally lasts much longer and will tend to come in waves. However, if a compulsion is fought off, Negs will eventually back off and try something else. But Negs will always rekindle old compulsions and bad habits from time to time, testing long-term resolve.

Negs do most of their work while victims are asleep. They are generally more active at night and people usually sleep in dark, quiet places. Negs need dark and quiet to manifest at levels where they can more easily affect people's minds. The presence of light and sound will not, in itself, break a psychic attack, but it does make life more difficult for Negs. People are also far more receptive to Neg telepathic broadcasts when they are dreaming. Negs broadcast disturbing dream scenarios to cause bad dreams and nightmares. Most people are not aware while they are dreaming, and to the mind, dreams are as real as normal waking reality.

Traumatic dream experiences can generate core images in much the same way as real-life bad experiences can. Bad dream experiences are quickly forgotten, especially if dreamers do not awaken during them. But whether they are remembered or not, all bad dreams are stored in our subconscious memory, and all have the potential to become core images.

Out of all the emotions or states of mind that can be generated by dreams, three stand out as the most significant in core image-producing dreams: fear, sexual desire, and guilt. Fear of death is the strongest primary instinct there is. Fear for the death of a loved one is also particularly strong and guilt inducing; fear of being pursued and powerless to defend oneself is also strong. Variations on these themes are frequently used by most Negs.

Fear has many levels, but at its highest, it terrifies, numbing the mind and paralyzing the will. This level of fear can cause natural psychic shields to drop completely. If this level of fear is experienced in the waking state, it can cause physical paralysis—one becomes "frozen" with fear. Negs induce terror through telepathic dream manipulation as well as by broadcasting a fearful presence that can be sensed.

Neg-induced dream sex causes a similar compromised psychic shield condition, as does extreme fear. A submission of will and permission of sorts causes shields to be lowered. Most people dream about sex occasionally and will sometimes experience orgasm during sleep. This is natural and does no harm, but Neg-induced sex is different. It is always guilt-inducing, often involving perverted, forced, or socially unacceptable forms of sex.

Guilt is a powerful weapon and most Neg-related dream interference produces some measure of guilt or remorse. Whether guilt is acquired in real life or unconsciously in dreams, it will always exist on some level of memory and can thus be used to empower core images. Guilt undermines everything positive in a person and creates negative mental conditions. For all these reasons, it is clear why guilt plays such an important part in Neg operations.

Negs use mixtures of these devices in conjunction with more direct methods of psychic attack. Every person's psychology is different and what affects one person may not affect another. Variations in psychic attack patterns arise from Negs identifying and attacking weak points in individuals.

The average psychic attack lasts about thirty days and then fizzles out. Subsequent attacks may, or may not, occur afterwards. This depends largely upon the source and nature of an attack and the reason behind it, and also upon the strength and resistance of victims. For example, if a living person is angry with the victim and is causing the psychic attack, it may be short lived. But Negs are opportunists, and if they succeed at implanting significant core images and energy body attachments, they will usually return. This can result in repeat attacks over time.

Some Negs will attempt to form long-term symbiotic or parasitic relationships with people. Whether attempts to do this are made or not depends upon the type of Neg involved. Some live vicarious existences roaming from person to person, while others like to move in and settle down. If a long-term "relationship" is planned, attempts follow to evolve a network of core images and energy body attachments.

Negs follow fairly predictable patterns when carrying out psychic attacks. Why Negs employ the same methods time and again is something I have pondered for many years. All things being equal, whether it involves direct psychic attack, symbiosis, or possession, all Negs use similar methods. I think the main reason for this is that these methods have always worked for Negs, possibly for many thousands of years, so why should they change their ways? I also think that, because many Negs are ancient, these methods may have become habitual. This factor is extremely important to understand when analyzing and working against Neg-related problems. That their psychic attack campaigns are predictable is one of their greatest weaknesses.

Negs are not good at adapting to changing circumstances. While often intelligent and always cunning, they are not original "thinkers." When they do not get expected results from their actions, they are often bamboozled. If changes made by victims circumvent expected results, they may try another set procedure, but they will not experiment with new methods. Negs may influence people to stop doing whatever is causing the Neg problems, or they may switch from fear to sex or vice-versa, but they will not come up with a new approach. They will doggedly keep applying and reapplying the same procedures. Many of the countermeasures are based on taking advantage of Neg inflexibility.

The most powerful "weapon" I have in my anti-Neg repertoire is education. The knowledge of what can happen and how Negs work can help armor people against their effects. For example, believing that bad thoughts and compulsions come from inside your mind is disempowering and guilt-inducing. Negs use this to their advantage. But knowing the potential for Neg involvement with these mental states can greatly ease the guilt factor. Once guilt is assuaged, Neg control devices are significantly weakened, and this is a good start for living a Neg-free existence.

In this chapter, we have examined some of the underlying factors involved with psychic influences and attacks. Ahead, we expand upon this and look at signs and symptoms that can indicate Neg-related activity. We shall examine other factors like sleep disturbances, Neg seduction and sexual assault, plus the mental instability, bad luck, and health problems that Neg activities sometimes cause.

7

Recognizing the Signs of Supernatural Activity

The signs and symptoms of supernatural activity, either environmental or personal, are many. What can happen is influenced by many variables, such as the environment; the sensitivity, strengths, and weaknesses of people involved; whether or not children are present; and the strength, experience, and nature of the Negs involved. This chapter reviews the detectable signs of supernatural activity and psychic attack as I have come to recognize them after many years of study.

Mediumistic People and Ectoplasm

People who regularly experience supernatural phenomena are usually mediumistic. They radiate and are innately capable of producing more psychic energy than non-mediumistic people. This comes with greater psychic sensitivity and brings with it Neg susceptibility. Most people are unaware they actually *contribute* to the psychic phenomena they experience.

Mediumistic people attract spirits to them, both good and bad, like moths to a flame. The energy they produce and radiate can be compared with ectoplasm, albeit much finer. Ectoplasm is a vaporous, fluid-like substance that can be thought of as a condensed energy body derivative. It has many forms, visible and invisible. Varieties of this basic substance can be used by spirits to produce all kinds of phenomena. Ectoplasm is the active substance involved with all forms of physical mediumship such as transfiguration and materialization. With transfiguration, a cloud of ectoplasm covers the medium's head and shoulders; spirit faces build up on this ectoplasm mask and become visible. With materialization, a medium (usually in trance) produces copious amounts of ectoplasm, which spirits then use as a cover to make themselves visible.

Ectoplasm is usually a pale, creamy, glow-in-the-dark kind of substance that is cold and clammy to the touch. It can look and feel solid. This is why disembodied hands sometimes produced by spirits during psychic attacks feel cold and clammy. The production of ectoplasm causes tingling goose bumps in sensitives. I have sensed this effect at a distance of 60 feet during a transfiguration demonstration; I have also felt these symptoms during Neg manifestations.

Ectoplasm is sensitive to light and sound. It can manifest under low light conditions, but is destroyed by strong white light. This is why transfiguration and materialization séances are normally held in semi-darkness or under dim red light. Strong lights and sharp sounds are detrimental to all forms of ectoplasm. This is part of the reason why most spirit phenomena occur at night or inside buildings where it's dim and quiet. Light and sound thus make good countermeasures against ectoplasm.

Sensing Environmental Signs and Symptoms of Neg Presence

The words "haunting" and "haunted" are casually used to describe most kinds of supernatural activity, but a traditional haunting usually involves repeating phenomena of a predictable nature— the same ghostly apparition climbing the same set of stairs.

When examining a house, I stop in every room and hallway, closing my eyes and reaching out with my senses for cold spots of

Neg disturbances. If I find anything—most people can do this— it causes a prickling, tingling, or cold shiver on my back and neck; a strong Neg presence causes my mid- to upper-back to cramp. This type of muscular spasm is a common response to Neg presences, as noted by many healers and sensitives I have known.

Troublesome Negs "nest" in cold spots. These areas will often have a cold, creepy feeling to them that make sensitives anxious. These are always the darkest, quietest areas Negs can find. Negs will retreat to these places during daylight hours and/or use these areas to gather strength before manifesting and/or causing phenomena elsewhere. I have solved a number of household Neg problems simply by increasing the light and ventilation in dark, suspect areas. This can be accomplished by opening curtains, doors, and windows, or by installing new light fitting, stronger bulbs, or skylights.

You should also examine the atmosphere of an environment. Atmospheres affect some people more than others, depending on their sensitivity. If you walk through a Neg-troubled house, you will sense an uneasy, depressing atmosphere. This will have a creepy edge to it, similar to the uneasy atmospheres found at night in cemeteries, morgues, and funeral parlors.

Sensitives can have difficulties breathing in a strongly Neg-affected atmosphere. The risk of direct psychic attack in such areas is always high for sensitives, as their presence will be instantly noted by all Negs present. Sensing cold patches in a room or registering goose bumps and hair-prickling sensations on the body are common indicators of a Neg presence. Uneasy atmospheres always strengthen after sunset and weaken after dawn.

Strange noises, such as knocks and taps on walls, ceilings, furniture, and fittings, are the most common symptoms of paranormal activity. All buildings make noises as timbers and joints expand and contract through moisture and temperature fluctuations, and these noises are identifiable. But this does not explain the knocks and taps on walls, furniture, and fittings so often associated with supernatural activity. Many spirit noises seem to come from empty space. The word poltergeist means "noisy ghost," which is apt. They cause unexplainable noises and move physical objects, often in plain view. In my experience, a wide variety of spirits can be responsible for poltergeist activities, from earthbound spirits to Negs.

Psychokinesis, or PK, is the most likely means used to produce spirit noises and poltergeist activity. As all spirits are by nature telepathic beings, it is reasonable to suppose that some would have abilities such as PK. My field experience supports this. Sometimes poltergeist activity can be extreme, with heavy physical objects being moved or thrown about a house. This suggests some spirits such as poltergeists may have stronger PK abilities than others.

Spirit noises and poltergeist activity are always more intense during psychic attacks. Objects will sometimes go missing or be moved for no apparent reason. In areas of strong poltergeist activity, objects will often be thrown at people, indicating deliberate harm is intended. I have been present while sledgehammer-strength blows have occurred, damaging solid objects like doors, walls, and furniture.

Disembodied voices are another common symptom of paranormal activity, and are common during psychic attacks. These can be heard at any time, but are more frequent at night, especially during pre-sleep. Common noises include the traditional dragging of chains, heavy footfalls, and the wailing lament of seemingly tormented spirits—the familiar sounds of a haunted house.

Strange odors are common during paranormal activity. Anything from perfume to cigar smoke to body odor can be smelled, and even very mild manifestations can produce strong odors. Many spirits emit a particular smell, almost like a signature odor. Psychic smelling (the ability to detect nonphysical smells) is the strongest and easiest to use of all psychic abilities. Most people have some level of this ability, although it's rarely recognized as such. The most common smell noted during strong Neg manifestations is something like a mixture of rotting meat, feces, and cat urine. The stronger the smell, the stronger the potential for Neg manifestations.

Astral lights and tiny ping lights are common symptoms of paranormal activity. Pings are pinpoints of light, appearing and vanishing in a split second, and are often brightly colored. Good spirits and spirits of recently deceased persons will often cause colorful pings. Black pings indicate the presence of Negs and are not a good sign. This especially applies to clusters of black pings that look like swarms of black flies. This is a sign that a strong Neg presence is building up. Areas like this should be immediately evacuated until the manifestation ceases and appropriate countermeasures are taken to cleanse the atmosphere.

All paranormal light flashes are called astral lights, and these are well known to occultists and parapsychologists as indicators of supernatural activity. Sightings of large creamy blobs, or groups of blobs moving in groups, inside or outside affected houses at night, indicate a high potential for strong manifestations. Blobs of astral light stay visible much longer than pings, often for several seconds or more. Some blobs can be a yard or more across, but astral lights this size are rare and usually singular. Thick columns of pale light are also possible. Strong astral lights can be captured on video or photographic film; many unexplainable pictures of astral lights exist, and most books dealing with supernatural phenomena contain examples of these.

Apparitions—ghostly shapes and figures—are common spirit manifestations. The most common apparitions are seen with peripheral vision as momentary glimpses of movement. Another common type of apparition resembles an opaque or transparent person. Stronger apparitions can be seen with the eyes and often look like persons with glowing white sheets covering them, showing blurred features—the classic ghost.

Disembodied hands, faces, and other body parts are also common. Some apparitions can manifest strongly enough to be touched, or, they can themselves touch living people. Their touch always feels cold and clammy, as is the nature of ectoplasm.

Symptoms Heralding a Psychic Attack

Typically, psychic attacks start with some kind of nocturnal interference, like obsessive looping thoughts, nightmares, waking paralysis, cold shivers, and "things that go bump in the night." The incidence of phenomena like astral lights and pings, strange noises, and unpleasant atmospheres will increase. Seeing frequent shadowy movements in one's peripheral vision is a sure sign something is wrong. The more indicators there are, the more likely it is that some type of psychic attack or manifestation is in progress. The following types of phenomena can occur in any combination and degree of severity. However, some of these will always be experienced during psychic attacks.

The Classic Incubus Nightmare: The most common and well-known symptom of psychic attack is called the incubus nightmare. An incubus is an evil spirit visiting a sleeping person. During an incubus nightmare, the victim wakes up feeling a heavy weight pressing down on his chest, as if a heavy person were lying on top of him, making breathing difficult. This usually includes some measure of paralysis or difficulty in moving. The victim feels incredibly weak, as if his vitality were drained away, which is often what is occurring. A fearful atmosphere or evil presence will usually be sensed. A typical incubus nightmare lasts only a minute or two, but it can be a terrifying experience.

In my opinion, the incubus nightmare is misnamed. It's a generic term used to describe many forms of nocturnal Neg attacks. During a true incubus attack, there is always intense sexual stimulation. If there are no sexual elements to an attack, then some other type of Neg is involved, and not an incubus. An incubus (also called a succubus) is a particular type of Neg that specializes in draining life energy through the forced sexual stimulation of its victims.

Localized Atmospheres and Phenomena: Victims of psychic attack and/or possession will often have localized negative atmospheres following them about. This will spread whenever they stay in one place for any time, especially if other sensitives or mediumistic persons are present. Various phenomena will also tend to happen around victims wherever they are located. For example, if a person under psychic attack visits a house with a calm spiritual atmosphere, where no phenomena normally occur, it will not be long before pings of astral lights and knocks and taps of spirit noises begin.

Living Psychic Guard Dogs: Another sign of psychic attack, or of persons carrying Neg "hitchhikers," is that sensitive animals will tend to be wary of them. Sensitive animals will often act defensively and/or aggressively around such people. While not all animals are sensitive, psychic pets are invaluable. If sensitive pets are forced to live in Neg-contaminated areas they will act strangely, becoming depressed and anxious; they may also run away from home.

My dog, Gus, a German shepherd, is sensitive and impartially senses all visitors to my home. Some people are able to fool me, but they never fool Gus. I make it a rule never to invite people back if Gus does not like them. Like his predecessors (other sensitive dogs I have shared my life with), Gus has never failed me. Sensitive people attract and are attracted to sensitive pets, and animals grow in sensitivity by living with sensitive owners.

Psychically sensitive dogs can be trained to react to and warn owners of Neg presences, that is, to become psychic guard dogs. I have seen my dogs attack empty space for no discernible reason, barking and leaping at things unseen. The aggression, movement, and noise of a barking dog are good countermeasures, drawing attention to and distracting Negs, making their manifestation difficult. Early warning allows countermeasures to be applied sooner than would otherwise be possible; this is good, as Negs are always at their weakest when they first arrive on the scene.

Warning Bells: The energy body has a sensitive outer layer which extends several feet or more in all directions during the normal waking state, depending on psychic sensitivity. This is the outer edge of the human aura. The human aura reacts in the presence of spirit beings of any type, good and bad. This is a natural safety mechanism, similar to the way humans are naturally afraid of spiders and snakes, and this reaction varies from person to person, according to psychic sensitivity.

Cold shivers, goose bumps, hair prickling sensations, and anxiety are nature's warning bells, urging us to move to safety. Our minds can overcome this to some extent. For example, if one works with snakes or spiders, one slowly loses fear of them. Likewise, if one works with spirits, one eventually gets used to them and loses one's fear of them. But the warning bells always ring, so it's wise to trust one's sensations and move away when these "bells" are detected. No matter what you suspect is causing them, it's wise to move away until either the cause is identified or the danger has passed.

Warning-bell sensations do not indicate what type of spirit might be present. The same sensations are caused by good spirits, recently deceased loved ones, or astral projectors. Experience will teach you the difference between these and Negs. But until this is gained, it's wise to control wishful thinking and not jump to conclusions. I always advise caution.

Symptoms Indicating a Direct Attack

Direct psychic attack is heralded by nature's warning bells, but other sensations quickly follow these first signs. Most direct attacks begin with a noticeable patch of tingling in the spine, usually between the shoulder blades or in the mid-back area. If one has had minor spinal injuries, tingling will often be localized in a damaged area. This is a reliable indicator of direct Neg assault. This can happen at any time, day or night. When it does, it is advisable to immediately leave the room or area.

In its strongest form, a direct Neg attack seems like a massive panic or anxiety attack. This can cause one's whole body to feel pressure, have difficulty in breathing, and experience partial or full paralysis. Persons can be so wracked with shivering they become frozen to the spot. This level of direct assault indicates the Neg involved is not attached, but is trying to penetrate one's natural defenses. Some Negs will expend all their strength to do this quickly. Direct attack can happen anywhere, indoors or outdoors, but it is more common at night.

Other common symptoms include: goose bumps and adrenaline rushes with no discernible causes; muscular cramps; sharp pains; nausea; head pressure and headaches; pricking and jabbing sensations. These last feel like one is being stuck with pins or sharp objects; pricking and jabbing can occur anywhere, but they are especially common in feet and toes. I think this is why demons are traditionally depicted as small, horned devils carrying sharp tridents, and why Hell is depicted as existing below ground. If people suddenly feel sharp pricks and jabs in the soles of their feet while walking, it would seem as if unseen beings underground were jabbing at their feet.

Associated symptoms include: localized areas of buzzing (as if a fly were buzzing next to one's skin); localized tingling or tickling; hot or cold patches of skin; throbbing and fluttering sensations in the skin. These are more common at night, while one is resting or during pre-sleep.

Strange Noises and Voices: Astral noises and voices, most often heard during pre-sleep, will be more intense and more frequent during psychic attacks. The types of astral noises vary enormously as does their volume. It is common to hear furniture being dragged, spirit knocks and taps, growling, muttering voices, or strange voices talking among themselves. Sometimes, you will hear voices clearly addressing or discussing you directly, often in critical or intimidating ways. Noises and voices are scare tactics to unnerve you, but they cannot do you any direct harm. Ignore them as much as possible.

Circular Thoughts and Core Images: Have you ever lain awake half the night, your sleep disturbed by endlessly looping, repetitive thoughts? This is understandable if genuine problems are bothering you, but when the subject matter is trivial or imaginary, it's likely to be Neg-induced. Often, the only reason people experience this is because they wake up or have trouble sleeping in general. The circular thoughts would have happened without them knowing anything about them if they had stayed (or fallen) asleep as usual.

Induced circular thoughts are an insidious form of psychic attack and/or subconscious programming. They can deprive people of sleep and weaken their natural defenses against Neg influences. The subject matter of these thoughts can also be related to core image creation, carried out by Neg telepathic, hypnotic broadcasts. Always note the subject matter, then check and treat for core images later when you are less tired.

Visions and Nightmares: Disturbed sleep, bad dreams, and touches by unseen hands are common during psychic attacks, as are glimpses of movement from the corner of one's eye, or even from behind closed eyes. Spontaneous visions are also common, especially if one has some level of inner vision ability, either dormant or realized.

The most common time to see things is in between sleeping and waking, that is, during pre-sleep or while waking. Sometimes you will see visions of accidents, often involving friends and loved ones, or leering demonic faces; sometimes people will wake up from bad dreams and see the content of their dream as if it were hanging before their eyes. This last is an indicator Negs are trying to implant core images.

It is a mistake to think this type of vision is prophetic, as it can lead to worry, guilt, and torment, conditions that will be used by Negs. Remember, Negs are cunning: they will sometimes show genuine prophetic scenes from the near future, such as visions of natural disasters and airplane crashes. When these come true, the validity of other visions that are inaccurate and worrisome is reinforced. This is why it is wise to discount *all* dreams and visions you have during suspected psychic attacks, no matter how startling or persuasive their content. Dreams of sudden wealth and winning the lottery are also commonly used to gain attention and to torment people. Like circular thoughts, all of the previous can be telepathically, hypnotically implanted by Negs during the sensitive dream state.

Addiction and Weakness Exploitation: During psychic attacks, all existing weaknesses will be exploited and used against you. For example, if you have a minor problem with alcohol, the urge to drink will suddenly grow strong. Urges will come in waves, always strongest at the worst possible times, such as when you are under temptation or stress. This is often an intelligently orchestrated trap, encouraging people to activate Neg control devices.

It can aptly be said that the fear and stress caused by psychic attacks can drive even a saint to drink. But urges and addictions can be worked against, if one is aware of what is happening, and *why*. Substance abuse, especially of alcohol, weakens energy body defenses by eroding natural psychic shields. Induced alcoholism is probably the most common long-term attack used by Negs against natural sensitives. When one's natural shields are weakened, this opens one to further Neg invasion and influence. Any damage that excessive alcohol use causes will slowly repair itself, but only if alcohol is avoided and long-term healthy lifestyle changes are made.

Waking Paralysis: Waking paralysis (also called sleep paralysis) is a peculiar condition that many people will experience at some time in their lives. When it strikes, a person wakes up paralyzed, unable to move a muscle or even blink. Although this condition usually only lasts a minute or two, it can be terrifying.

There is more to the waking paralysis state than is commonly believed. Unknown subtle mechanisms relating to how the mind animates the physical body are involved. Studying waking paralysis through the examination of case histories is not enough; other types of related experience phenomena must also be examined for common factors. Waking paralysis is well known to be associated with out-of-body experience. During waking paralysis, some type of OBE and mind-split effect will always be in progress. Natural OBE-ers usually suffer frequent bouts of this during their lives, but waking paralysis is complex and no single explanation covers the whole field.

The physical body is not truly paralyzed during waking paralysis. Nerve connections between the physical brain and body remain intact; the mind is simply disassociated from the body and unable to reanimate it. Therefore, waking paralysis is as much related to OBE as it is to overshadowing and possession.

Waking paralysis usually brings some level of astral sight. This means a person in this state is often able to see through closed eyelids into the astral dimension around him. When this happens, they are sometimes able to see spirit entities, which can be unsettling and frightening.

I suspect that waking paralysis may sometimes be caused by Neg telepathic interference as core images and energy body attachments are created. Waking paralysis episodes could even be deliberately induced by Negs to cause trauma. However, most Negs seen during waking paralysis episodes act surprised and retreat from sight immediately. Keep in mind that Negs go to great lengths to hide their presence, activities, and intentions.

Many waking paralysis episodes are accompanied by unexplainable feelings of dread; often there is a tangible presence sensed to be coming from a particular direction. However, this feeling of presence can be accidentally caused by the mind-split during an OBE such that the presence sensed is often that of a person's *own* projected double. The feeling of dread is often caused by anxiety and fear produced by the astral feedback phenomenon—that is, the shock of telepathically connecting with one's own astrally projected double while it is out of your body.

To cause waking paralysis, Negs would need to induce fear in multiple aspects of a person during sleep and during the mind-split to generate the emotional feedback necessary. In theory, this process should be no more difficult than causing circular, repeating thoughts through telepathic, hypnotic broadcasts. Such a broadcast during sleep would have a pronounced effect upon the dream mind, projected double, and the energy body and physical mind, especially if one woke up in the middle of it. Generally, in most cases, waking paralysis is not deliberately caused by Negs, but is an accidental side effect of hypnotic, telepathic broadcasts designed to implant core images.

Overshadowing: Overshadowing is a mild form of temporary possession, although terms like "heavy influence" or "spirit control" can be used instead. Episodes of overshadowing can last from a few seconds to many days, although they usually only last a few minutes. It can happen unnoticed, and its cause is usually unsuspected, but it can cause slight changes of mood to major personality alterations. Familiar sayings actually reflect the overshadowing experience: "I'm not myself today;" "I don't know what got into me;" "He's got the devil in him today;" "I don't know what came over me;" "I don't know what possessed me."

Overshadowing can happen frequently during psychic attacks. It is one of the main control devices used by Negs. Not only the target person will be affected, but those around him. Overshadowing is used to affect situations in negative ways, to damage relationships, cause arguments, and disrupt harmony. It unbalances and thereby weakens the target by spreading discontent, causing negative atmospheres, and by reducing emotional support from friends and loved ones. All of this alienates and weakens the intended victim.

The most common signs of overshadowing are sudden mood swings, marked changes in personality, and loss of self-control, all of which are of a temporary nature. These can happen very quickly and persons experiencing them will go from a congenial to an argumentative state in seconds. The change is quite noticeable, if one learns to *recognize* the symptoms. Facial aspects can also change, with eyes deepening and even changing color; often it will appear as if a shadow has fallen over the victim's face.

Overshadowing is similar to what happens to channels and trance mediums, when they go into trances and channel spirit beings. Sometimes this is so heavy that channels will not remember what happened or what was said through them. As there are marked similarities among overshadowing, channeling, possession, and waking paralysis, it is likely the same mechanisms are involved in all.

Spectral Hands and Hitchhikers: A variety of peculiar phenomena can occur during dreams, lucid dreams, and OBEs that can indicate Neg attachment to one's energy body. When you look at your hands during an OBE, they will begin "melting" within moments, like white ice under a blowtorch. However, if a strong Neg is attached to you during an OBE, your hands may sometimes look ghastly, elongated, and spectral. This can also indicate overshadowing or possession.

Another symptom of Neg attachment is that during dreams and OBEs you feel you are carrying around another body, as if someone were riding you piggyback. This is an astral hitchhiker. Some hitchhikers will appear to be asleep, others awake; some will attempt to frighten you while others will ignore you. The sleeping hitchhiker phenomenon may also involve a sleeping spirit you have accidentally picked up. I am fairly sure both spectral hands and hitchhikers are Neg-related.

Seduction and Sexual Assault: Sex does not always form a part of psychic attacks. However, while people sleep, they may not even be aware this is happening. It depends on the nature of Negs involved and whether or not sex forms a part of their makeup and/or habitual procedures.

Erotic dreams are common, normal, healthy experiences and most people will experience these at some time during their lives. But seduction and sexual assault are devices Negs use during psychic attacks. Whether these devices are used or not depends on the type of person being attacked and on the type of Neg involved. Heterosexual as well as mixed-gender varieties of sexual assault are possible.

Neg-induced seduction is accomplished by hypnotic, telepathic broadcast, plus direct energy body stimulation of the genitals and the primary energy center (or chakra) situated in the genital area. When stimulated in this way, people can wake up highly aroused, sometimes remembering an erotic dream. An erotic broadcast will often begin during pre-sleep, but unlike erotic dreams, genital stimulation does not stop when the dreamer awakens. It continues until that person experiences orgasm. The genital energy center stimulation causes this to be a more powerful orgasm than usual.

During an entity seduction, several things happen: erotic thoughts and imagery are hypnotically, telepathically broadcast into the mind; the genital center is stimulated; the energy body expands and its natural defenses weaken; some form of permission is sought; and sexual energy is drained. Many Negs seem to solicit permission or submission from victims, and this appears to enhance their attacks. By complying with psychic seduction, one gives emotional permission for further Neg interference. This can develop into a long-term relationship. I have known several people to become sexually addicted to unseen spirit lovers. They have no idea what these beings are but cannot resist their sexual advances. In time, Neg seduction no longer requires the victim to be asleep; Negs begin approaching during pre-sleep and eventually during waking hours.

Neg sexual assault is different from seduction. It can be a terrifying, soul-destroying, painful experience, like rape. I have experienced versions of this and seen it happen to others. It is usually combined with waking paralysis and is doubly disturbing when it opposes one's natural sexual orientation.

The unseen, unfelt part of Neg sexual assault is that a victim is forced to endure traumatic experiences in the waking state. Most people try to forget it by driving the memory into their subconscious, but the result is a natural core image that Negs can use to strengthen their controls.

Sexual Fantasies: Teenage hormonal enthusiasm aside, for many people spontaneous sexual fantasy is their greatest weakness. Neg-induced sexual fantasies are a powerful control device. The main thing to watch for is when sexual fantasies arise *spontaneously* for no apparent reason, unaccompanied by any mental association that could reasonably have triggered them.

For example, if a sexual fantasy arises in the middle of a soccer match, one should be suspicious of its source. If the urge to act sexually on such a spontaneous fantasy is strong, the possibility that this is a Neg-induced compulsion should be considered. If spontaneous fantasies are frequent and powerful, occurring many times each day, one should be suspicious of Neg involvement.

Group Interference and Strife: An important aspect of psychic attack is the length to which Negs will go to spread disharmony and strife. In groups or families, people will be used against one another to disrupt harmony. This type of interference will tend to follow the intended target, negatively affecting everyone he interacts with.

This is especially true if victims manage to withstand other aspects of psychic attack. They will often find their friends, family, and work associates causing them problems or turning against them for no apparent reason. For the target of psychic attack, anything positive they do will be worked against by Negs. For example, if victims are successfully dieting, they can expect more invitations to fattening lunches and dinners than usual.

Mental Instability: In my experience, psychic attacks always cause some degree of mental instability in victims, and often in the people around them. During psychic attacks, many strange influences and pressures are at work, and often a great deal of fear and tension are involved. This is especially so if direct psychic attacks and heavy phenomena are occurring.

Dealing with unknown and unseen forces is destabilizing for anyone. These days, many people do not believe in spirits or Negs, so the advice and support of friends and loved ones is usually minimal. This alienates victims of psychic attack and fills them with self-doubt; most think they are having breakdowns or delusional episodes.

When this happens, it's time to slow down and take some time out, to have a good think about what is happening. Write everything down; list all the events and phenomena; examine your thoughts and actions as they relate to the situation; apply logic and common sense. If you can examine the situation calmly and honestly, without becoming emotionally charged, this can be helpful.

Bad Luck and Ill Health: Bad luck and ill health are common but subtle symptoms of Neg interference. The presence of Negs within people changes the way they interact with universal law. One's natural set of attractions and repulsions (those unseen forces that guide us through life) are corrupted by the presence of Neg influences in one's space.

I have found it common for people under psychic attacks to lose money or jobs, have cars stolen, make bad investments, break things, have relationship problems, or suffer a string of minor accidents, illnesses, and injuries. Basically, nothing in life can be expected to go smoothly when one is under psychic attack; one is as if cursed or crossed with negative influences.

Yet it is wise not to overreact to unpleasant life events and thereby give Negs more ammunition to use against you. Look upon significant negative events in your life—losing a job or partner—as openings for change. It might hurt, but if you can do nothing about it, being optimistic helps. I have had times during psychic attacks when I experienced bad luck in the extreme. This is especially noticeable while driving a car. At such times, it seems every other driver, child, and pet I encountered had suicidal tendencies. Being aware I was under psychic attack, I have resorted to slowing down to a ridiculously slow speed, yet even then people and pets seemed to launch themselves suicidally at my wheels.

Understanding what can happen and *why* helps you weather this type of problem, as does slowing down and being cautious. While it's unhealthy to expect strife, it's wise to take extra precautions if Neg influences are suspected in your life.

8

Spirit Activity Problems Common to Children

While I wish it otherwise, children are not immune to Neg problems. Most children are more sensitive than adults and thus more open to psychic attacks and influences. There is no age of consent: Neg problems can begin at any age, even in infancy. Adults were once themselves children, and many adult problems stem from childhood Neg problems. Negs do not suddenly let go when children grow into adults.

When faced with supernatural phenomena, many people slip into denial. Many will deny spirit-related phenomena, even while repeatedly witnessing it firsthand. Many adults also disbelieve their children when they complain of supernatural problems. "It's all in your imagination" is the usual response. Adults' or parents' lack of belief and closed minds when faced with the supernatural gives Negs better access to children. No matter what Negs do to children, those children will not be believed if they report negative activities. Children are often punished for worrying their parents so that parents may avoid the unsettling consequences of having to believe in the children's stories of monsters under the bed.

Some people will twist things around to suit themselves. Many parents will not entertain the possibility that unseen forces might be able to harm their children but they will often claim their children are protected by angels while they sleep. Angels are about as supernatural as it gets. The belief that all children are protected by guardian angels day and night is, in my opinion, unrealistic wishful thinking. Angels definitely exist. I have seen too many not to believe. But in my experience, angels will only rarely interfere in the affairs of humans. They have their own agendas and generally keep to themselves. They will only intervene in very special cases. To rely on angelic protection by default, without so much as offering a prayer, is imprudent.

The only thing standing between children and Neg-related problems is the parents. Family lifestyle and associations, the home environment and parenting methods are important factors, and these have a lot to do with how exposed and vulnerable children are to Neg-related problems.

While some people freely admit to Neg problems with children, no one knows what to do about it. I have questioned many learned spiritual teachers about psychic attacks on children. While I have heard a lot of philosophy involving children's karma, I have not heard any practical advice.

The bottom line is that no one knows what to do when it comes to helping babies and very young children under Neg influence. Eventually, everyone falls back on the karma explanation, the only thing in the new-age paradigm that offers a reasonable explanation. According to karma belief, Neg attacks are caused by bad karma, which results from bad deeds performed during previous incarnations. It has also been said to me many times that people should not interfere with children's psychic attacks, that children's karma should be allowed to work itself out undisturbed. I do not agree with this, fortunately for the many children I have helped over the years.

One could apply the karma theory to the experience of encountering a tiger. One could say it's "natural" for a tiger to take and eat a child, that the child's "karma" plays a part in causing this to happen. But we do not allow tigers to roam our towns; we shoot, fence off, and drive them away; we do not sit meekly by citing "karma" while our children are taken by tigers. This same logic should apply to the "tigers" we cannot see: something can and should be done to protect our children from these unseen predators.

An Example of a Psychic Attack on Children

I have had a lot of experience with children suffering psychic attacks, Neg interference, and possession. I began shifting my focus to children many years ago because more can be done for them than for adults. Most adults, I have found, want someone to wave a magic wand and make their Neg problems go away. Most have enough difficulty making small changes, let alone major lifestyle alterations. But if one stops *early* Neg attachments from happening, children will grow up relatively Neg-free—decidedly a good start in life.

The youngest child I have seen under direct psychic attack was a nine-month-old boy. At the time, several adults and older children were in the house with us, but no one sensed anything out of the ordinary. The Neg in question was definitely singling out the baby. Babies cannot talk, but I know the symptoms of infant attack. The mother had not suspected Neg invasion, but her son had been having screaming fits and had not been sleeping well for several days. Several visits to a children's hospital, and a diagnosis of colic, had not helped.

The attack began soon after they arrived at my home for an early evening visit. The baby was sleeping peacefully when suddenly he screamed, his face red, eyes closed, fists clenched, his body spasming and rigid. I sensed a presence and picked up the baby. It was like picking up a lump of wood: the poor chap was rigid. A wave of cold, prickling shivers and cramps in my upper back confirmed my suspicions of Negs.

With his mother's permission, I took the infant outside and turned on the garden hose, gushing water along the ground. I held him by his arms and walked across the running water, dangling him like a stiff puppet, his little feet just brushing the water. The instant we crossed the running water he stopped screaming and his body relaxed. I lifted a happy, squirming, smiling, and now yawning baby into my arms and cuddled him. He fell asleep in seconds and I returned him to his mother. Exhausted, he slept until midday the next day.

I have used this water countermeasure countless times with children and babies under direct Neg assault, always with the same instantaneous results. By "instantaneous," I mean relief is obtained the moment running water is crossed. Many other people have used this method on their children with similar good results.

Natural Defenses and Weaknesses of Children

Children can be exposed to Negs in many ways, through chance circumstances beyond anyone's control or exposure to playmates, family members, and family friends. A child's primary defense against Neg influence is mental activity. A child is a hive of mental activity during waking hours. Even though children are sensitive, Negs cannot easily exert influences because of this activity. But children have weak moments, sleep being their most vulnerable time; therefore, early symptoms of Neg interference usually involve sleep or pre-sleep disturbances.

Children are soft, yielding, and easily frightened. Their personalities have not yet congealed and they have little defense against hypnotic, telepathic, and psychological pressures. Even though children's active minds protect them to some extent, they still can become exposed to these pressures while playing, especially if they are tired. If you watch a group of children playing, you'll see they soon form a group mindset similar to the group mind that forms in excited crowds.

Crowds are easily influenced and controlled, and it is well known that crowd violence can be orchestrated by a few key agitators. If an idea is presented to a crowd at the right time and in the right way, the crowd will act on the idea as a group, without thinking. Crowds will often do terrible things that no individual within the crowd would ever do alone.

My point here is that when children play in a group, they develop a pack mentality. Individuals are thus psychologically exposed to other members of the pack. In this way, they also become exposed to any Negs attached to other children. Group behavioral changes and peer pressure are only the tip of the iceberg; much is going on beneath the surface that we barely understand.

When children have nothing to occupy them, they become bored and daydream; and their minds slow down. This increases their susceptibility to Neg influences. Television viewing is a good example of this and is a curse for some children. They enter a passive, trance-like mental state and become highly susceptible to Neg influences, especially when tired. Playing computer games is preferable to watching TV and videos, as games require active mental participation, and they keep the mind busy. Keeping children fit, active, and busy in a healthy way are important in reducing Neg influences.

Moreover, the quality and activity of family life have a lot to do with whether or not children are at risk. The company parents and children keep is an important factor, and disreputable company should be avoided. Adults will often pick up Neg "hitchhikers" and carry them back into the family home, exposing their children to Neg influences.

There are three key signs to look for as indicative of Neg attacks on children: sleep disturbances, night terrors, and sleep deprivation.

Sleep Disturbances: The reasons Negs actively target children are not hard to understand. Children are easy, uncomplicated targets with an abundance of life energy. They are a prime resource for Negs with few mental defenses; their minds are easily influenced. Some Negs seem to specialize in targeting children, attaching to and integrating with them. This is a kind of "illegal" reincarnation, appropriating life after life down through the ages. For these reasons, any type of sleep disturbance in children should be carefully examined and never left unattended.

Once a child is targeted by Negs, a predictable campaign begins. With all children I have studied in these situations, I have encountered few variations. Negs are not good at adapting to change, and this is their major weakness. If Neg processes are interfered with severely and for a long enough time period, Negs will often go away and look for greener pastures.

Night Terrors: Nightmares and night terrors are the most noticeable indicators that Neg events may be occurring. These are serious matters that should never be ignored. It's estimated that twenty percent of children and ten percent of adults experience nightmares. Children should be gently questioned after nightmares to help identify the source of their problem. This will often involve nothing more than images from a movie or TV show, but keep in mind that anything capable of frightening or troubling children can be used by Negs to create core images. REM (rapid eye movement) is always present during nightmares, showing the dream mind is active and causing problems. Children can be easily wakened from nightmares and will often remember the details.

Night terrors (also called sleep terrors) are different from nightmares. Five percent of children and one percent of adults suffer night terrors. With night terrors, no REM activity is present, indicating the dream mind is not the cause. Children may cry out, but are difficult to wake. When woken, they are often distraught, bathed in sweat and exhibiting a rapid heartbeat. The cause of night terrors is never remembered. While the cause of night terrors is unknown, they are often hereditary.

Children also experience the incubus nightmare that involves paralysis, fear, difficulty in breathing, and the sense of a heavy weight on the chest. They will often whimper or cry out in their sleep. Parents can usually tell if their children's sleep is disturbed; if it is, they should be wakened to break the disturbance. If they cannot be easily wakened, the water-crossing countermeasure should be used. It is generally safe to wake people from any sleep disturbance, including sleepwalking.

Children should not sleep alone when having episodes of nightmares or night terrors. If Negs are involved, sleeping between the parents is the best way to protect children. If disturbances continue even in these circumstances, parents should take turns watching for a sleep disturbance, waking the child whenever it happens. If disturbances are frequent, parents should concentrate on protecting their children; active and passive countermeasures should also be applied as necessary.

Sleep Deprivation: After Neg-related bouts of nightmares and night terrors, a sinister process of sleep deprivation might begin. Negs may hold children in the trance-state throughout much of the night; their bodies may be allowed to rest but their minds are held awake and active. During this time they are shown a string of animated visions. I learned this by observing and questioning many children; I also drew on my own childhood experiences with this.

Children's eyes will often be open and moving rapidly during this process (REM). Rapid eye movement indicates dream activity, but there is more to this than bad dreams. Children are difficult to wake during the open-eyed REM state; they are often sweaty with a rapid pulse, and phenomena such as flashing lights and spirit noises may be noted in the room.

This sleep deprivation process is similar to military-style brainwashing. During brainwashing, a person is denied sleep until his mind is weakened to the point where he becomes highly vulnerable to suggestion. He can then be reprogrammed; memories, beliefs, and personalities can be dramatically altered in this way.

It is wise to check your children's eyes as often as possible during and after bouts of nightmares and night terrors. Use a small flashlight to see if their eyes are open. If they are open, children should be wakened and made to walk over running water; other countermeasures should be applied as necessary. Children should also be gently questioned after being wakened, as they may be able to tell you what happened.

Even if symptoms of night terrors have not been noticed by parents, it's a good idea to check your children for this if behavioral changes occur or if your children appear tired and listless during the day. If children are getting plenty of sleep but appear tired during the day, something is wrong. While a medical checkup is recommended for problems that might contribute to this, nightly eye checks are advisable; checking a few times during the first three hours of a child's sleep is normally sufficient.

Integration Process: Negs Implement Their Controls

After the stage of night terrors and the sleep deprivation process, Negs will often coexist benignly with children while slowly improving their controls. Children will often be aware of Negs around them, seeing them and/or hearing their voices. Negs will often try to gain a child's confidence by *pretending* they care for them. Sometimes Negs will pretend to be invisible playmates, often pretending to be a child of a similar age to the child they are working on. Negs use rewards and punishments to condition children to respond to their prompting.

This is the same basic conditioning device Negs use on adults. Children feel bad when they disobey and feel good when they obey. Children quickly learn to keep such things to themselves as adults seldom believe children's tales and often punish them for making up disturbing stories. But the Negs will continually get children into trouble by influencing them to misbehave. It's in the nature of Negs to lie and deceive.

While some invisible playmates seem harmless, seeming is not a good indicator of intent. Invisible playmates should be judged on the *effect* they have on children. But convincing children to turn away from invisible playmates can be difficult, often driving the problem underground. Even so, parents are in a better position to influence their own children than are Negs, and good parenting can do much to circumvent problems that might arise from this type of association.

Some Negs, once successfully attached to a child, will back off until the child grows into an adult. However, other Negs will move in and begin integrating with a child's personality immediately. When this happens, Negs begin forming the dark side of a child's personality. Marked behavioral changes will usually occur at this time. For example, a once kind, generous, sociable child may suddenly become cruel, selfish, and critical.

Behavioral Changes Observable in Neg-Attached Children

Changes in child behavior are a warning sign that something is wrong. But keep in mind that children can be influenced by many sources—TV, movies, schoolmates, and friends. These are parenting problems and should be dealt with accordingly. But if no reason can be found for behavioral changes, others causes should be explored, and you should consider Negs.

Children with Neg-related problems can exhibit a wide variety of physical and behavioral problems. These may include becoming tired and listless, withdrawn, and frequently daydreaming; children may become cruel, selfish, emotionally demanding, and aggressive. They may also show signs of obsessive compulsive disorders, or a variety of other psychological problems, including attention deficit and hyperactivity disorders. While these changes can all have natural causes, they are also indicators of possible Neg interference.

If some of these symptoms come on suddenly, including nightmares, a well-known psychological profile begins to appear. These are the classic symptoms of child abuse, but what is actually happening is child abuse by *Negs*. Psychological pressures and abuses from any source have predictable consequences, and regardless of whether the source of abuse is physical or nonphysical, children will react in predictable ways.

Behavior Changes Due to Negs: I recently came across a case of child behavioral changes relating to night terrors. I visited a neighbor over a small matter and we got talking. It was not long before the subject of night terrors came up. My neighbor's five-year-old-son bounced off me into a brick wall, before charging off on some high adventure. He was laughing and yelling in play and did not realize he had cut and bruised himself.

His mother was worried about him. She said he had not been the same since he went through a string of night terrors several months before. During this time, he would scream and cry and partially wake up, soaked in sweat, but he would not fully wake even when they tried to comfort him. She said he pushed them away and seemed to think he was somewhere else, still dreaming. Nothing seemed to help so they carried him around the house until he quieted and fell back to sleep.

His basic behavior changed during this patch of night terrors. He became more demanding, hyperactive, and difficult to control; he had mood swings and his emotions seemed blunted. He became more controlling, demanding to be the center of attention all the time and becoming loud and aggressive if ignored. He also became more single-minded and less aware of the world around him. An example of this was how he hurt himself running into the brick wall, but did not notice the injury. He had recently been diagnosed with Attention Deficit Hyperactive Disorder and had been medicated accordingly.

It is not difficult to work out what may have happened to this child. He had been through the night terror process and the resulting Neg influences were affecting his personality, behavior, and self-control.

Overshadowing and Possession in Children

Incidents of overshadowing will sometimes happen unnoticed in children. Children undergoing Neg-related abuse and sleep deprivation are particularly vulnerable to this problem. Apart from sudden behavioral changes and mood swings, overshadowing is most likely to happen when children are mentally inactive and/or tired. This will often happen while they are watching TV or eating dinner, both of which require little mental activity.

When overshadowing starts, children go quiet and slide into a trance-like state. Their eyes droop and they stare fixedly for a few moments; then they take a deep breath and straighten up, as if waking themselves. Their facial aspects alter slightly, eye colors darken, and an indefinable shadow falls over their faces. From this moment on, children are capable of anything because they no longer have full control of themselves. They may move and walk differently than normal; their responses to stimuli will be changed and unusual, as will be their behavior.

I came across a case of child overshadowing while helping a family. Their four-and-a-half-year-old son had recently been through the spectrum of Neg invasion and conditioning—night terrors, pre-sleep problems, sleep deprivation, open-eyed REM, mood swings, behavioral changes. He even had an invisible friend. He also had a history (since the age of one) of paranormal activity centered on him, including poltergeists. In fact, I witnessed some of this activity while I was with him.

These problems had been going on for some time before I got involved. The boy had developed dangerous habits and his parents were at their wit's end. The boy would pour drinks into electrical appliances and suck on power extension cords. No matter where he was, he would find something electrical to play with or suck. He destroyed several appliances and had several electric shocks. It was a miracle he had not killed himself.

The boy's father was a good parent and had been trying to break these dangerous habits the old-fashioned way, but all reasoning and other passive methods had failed, including visits to child psychologists. Every time the boy sucked a power cord, his father smacked him hard, and these smacks got progressively harder.

I saw one incident in which the boy was caught red-handed. The father yelled, took the power cord off him, smacked him, and forcefully explained how dangerous it was. But before his father left the room, the boy had the same cord back in his mouth again, grinning openly back at his father. His father repeated the warning and smacked the boy even harder. This happened several times in a row, until the boy's forearm and hand became red and swollen.

Finally, the father stood over the boy, his hand raised, shouting and threatening him. It was then I witnessed the clearest case of overshadowing I have ever seen. A titanic battle raged within the boy's mind, with his eyes, facial aspects, and expression changing every few seconds. He switched from a scared little boy nursing an injured arm, to something that glared at his father with a wide, sickening grin as he reached for the power cord again. But before he could touch it he would change back and quickly retract his hand, tears rolling down his face. He changed back and forth a dozen times in a row, battling the Neg influence.

Finally, the boy won the battle, folded his arms, and did not touch the power cord again. Apart from his bruised arm, one would not know anything had happened a few minutes later. The boy played happily and was loving, polite, and helpful at least for the rest of that afternoon.

The final episode of overshadowing with the same boy came a few days later at dinner. We had sat down to a dinner of spaghetti (the boy's favorite) when it happened. His eyes drooped and flickered, and his face darkened as he was overshadowed. He glared at his father and with a sickly grin tipped his plate over his head and rubbed it into his hair. He then began throwing spaghetti at everyone, including his father. The father put his son under a cold shower, after which the boy sat watching TV, happily eating a spaghetti sandwich. I gently questioned the boy. He had no memory of the incident at the table and was well behaved for the rest of the evening.

This case happened many years ago and was part of what motivated me to begin investigating Neg influences in children. I tried my best to help at that time and had some success, but unfortunately the boy was so enamored he kept calling the Neg back. Under my careful questioning, he admitted doing this. He claimed to be lonely and to miss his "secret friend." Nothing we did shook his faith in his friend, even though he freely admitted it lied, tricked him, and got him into trouble all the time.

Children's Mystery Maladies

Children's mystery maladies are apparently serious medical problems that suddenly arise in the middle of the night, but disappear on the child's way to the hospital. Most parents are familiar with this scenario: a child wakes at 2 A.M. screaming in pain, often with a high fever. Parents rush the child to the hospital only to find themselves presenting a healthy, sleepy child to the ER doctor.

Mystery maladies can present a variety of symptoms: earaches, stomachaches, sore throats, headaches, asthma attacks, toothaches, croup, whooping cough, any of which may be accompanied by fevers high enough to panic any parent. If a condition is Neg-related, it will disappear rapidly on the way to hospital. If this happens, it's a fair indicator that children are being interfered with by Negs during sleep, and appropriate countermeasures should be applied.

The reason mystery maladies disappear so quickly on the way to the hospital is that water mains get crossed many times along the way. This forcibly removes the Neg and/or disrupts whatever energy body interference is causing the child's physical symptoms.

I have witnessed this phenomenon countless times over the years. I have also seen my own children go through this many times. This seemed to happen at random, but was most likely to occur while I was meditating late in the evening. This was especially likely if I achieved a high level of altered consciousness or had a mystical experience. At first I thought this was coincidence, but this happened time and again, always at the exact moment when I made a significant breakthrough, such that it soon became predictable.

Logically, either my high-level altered states were attracting Negs, or they were already resident in my house. Further, they were either trying to stop me, or they were simply attacking the weakest person in my house. But the timing of these attacks on my children was too precise for them to be random, so I think I was the cause.

The first few times this happened, we quickly dosed our child with pain/fever reducing medication and rushed him to the hospital, only to find ourselves presenting a sleepy but otherwise healthy child to the ER staff. It was not long before I realized what was happening. We were faced with a variety of complaints, such as earaches, croup, and stomachaches, and always with high fever past the point where seizures should have occurred. Once I realized what was happening, I used the running-water countermeasure *before* giving medication or driving to the hospital. Every time I did this, without exception, the pain and screaming stopped instantly, and the fever disappeared within a few minutes.

I am not suggesting parents delay seeking proper medical attention if their children become sick in the middle of the night. But I do recommend as a precaution that parents walk their children over running water (a water main or garden hose gushing water along the ground) on the way to their car and that they check their child's condition on the way to hospital.

Prognosis on Children's Afflictions by Negs

What will happen if a child experiences, or has experienced, psychic attacks, night terrors, and other Neg-related symptoms is difficult to say. The prognosis depends on a great many factors, including parenting, family lifestyle, and the child's natural strengths and weaknesses. Everyone is different and, while typical patterns exists, every situation will unfold in a different way.

Neg-human relationships have existed for many thousands of years. One could say this is a natural part of growing up and of the human condition itself. Negs, especially parasitic and symbiotic types, can form dark sides to some children's personalities. These are in turn opposed or countered by all the positive influences children are exposed to while growing up. More than anything, good parenting and parent/child communications can do a great deal to counter the bad effects of Neg interference. Parents are in far stronger positions than Negs to influence a child's development.

Here is a way of looking at this situation: Imagine a child with an angel on her right shoulder (whispering encouragement and right action) and a little devil on her left shoulder (whispering discouragement and bad action). With good parenting to help, these opposing influences usually balance out. This struggle between good and bad is the natural way of things, as is overcoming one's negative side and growing up to become a good person.

The Neg countermeasures described later in this book can do a lot to ward off and/or ease Neg-related problems. In my experience, breaking the initial attachment process (night terrors, sleep deprivation) is the most successful way to achieve a Neg-free existence. If Neg activities are recognized and countered early enough, Neg attachments and symbiosis with children cannot take place.

This does not mean nothing can be done for children and adults who have already lived through Neg-troubled childhoods. Much can be done, but it can be more difficult. Self-discipline and self-control must be developed, and other countermeasures used to counter and remove Neg influences. While it's more difficult than catching it in the bud and stopping the initial attachment, it can be accomplished.

9

Possession: The Ultimate Invasion of Privacy

Possession is the ultimate invasion of privacy. It's a ghastly thing to consider, let alone experience. Most people cannot deal with it and slip rapidly into denial when it's mentioned. Consequently, most deny even the possibility that something as horrific as possession could ever happen. This is understandable, but it does not help matters when you have to deal with it.

Call them evil spirits, Negs, demons, or earthbound spirits, they do exist, and some are capable of possessing humans. Exactly what they are and where they come from is a vast subject needing much further exploration. But the details are less important than the need to do something effective about it. Knowing possession is a real possibility makes you more alert to the dangers. This not only makes it a recognizable condition, but reduces the likelihood of it happening.

Negs possess people by conditioning their bodies to respond to their controls. This is achieved by Negs working through unconscious levels of the mind that relate to the autonomous nervous system (reflex system) and requires significant preparation and conditioning before full possession can take place.

Both Sides of the Possession Coin

I understand possession in an unusual way. I have been possessed myself and know what it is like. The observations I made during my own possession were invaluable to me later in my work. I also understand possession from the other side of the fence. Years ago, I accidentally discovered how to enter the bodies of awake people during real-time OBEs. This discovery was accidental and I will not go into details for obvious reasons.

During a series of daytime experiments involving twelve powerful wake-induced OBEs, I deliberately entered several awake human beings; they were strangers picked at random. With a crowd of people to choose from, I could enter some, but not others; some could be influenced, some could not. This is a type of overshadowing, a low level of possession, but it was done with the best of intentions. I did no harm and the knowledge gained has been invaluable to my work. But I strongly advise this *not* be repeated by OBE-ers, as my intuition tells me this could be dangerous to both parties.

To my reckoning, approximately ten percent of people are susceptible to this kind of direct OBE penetration, but generally, strong-minded people are not susceptible. Sensitives, of course, are more susceptible and thus easier to approach; people who are weak-minded also are wide open to this. There must be an existing inclination before a person can be made to act on it, weak-minded or otherwise. One could, for example, make a dieting person buy and eat a candy bar, but one could not make a non-drinker buy alcohol, nor a non-smoker buy cigarettes. Most people have invisible shields surrounding them of varying depths and strengths; with some people, this is like an invisible brick wall extending a dozen feet or more in all directions.

It's also possible to sift through the memories of susceptible, weak-minded people. This is difficult to comprehend unless one has experience with visual clairvoyance. Imagine flipping rapidly through the pages of a photograph album and being able to enter and experience any photograph by concentrating and willing yourself inside it. You see a confusing blur of symbols and metaphorical imagery mixed with real-life memories.

No astral projector, including myself, gets more than a few minutes of worthwhile operating time in the real-time zone. Working at this level, it does not take long before reality fluctuations destroy the real-time aspect and you enter the astral planes, which do not resemble the real world. Therefore, this is not an ability that can easily be misused, even if one knows the technique. The reason I am explaining this is because it relates to possession. It struck me while doing the previously mentioned experiments that if an OBE projector could do this much in such a brief time span, an entity living full-time in the astral environment should be very good at taking advantage of its position.

Details on My Possession Experience

In my early thirties, after many years of exploring the supernatural, I thought I had seen just about everything. I had helped many possessed people and fought off many psychic attacks. But I had a false sense of security concerning my psychic shielding and strength. Through experience, I had come to believe I could take on anything face-to-face and live to tell the tale. But I was about to get a hard lesson that would change my life.

The details of this incident are too horrific to render in much detail. In brief, while trying to free a small boy from a possessing Neg, I opened myself and gave it direct permission to enter me. This was a "take me and leave the child" act of desperation on my part. Naively, I planned to free myself of the Neg later, thinking I had a better chance of doing this than did the boy. But the entity struck like a snake the instant I gave permission. It hit me in the mouth and latched onto the right side of my lower lip, making it swell and bleed within seconds, as if I had been punched in the mouth. This also paralyzed me. I was held in my chair and tortured (this is the only way to describe it) for several minutes before I collapsed.

I recovered from this incident, but that was not the end of it. The swelling in my lip grew into a gristly tumor, the size of half a walnut, in a few days. This indicated that a strong Neg attachment point had been inserted into my lip. But this was the least of my problems. Soon, I began losing control of my body, one part at a time. The first episode of this was while reading; my arm moved on its own, picked up a book, and tossed it on the floor. This shocked me, but I still felt okay. I did not sense anything evil or threatening in or around me. Incidents of brief loss of control increased over the next two weeks. It was not long before I knew I was in deep trouble.

The episodes of loss of control culminated in an incident in which I lost control completely. I was on a roof-top car park, lifting my baby son from my car. As if a switch had been thrown, I suddenly lost control of my body. Powerless, I was marched like a puppet carrying my son to the edge, even while I was fighting my own muscles every step of the way. I suspected the Neg in me was going to make me throw my son off the roof and then have me jump.

The strength of the mental pressure I felt was unbelievable. I did not hear voices or experience insane thoughts. This was not a compulsion. I was sane and rational. I just had no control over my body, as if I had been suddenly struck with physical paralysis and someone else was now running my body. Thankfully, with a supreme act of will and some much-needed luck, I broke free of the puppet-like state at the last possible moment. But I no longer trusted myself after this event.

A couple of days later, I woke up (I seemed to have been sleep-walking) and found myself in the nursery with a raised ax. I got rid of the ax. I found myself back there the next night with a carving knife. I tried everything I knew of to rid myself of this Neg, but whatever I did was not enough. I was faced with only two "logical" choices: I could turn myself into a mental hospital or commit suicide. Then, I came up with a third option: I could surrender to my higher self and let it lead me out of the darkness rapidly overtaking my life. I sensed this would be difficult and probably kill me in the process anyway, but I had nothing to lose and everything to gain. I chose the third option. I could always kill myself later.

I had only the vaguest idea of what to do. My intuition told me I had to go away somewhere and do something, but I had no idea where or what. I decided to dive in and let it happen. Everything I knew and believed in told me my higher self would try to get a message to me. I left home and went for a walk (it was storming) with the conviction I would find the message, or die trying, and that no matter how it came, I would follow its instructions to the letter.

I slogged through the rain-drenched scrub. I cleared my mind and prayed, filling myself with the intention of finding the all-important message my life depended on. Everything I believed in told me this would happen, but I had never put this belief into practice. After hours of walking in the wet darkness, I was soaked to the skin and freezing. I started jogging to keep warm, but ran head-on into a tree. I rebounded into a ditch full of dirty water and rubbish. Climbing out, I regained my footing. Brushing myself down I found a piece of newspaper stuck to my leg. This was it, I thought as hope surged in me. I had the message at last. That scrap of paper saved my life.

I nursed that scrap all the way home, trying not to damage it. When I had some light, I saw it was a scrap of burnt, rotting, mud-stained newspaper, but with a magnifying glass, I made out a few words from an ad: "Come to . . . garden nursery . . . nestled . . . Jarradale . . . hills . . . open . . . 7 . . . days." I knew where these hills were. They were a few hours drive out in the bush (Australian for wilderness). I had no option but to follow the directions in the message. I packed a small bundle: a couple of old blankets, a ground-sheet, some warm clothes, a couple of canteens, an old kettle, and some tea.

I spent several days and nights wandering those hills, fighting the Neg inside me day and night, especially at night. At times I thought I was going mad, almost dying of thirst and exposure in the process, wandering during the day and sleeping on the ground at night. I had vowed to free myself of the possessing Neg or die. There was no way I was taking the evil thing back home with me.

Unbeknownst to me at the time, the place I chose to sleep my last nights in the hills was directly over an underground spring.

This was, I discovered later, an important factor in freeing myself from the possessing Neg.

On the second-to-last day there, I awoke as usual at first light. I was weak from hunger and feeling sorry for myself. I was half-expecting to die soon but was not afraid. For all that I was in good humor. I figured if I died I would have won the battle by default. I walked towards the small spring near my camp to get a drink. All of a sudden the gristly tumor in my lip burst. At the same moment, a huge weight lifted from me. I suddenly felt wonderful, even though I was spitting blood and bits of gristle. The lump was completely gone, leaving a bloody hole inside my lower lip.

About thirty seconds after the lump burst, I experienced the most painful Neg attack of my life. I dropped screaming to the ground. My body felt like it was tearing itself apart from the inside, all my muscles working overtime against themselves. This lasted for about a minute and then stopped as suddenly as it began. Too weak to walk, I crawled to the spring and cleaned myself up. I had some torn muscles to contend with, but I felt wonderful. The dark thing inside me was gone.

The results of this cleansing experience were lasting. For several days after this, I lived in a kind of spiritual grace and purity. No insect annoyed me and no wild animal ran from me. They seemed to sense that I was no threat to them. This grace slowly left me a couple of days after I returned home. The Neg did not come back.

In hindsight, I now know that the deciding factor in my release was that I was sleeping above an underground stream. These generate large amounts of positive energies that are detrimental to Negs.

You might wonder, as I did, how angels fit into a possession scenario. I will share another part of the experience relevant to this.

On the second day of my quest to rid myself of possession, I ran out of water. The Australian bush is a very unforgiving place. Especially in summer, one mistake can cost you your life. My mistake was to lay my waterbags on bare rock. During the night and next morning, the water leached out into the dry, porous rock. By mid-afternoon I was in serious trouble. At 110 degrees Fahrenheit in the shade, it does not take long to dehydrate, especially when you are climbing through steep, rocky hills. I searched for water, but the bush has little surface water.

I climbed to the peak of the biggest hill within range. I leaned back on a lightning-blasted gum tree that offered a spot of shade and a magnificent view. As far as I could see were rolling hills and there was not a sound that did not come from nature. I had decided to die rather than go back to civilization in the state I was in. I did not trust myself anymore and would rather end the game than risk hurting others. I settled back, smoking my pipe while I wrote short letters to my family, then I sealed them in a plastic bag. I figured my body and the letters would be found, eventually.

I prayed for help and made my peace with God as best I could under the circumstances. Deep inside I half-expected a miracle, but the logical part of my mind did not hold out much hope. Only a miracle could save me now. Even if I tried for the highway, several miles away through thick scrub, I would never make it. But I was, surprisingly, happy, at peace with myself. Regardless of what happened to my body, I would beat that foul presence inside me. By dying, I would win by default. I found this both ironic and hilarious, and then it happened.

There was not a cloud in sight, only a clear blue sky with the mighty Australian Sun beating down, sucking moisture from my body. Then, a cloud formed above the valley in front of me. This grew in seconds from wispy strings of vapor to a solid dark-gray cumulus. It was fairly low for a cloud, only a few hundred yards above me. The cloud formed quickly into the shape of a man's head with a massive bejeweled turban, so that a perfect cloud sculpture of an exalted being now looked down upon me.

This was not my imagination; I was dehydrated but I was not hallucinating or dreaming. I know the difference. I stood and spread my arms. I think my words were, "Hey, big guy, I could really, really, *really* use a little help down here about now!" Not the most esoteric salutation, but fitting for an extremely thirsty Aussie. Then, an amazing thing happened. The cloud grew, shoulders and arms appeared, bending a great bow and arrow. An arrow of cloud shot out from the bow and hung in the air over the valley before me. The cloud sculpture quickly disintegrated, leaving the arrow hanging in the blue sky.

The giant cloud arrow was perfect in every detail. Probably fifty yards in length, it was straight with a sharp, triangular arrowhead and neat feathered flights. It pointed slightly downwards into the valley. Hope surged and I studied it carefully. Could it be a sign? In my mind I drew a line through the arrow, extending it down into the valley. Amidst myriad drab bush colors, the arrow pointed to a very faint green line that snaked through the bottom of the valley. As hope and realization flared, the cloud arrow quickly disintegrated. Nothing but cloudless blue sky remained anywhere.

With hope giving me strength, I took a bearing, grabbed my pack, and started down into the valley. It was a long way off but mostly downhill, so I made good time by sliding and tumbling down rocky slopes. It was brutal going and I was amazed I did not break anything in my body. Two hours later, almost collapsing with thirst and exhaustion, forcing my way through thick, chest-high scrub, I fell into a tiny stream of water. This was so well hidden and overgrown I would never have found it without the cloud arrow. I remember lying back, laughing, and rolling around in the narrow creek. I cannot remember a time in my life when I was happier. Man, that muddy water tasted good.

So, how often will angels intervene in our problems? The only limitations angels have are moral and ethical. Like most high-level good spirits, they will seldom interfere with humanity. They will occasionally bring messages of hope to people in need; more rarely will they intervene. This does happen, but it's rare. If angels do help directly, it may be because the person they are helping has a special destiny to fulfill.

I have sighted angels several times during high-level OBEs, and have been visited by them three times while I have been fully awake. Three angels visited me when I was thirteen. I was home in bed recovering from influenza. My room was fairly dim but I had a good reading light on. I was propped up in bed eating lunch, halfway through a cheese and tomato sandwich and avidly reading.

A heavy atmosphere flooded my room, much like how a church feels. An angel, flanked by two other angels, walked through my bedroom wall. They were lightly glowing, adult-sized, floating about twelve inches off the floor, and dressed in full length, creamy white robes. Neither male nor female, they had fine, curly, pale gold hair about shoulder length, and no wings. I could see hands but no feet. The lead angel was larger and taller, looked slightly older, had more of a glow, and was obviously in charge. The angel on the right carried a massive tome of a book; it was more than a foot thick.

With the lead angel's head near the ceiling, and the other two angels slightly back and below, they looked at me expectantly. My mouth fell open and half-chewed sandwich joined the cold juice spilling into my lap. I rubbed my eyes and slapped and pinched myself hard several times (I wore the bruises for days afterwards). I shrunk back against the wall, waiting to see what would happen.

It was no good calling for help as I was the only one at home. I started praying for help but then thought that a bit silly, seeing as there were already three angels in my bedroom. I was shocked and awed but not scared. I knew what they were but had no idea why they were there.

For a moment I thought I was dying and that these angels had come to take me away to heaven. I was a still a bit weak after the influenza, but otherwise I felt fine. The lead angel took the huge book from the other angel. The book floated in midair before the lead angel as if on a reading stand. The lead angel opened the book and slowly turned the pages. After awhile it found the page it wanted. It then moved its hand slowly down the page as if looking for something. I had the sense it was looking for my name.

Holding a hand on the page, the angel lifted its head and looked me in the eyes. It gave me a loving, compassionate smile, one somehow tinged with a little sadness. For the briefest of moments I felt connected with this angel and my spine tingled with energy and tears sprang into my eyes. The lead angel then handed the book back to the other angel. With one last smile they floated majestically back out through the wall. The whole experience lasted only a few minutes.

For many years, I had no idea what the angelic visitation meant. But the memory of it helped greatly with my personal spiritual development; it gave me tangible proof of a greater reality. It also sustained me through many traumatic and heartbreaking times in my life, when, without this memory, I would not have survived.

On the matter of angelic help against Negs, angels do not regulate the behavior of lower spirit beings (Negs) and will rarely intervene. Angels exist at higher vibrational and dimensional levels than bad spirits. One might think this is why they cannot intervene, but it's not that simple. I have heard many people state this as the reason for angels' noninterference, but angels have the power to operate in any dimensional level, high or low. They can also manifest in the physical dimension, appearing visibly before non-sensitives. They do not interfere unbidden because they are ethically bound not to.

Angels are not an exalted police force. They are messengers of God. They have awesome powers but will seldom intervene in human affairs. This may sound cruel to some people, thinking there are exalted spiritual beings capable of saving people from suffering and death. But this would take destiny out of the hands of humankind. It would grossly interfere with universal law and freedom of choice.

If God wanted to insure our safety from harm from Negs, He would not have created the physical dimension and placed us within it in the first place. If there is a purpose to our physical life, then there is purpose in living it, warts, Negs, and all. Living often involves making mistakes and suffering in order to learn life's many lessons, including problems with Negs.

A Case Study of Possession

This next case history illuminates more aspects of possession. It is based on the experience of a young man I have helped for some time. Paul lost his father and older brother in a car wreck when he was five. He was traumatized by the memory, and his life began taking on a strange flavor later that year. Paul's mother doted on him, so he was well-loved and wanted for nothing. He was never exposed to pornography, yet Paul began having adult heterosexual fantasies at the age of six. This is psychologically impossible without having some kind of exposure to adult sexuality or pornography. Paul vividly remembers having dreamlike, waking sexual fantasies involving groups of beautiful young women.

Paul also experienced frequent night terrors. By the age of seven, he began having sadistic and murderous fantasies. With the onset of puberty, Paul became obsessed with his fantasy world. Riddled with guilt and self-loathing, he never acted on these urges, but they plagued him into his adult years. Along the way, Paul developed obsessive-compulsive disorder, speech problems, and a variety of other psychological disorders, all of which responded to treatment. Yet night terrors and regular nightmares also continued.

Paul was eighteen when I met him. The most soul-destroying part of his problem was his belief that these thoughts came from within his own mind. This resulted in low self-esteem and self-destructive tendencies. Amazingly, Paul did well at school. He used study as a way of keeping his mind occupied, to keep the fantasies, thoughts, and compulsions in check.

I convinced Paul his problems did not derive from himself, and I proved it by forcing his resident Neg to show its hand. I could not remove it, but one night I disturbed it enough so that it made a grab for control. This resulted in severe momentary loss of control for Paul and a change in his appearance. Murderous thoughts filled his mind and were directed at me. Although only a momentary experience, this shocked Paul to the core and left him with no doubt as to the cause of his problems.

With this realization, all the pieces began dropping into place for Paul. He saw his problems had an external source, and a great weight was lifted from him; he even visibly straightened his posture. The guilt that consumed him was now replaced by resolve and determination. Paul had been given something to fight.

I failed to exorcize Paul at the time because he was simply not strong enough to resist the return of his possessing Neg. Over the next few years, however, I taught Paul spiritual discipline and countermeasures. He also took up yoga, Zen meditation, and chi kung (Chinese-style energy work). Paul worked hard on improving himself. As his mental control and strength grew, his condition also steadily improved. A day came recently when I sensed it was time to deal with Paul's problem more directly, and I successfully exorcized his possessing Neg. The change in him was remarkable as his obsessive thoughts and compulsions suddenly disappeared.

The end result of this case is that *because* of his possession and release, Paul became stronger mentally, and more focused and well-balanced, than he might otherwise have become had possession not occurred. His condition had a positive outcome in that he now has great potential for good and the strength and drive to achieve anything he desires.

Having something to fight significantly helps a person when coping with strong Neg problems. Once the cause is realized, self-esteem increases and Neg controls are significantly weakened. It's for this reason that Negs make great efforts to *hide* their existence. Informed, outraged, determined people are far more dangerous to Negs than frightened, uninformed ones. If you cannot beat Neg influences, you can learn to work around them. Some people may never rid themselves entirely of Neg influences, but they can learn to control them, and in controlling them you will grow steadily stronger while Negs grow weaker.

The Different Levels of Possession and Virtual Puppetry

There are many levels and degrees of Neg influence and controls that comprise possession and many different ways these can occur. My life experience has taken me through the gamut from mild influence to extremes of pressures and urges, compulsions and obsessions to the point where my control was temporarily lost. I call this condition virtual puppetry. Virtual puppetry is a heavy form of overshadowing. One loses conscious control of one's body and becomes a powerless observer in a surreal world.

This is much like waking paralysis (sleep paralysis), only here one's body is animated and controlled by another mind.

The term possession is poorly understood. It typically sparks images of raving lunatics running amok. But possession itself does not mean insanity or total loss of control. Most possessed persons are not insane, nor are they Neg-controlled all the time. Mostly, they appear normal.

By and large, possession is usually a progressive process, whereby a Neg gains control over its host in stages. Humans have several levels of resistance and natural shields against possession, and Negs have to overcome each of them to gain control. The length of time this takes depends on the strength and experience of the Neg and the strength of the person. In the average case of possession, supernatural disturbances come first, then obsessions and compulsions, then various levels of overshadowing; only after this is virtual puppetry possible.

Neg influences may rise and fall, come and go, seemingly as manifestations of the darker side of one's personality or as personality disorders, or they may exert influences only at certain times, when people are weak and vulnerable. Possessing Negs seem to enjoy tormenting their hosts, taking advantage of every opportunity to damage their host's lives.

A possessing Neg will not normally take full control unless it plans to destroy its host, or if its position is threatened by exorcism. Most Negs are content to sit back and go along for the human ride, to share a life and exert a hefty influence over it. A possessing Neg mind cannot function unaided in our society. It needs a human mind and memory to take care of all the boring details—travel, work, socializing, relationships, etc.

It is common for possessed people to react violently when their possessing Negs are threatened. This only happens, and usually does, when they are faced with some form of exorcism. When this happens, the situation can suddenly become dangerous for all concerned, especially the exorcist.

Generally, though, possessing Negs will actively hide their presence. Consequently, most possessed people are not aware they are possessed. The reasons for this are clear: if victims suspect Neg presences within, they are given something to fight and will thus actively oppose Neg influences and controls. Aware victims may also seek outside help that could damage or remove Negs.

For example, people have often reacted violently when I have tried to remove possessing Negs from them. People can lose control, fight, and scream hysterically when someone tries to help.

Here is a case involving a four-year-old boy. His mother said he had always been a jovial boy, but over the last several months he had become devious, cruel, selfish, and uncontrollable. Even his eyes had darkened in this time. I relaxed, prayed, and entered the full trance state, and it was not long before I felt the gentle rising inside that heralds a manifestation of my higher self. (When this happens I enter a cloudy, almost surreal state, but can still move and function, albeit slowly and carefully.)

I gestured for the boy. As I had half-expected, the boy exploded. Struggling violently, he screamed and begged his mother not to let me touch him. His mother struggled to drag him within reach. I pulled him to me and immobilized him. He screamed, scratched, and bit, begging his mother to save him. But I was too strong for him; with an adult, of course, this would have been dangerous. He fell limp the moment I started the deep healing. This continued for less than a minute and then ceased, then I gave him back to his mother, who put him to bed.

He awoke two hours later, hungry, but with no memory of what had transpired. He had reverted to his old self. He was jovial, kind, and funny, and his eyes had changed color, brightening considerably. His mother was so happy that she cried, saying she could not remember the last time she had heard him laugh.

Typical Symptoms of Possession

In most cases, people are not aware they are possessed. The saying "Ignorance is bliss" is apt here. Often, the human host is too strong mentally for full possession to occur immediately, so other control methods are used. It can take many years of behind-the-scenes conditioning before the average Neg is capable of possessing its host. Above-average Negs do exist (the one that took me, for example) but instant possession on first contact is rare.

The mental symptoms that can be involved in possession are many, covering nearly every aberrant psychological condition there is. The main things to watch for in others are: sudden, unpredictable, and unusual changes in personality, reactions, and behavior. Things to watch for on the inside (that is, in yourself) are obsessive thoughts and powerful compulsions to do or say things that are unnatural or out of character. With possession, the key thing to note is the *strength* of the pressures involved.

The symptoms of possession are difficult to define because of two factors. First, there are different types of Negs that may be involved and each elicit different symptoms. Second, victims differ in the weaknesses that may be exploited by Negs. The result of this is that a level of psychic influence that a strong-minded person struggles against and overcomes may be sufficient elsewhere to possess a weaker-minded person. Because of the operation of telepathic influence in both persons, it may be said that they are both technically possessed, but the end results are different. The stronger-minded person may only become *troubled*, while the weaker person becomes *controlled*.

The classic symptoms of possession are just as the Christian Church defines them: violence, lust, greed, and unnatural powers of persuasion. These symptoms can be progressive or come and go in waves. Of course, all these symptoms can occur naturally in people who are not possessed, but it is the *sudden* or unnatural *exaggeration* of the symptoms that can indicate possession.

Violent thoughts and the urge to do violent things, if out of character to a person, are symptoms of possession. An unusual level of lust, especially perverted lust, is another symptom. Greed (including selfishness) is another sign. An unusually strong power of persuasion is another strong indicator. This last is unlike normal persuasive abilities resulting from good salesmanship; rather, it's the unnatural ability to mesmerize and coerce normal people into doing things, contrary to their nature, that would normally defy their sense of logic, reason, and common sense. A good example of this is Charles Manson, who was responsible for the Sharon Tate murders, and his unnatural ability to influence people.

The activities of possessing Negs affect the energy bodies of their hosts, and in turn, affect their nervous systems. When resident Negs are active, peculiar symptoms can arise. While many of these symptoms can have normal medical causes, and these should always be considered and eliminated first before relating them to Neg problems, don't overlook the possibility that Negs are behind them.

Involuntary Movements: A sure sign of trouble is when one's body begins performing actions on its own. For example, your hand might reach out and pick up something for no apparent reason. This symptom indicates Negs are working through autonomous levels of unconscious mind.

Muscular Cramps: These usually come on suddenly and can occur anywhere in the physical body. They can be very painful and even cause physical damage like bruising and torn muscles. One might, for example, get a cramp in the right bicep, the left calf, the right shin, a small area of the chest, back, neck, or stomach, a single toe—anywhere on the body.

Hernia-like Attacks: Sudden, painful hernia-like swellings may occur for no reason. For example, a hernia might suddenly appear in a chest muscle while one is resting or sleeping, something I have been told is medically impossible. These can happen in any parts of the body, but are most common in the stomach and chest areas.

I first experienced hernia attacks during the time I was possessed, but I have also experienced them during other strong Neg attacks since. Several months ago, after suffering several consecutive psychic attacks, I consulted my doctor about the hernia attack problem. I could not, of course, explain what I thought was causing it. He said it was impossible to cause a hernia during sleep or while one is deeply relaxed in bed. He prescribed quinine and vitamin supplements and advised me to use a relaxation technique should it happen again.

That same night I came under another psychic attack that

woke me at 2 A.M. I experienced severe cramping and bulging in my lower right stomach muscles. Fighting the impulse to roll onto my fist to stop my stomach from tearing itself apart (that's what it felt like), I followed my doctor's advice and used a relaxation technique. This failed, and a minute later I experienced a painful stinging sensation as the muscle or membrane concerned slowly tore. This was very painful, and my doctor could not believe what had happened, when I told him the next day. The bruising was quite evident and I had to wear a truss for a month until it healed.

Stomach and Bowel Problems: Nausea, vomiting, stomach and bowel cramps, diarrhea, unexplainable bouts of flatulence, and belching all can be caused by Negs. These problems are particularly common when resident Negs feel threatened. I once gave a healing to a woman of thirty-five who began belching loudly and continually. The healing lasted less than a minute. The belching began the moment energy began flowing into her and continued loudly for several minutes with no letup, then stopped as suddenly as it had begun. While a medical explanation is conceivable, the woman had eaten nothing unusual and had no history of belching. Given an absence of other symptoms of illness, to suddenly erupt in a belching attack at the moment healing begins seems beyond medical explanation.

Sexual Arousal: Unusual sexual arousal is a reward and punishment device used by many Neg types, depending on host susceptibility. Telepathically stimulated fantasies are reinforced with direct stimulation of the genitals. Negs can have more than a little to do with a person's sexuality. One's sexuality over time can even be altered by Negs, who reinforce particular types of sexual fantasies and weaken others. Natural sexual inclination, orientation, and behavioral triggers can be compromised.

The physical symptoms of direct Neg stimulation are different from normal sexual arousal. Sensations are deeper, more intense and urgent, often accompanied by deep genital burning sensations. Neg-induced sex compulsions are rewarded with heightened sexual arousal, enhanced orgasmic pleasure sensations, and feelings of comfort and well-being. Pursuing Neg-directed sexual activities can become obsessive in some people.

Sex addictions can result from this level of Neg interference. Sexual interest can become heavily reliant on Neg involvement, causing serious life and relationship problems. Succubus- and incubus-type entities are well known Neg sexual energy predators. However, these are not the only Neg types capable of causing extreme sexual arousal and utilizing sexual energy.

The Experience of Rewards and Punishments: By far, the most common control device used by Negs is energy body-stimulated rewards and punishments. Neg hosts are rewarded for obedience and punished for disobedience, both in response to Neg urges. Reward often entails energy body-stimulated endorphin releases, adrenaline rushes, heightened sexual arousal, feelings of comfort and well-being; punishment entails feelings of pressure, confusion, depression, and loss of desire.

Neg-motivated alcoholics and drug addicts are rewarded by Negs in the form of short-lived endorphin and adrenaline surges, plus feelings of comfort and well-being. With alcoholics, this occurs when those first drinks are taken, when they get what alcoholics call a buzz or a charge. With all forms of substance addiction, the psychological pressures exerted on addicts are massive, far stronger than the pressures caused by chemical addiction and withdrawal. In general, pleasurable endorphin releases and feelings of comfort and well-being are common to all Neg-related reward stimulations.

Neg conditioning and control devices can involve any type of aberrant behavior. Some people are known to experience sexual pleasure while shoplifting, for example. I once witnessed a woman have an orgasm during a sudden compulsive spending spree. I gave her a lift into town to pay the airfares for a family holiday. Within sight of the travel agent in the mall, she suddenly darted into a jewelry shop. Her facial aspects changed, her eyes glazed over, and she breathed heavily. She would not listen to reason, but proceeded to purchase several expensive items she did not need. As she handed over the last of her money, she half-collapsed and slumped panting over the counter.

She said it was a dizzy spell, but my senses and her symptoms suggested Neg overshadowing, possibly accompanied by orgasm.

She cried all the way home, devastated by what she had done. Fortunately, her husband was able to return the goods the next day.

Hearing Disembodied Voices: Hearing disembodied voices is a symptom more often related today to mental illness than to supernatural problems. This is understandable, but I believe auditory voice phenomena stem primarily from Neg interference. Neg problems can cause mental illness, but mental illness can also open one to Neg problems such as hearing voices. Hearing disembodied voices is a common symptom of possession; however, voices do not always indicate possession, and possession can occur without voices being heard. While I have experienced objective voice phenomena on several occasions, I did not hear any voices while I was possessed.

There are two distinct types of voice phenomena: subjective and objective. The subjective voice is heard inside the head, much like one's own thoughts, but it sounds different; the objective voice is heard with the ears as a normal voice.

Little scientific study has been done on objective voice phenomena, but here are some observations and assumptions, based on what I have experienced and observed in others. When the objective voice is heard, the parotid gland (the gland beneath the ear) pulses and vibrates; this vibration spreads through the mastoid bone behind the ear. Mastoid vibrations can be felt with the fingertips, much like the vibrations given off by audio speakers. The mastoid vibrates in tune with the voice being heard, transferring vibrations into the ear canal, making the eardrum vibrate to produce a voice that sounds real.

This experience is the result of energy body manipulation by a spirit. A spirit manipulates the energy body to produce the voice-causing vibrations in the parotid gland and mastoid bone. Everyone I have questioned has verified the parotid/mastoid involvement with objective voice production. However, I think it is also possible for the objective voice to manifest from out of "thin air," as if a real voice were talking near the ear.

Dream Indicators: Dreams can provide a wealth of information about one's current state of spiritual and psychological well-being, but Neg interference can cause noticeable changes in dreams. You might, for example, dream you are being hunted by a vampire, or dream of snakes and spiders. Nightmares and dreams with abnormal content are indicators that something is wrong. These can result from telepathic dream manipulation during the sleep state. This is especially noticeable when a major psychic attack is in progress, and/or when a Neg is in the process of breaking down a person's natural defenses. It can be useful to keep a journal of dreams, including the bad ones. These can help identify the human source of a psychic attack and provide keys to unearthing core images.

Changes in Eye Color and Facial Aspect: Eye color and facial aspects can darken and change rapidly in response to a strong Neg presence. This is particularly noticeable when a possessing Neg rises to the surface and overshadows or takes control of its host. During the time of my possession, my eyes turned dark gray. After my release from the Neg, they turned a clear sky-blue and stayed this color for several days, before slowly returning to their normal light blue-gray color.

Physical changes can occur during heavy episodes of possession. During such times, the aspects of a face can transfigure as facial muscles try to match the face of the possessing Neg. In extreme cases, the face can become clouded by a murky green discharge of ectoplasm. When this happens, the Neg's true face and eyes can be seen by the human eye as superimposed over the physical face. The eyes, in this case, will often appear as black holes or red orbs.

Strange Medical Problems: Strange infections can occur during strong psychic attacks and possession. Often localized to particular areas of the body, these can flare up suddenly and strongly. For example, the elbow, knee, nose, coccyx, toe, or ear might suddenly develop a virulent infection, even though no break in the skin or other cause may be apparent.

During a Neg attack, I once developed an infected elbow. There was no break in the skin and my doctor was perplexed as to its cause. The infection spread rapidly and soon had me in hospital. A few days later, as my doctors discussed amputation, the infection finally responded to antibiotics. I have experienced several such Neg-related, medically perplexing, virulent infections; these all occurred during strong Neg attacks or while experimenting with Neg countermeasures.

Severe headaches and other violent pains are common symptoms of psychic attack and possession. This type of headache will often come and go in the hour. Pain can be widespread, or localized to a part of the head, perhaps centered over one eye or in half the brow only. The sudden onset of allergies and dietary intolerances can also be side effects of Negs.

For example, afflicted persons might suddenly find they become intolerant to wheat or dairy, or develop asthma around cats, even though there was no prior history of these conditions. These can be caused through Neg activities interfering with the energy body, which can result in biochemical changes in the physical body. Given these symptoms, qualified medical opinion should be sought immediately. Medical and pharmacological treatments are invaluable when weathering Neg-related side effects.

The Mechanics of Possession

There are two types of possession and their mechanics I will discuss here—instant possession and virtual puppetry.

Instant Possession: For a Neg to possess a new host in a short time indicates great strength and experience on its part. But Negs of this caliber are rare, in my experience. Many other factors must also be considered, including the strength of mind of the victim, the victim's state of physical and spiritual health, sensitivity and susceptibility factors, whether or not permission has been given, occult dabbling, and alcohol and drug usage.

The only case of instant possession I have studied in any detail, including its long-term effects, has been my own. Knowing my history, strengths, weaknesses, and all other related factors, provides me with a clear picture of what happened. The Neg that took me orchestrated a situation in which I would open myself up to it and give it permission to enter my space. This denotes intelligent planning on the Neg's part.

Once I foolishly gave permission and exposed myself, the Neg struck instantly. Although it firmly attached to me, it seemed unable to take full control of me at that time. Several days passed before it began attempting control. In the beginning this was limited to occasionally moving an arm or a leg. It was as if the Neg were learning how to control me one piece at a time.

When it did attempt control, on the rooftop car park, it chose the perfect time to do maximum damage to my life, and possibly kill me in the process. This denotes intelligence and cunning. I am sure it could have tried to grab control earlier than this, but it waited until just the right moment. Most possessing Negs seem capable of taking significant control when necessary, but only a small minority will do this, or only attempt full control when threatened.

It's difficult to ascertain whether a given case of possession results from a preexisting Neg residency or from a fresh Neg invasion. Either way, the symptoms experienced when Negs take control are the same. However, if a new Neg is involved, a major Neg-related event or episode of psychic attack usually will take place before actual possession occurs. If this has not occurred, then the possessing Neg likely stems from a preexisting condition.

Virtual Puppetry: I have experienced this state several times myself, but only for a minute or two each time. I have questioned others with possession experience and found similar symptoms reported. In virtual puppetry, a Neg forces full mind/body disassociation and takes control over one's physical body. Logically, this is accomplished by Negs working through the autonomic nervous system (reflex system), using this as a back door to gain control over the physical body.

In principle, this mechanism is similar to how any set of complex actions is learned, such as learning to walk, do karate, play a musical instrument, or ride a bike. Through exhaustive, repetitive training, humans program themselves to carry out sequences of complex, delicately timed actions without having to think about them. Often, these actions are so complex that training the autonomic nervous system is the only way they can be done; if one thought about how to do them, one would be unable to do them.

This is why Negs habitually use psychological conditioning processes to gain control over humans. Advanced Negs know how to condition the human body and its autonomic nervous system in such a way as to gain full control. At the time I was possessed, while the Neg was conditioning me and learning how to use my body, some interesting observations came to light.

The occasional involuntary actions I experienced were fast, smooth, and precise; they were not muscular twitches. For example, my hand and arm would suddenly reach out, pick up something, then throw it; this was a fast, smooth, precise action. My controlled hand did not just lash out crudely and knock something over; rather, these movements had the signs of trained reflex actions.

Virtual puppetry is the stuff of which nightmares are made. Suddenly, your mind is forcibly disassociated from your physical body. Amidst feelings of whole body pressure, you float in a surreal, dreamlike world. You feel arms and legs moving of their own accord, and it's much like an OBE or lucid dream, but you have zero control over the actions or words of your physical body. Your mind feels numb, weak, under relentless mental pressure. It's very quiet inside and the world outside seems at a distance. You are a powerless observer.

It's easy to think this is a dream and give in to the pressure. You sense your physical body, but as if from a distance. You know when it is walking, but it's like walking on huge fluffy pillows. If your body picks up something, you are aware of this happening but cannot feel what is in your hand. It's as if your thinking mind has been forced outside your body.

The best advice I can give to anyone experiencing virtual puppetry is to stay calm and don't fall into the trap of believing it's just a dream. Fight it with every ounce of courage and mental strength you have. Never give in! Fighting costs the possessing Neg energy and weakens it. In principle, fighting virtual puppetry feels similar to fighting waking paralysis. The underlying principles and subtle mechanisms involved with virtual puppetry are likely related to those involved with the waking paralysis state. But this is not to say Negs are always involved in waking paralysis.

During an episode of virtual puppetry, you may feel powerless to move, but you are still in touch with your body. It will feel numb, vague, and unresponsive, even though it may be moving of its own accord. But you can regain control. The best way to do this is to concentrate on moving your big toe; fight to do this simple action with all your strength. The instant you succeed in moving your big toe, the possessing Neg will be evicted and your full control regained.

To beat the Neg on the rooftop car park episode, for example, I put everything I had into one simple action: I bit my tongue hard. I did not have time to think; the idea popped into my head and I did it. The pain appeared to surprise and distract the possessing Neg, allowing me to regain control. Then, I quickly put down my son, knelt, and splashed icy cold water into my face from a puddle (it had rained recently). This last act may or may not have helped, but it made me feel better. Being spontaneous and unpredictable is a big asset when dealing with serious Neg problems, especially possession.

To produce virtual puppetry in a human being, a Neg must forcibly disrupt the connection between the human mind and its brain, causing full disassociation between mind and body. It then controls the physical body in much the same way as the human mind does normally: like a hand slipping into a glove and flexing.

The human mind and will can interfere with and overcome Neg control devices. For this reason mental training and self-development are big parts of all spiritual and occult disciplines. The mind and will are like the muscles of the physical body. If regularly exercised and properly "fed," they grow strong and resilient; if neglected and starved, they grow weak and ineffectual. A strong, well-disciplined mind provides a strong defense against all Neg problems.

Dealing with Possession

The consequences of full-blown possession are dismal. If a person is having episodes of virtual puppetry, hearing voices, having unusually strong compulsions, and other symptoms relating to possession, his options are limited. Under these circumstances, training the mind and will to reduce their susceptibility and improve inner defenses will be more difficult, but not impossible.

The best advice for persons in this situation is to seek the help of a priest or occultist experienced with exorcism. If no other recourse is at hand, the police or mental health services can be contacted and arrangements made to be taken into custody or a protected environment. This reduces the risks of doing harm to yourself or others. Containing a potentially dangerous situation should always be a priority. Doctors can help a great deal. Many drugs are available that change the way the brain works, chemically overruling many Neg control devices.

1 0

Neg-Induced Suicide, Murder, and Accidents

If one weighs the evidence carefully, considering how Negs can influence and even possess people, it is clear that unsuspected dangers lie beneath the surface of society. While some Negs share human lives, some will use every device, weakness, and opportunity to corrupt, torment, and destroy humans. Some Negs can be likened to free-roaming predators, so when this type of Neg comes across susceptible people in potentially dangerous situations, they use their powers of influence to cause mischief, suffering, and even death. They do this because it is in their nature to do so.

Neg-Induced Suicide

Negs can exert telepathic, hypnotic influences over sensitives without having to possess them. Given the right circumstances, some Negs are capable of influencing people into taking their own lives.

It is easy to imagine scenarios in which Negs can influence people detrimentally. Some people have a precariously balanced psychology, such that self-esteem and self-worth can be shattered by a hurtful word or look. When people are hurt and disillusioned by life, they become extremely vulnerable to Neg influences. For some, all it takes is a little added pressure, some telepathically induced thoughts, a few trivial mishaps, a nudge in the wrong direction, and they are soon reaching for a bottle of pills, or a gun.

For example, a friend in Scotland recently told me a sad tale. His son had been depressed for months over various matters, including a failed semester at university, and money and relationship problems. Family and friends were worried, but these problems did not seem life threatening. Then, one day the boy scribbled a note, climbed to the top of a monument and leapt to his death. Neg involvement here is unprovable, but experience tells me it is more than possible this boy was the victim of a Machiavellian Neg campaign that culminated in his compulsion to suicide.

My friend in Scotland told me he climbed the same monument recently, to look down from where his son had jumped a year earlier. He had no intention of jumping. He was merely retracing his son's last moments, trying to understand what motivated him to take his life. As he was looking over the edge, he was suddenly consumed by a terrible compulsion. It took all his willpower not to jump. He staggered backwards and fell to the ground, panting for breath and not trusting himself to stand. He literally crawled to the stairway and then clung to the rail all the way down. The compulsion did not reduce in intensity until he got in his car and drove away.

It would be easy to think that this case may have been exaggerated by grief. But my friend has a strong, mature, well-balanced mind. He had never before experienced such a frighteningly powerful compulsion. Because of this, he suspected this compulsion came from a powerful Neg, and that this may have been the same one that caused his son's death.

I wonder how many people flirt with suicide, with no real intention of actually killing themselves, only to find an overpowering compulsion suddenly forces them to commit it. How many lives could be saved if people only knew about Negs and how strong their telepathic compulsions can be, and how these can arrive at the worst possible moment.

It is well known that being informed of what can happen in potentially dangerous situations can save lives. If sudden Neg compulsions are known about, people can armor themselves by not taking foolish chances with their lives. It is clear to me that Negs frequently influence people to do terrible things to themselves and others, things they would not normally do, but for which they need only a little negative encouragement at the right time. This includes every crime imaginable, from petty theft to mass murder. An understanding of Neg involvement here could revolutionize our society's approach to crime and antisocial behavior, to include how unseen Neg influences play a major part in causing and/or triggering these events.

Neg-Induced Murder: Some Negs will do everything in their power to cause pain and suffering to humans. The most common reason for murder is loss of self-control, and Negs excel at driving people to extremes where self-control is lost. In my opinion, many murders are Neg crimes against humanity. Whether it's a jilted lover, a depressed student turned schoolyard killer, or a disgruntled employee going on a killing rampage, these actions often grow from the seeds of personal failure, guilt, and blame, escalating into a killing mentality.

Some murderers seem to kill for enjoyment, and a few become serial killers, killing again and again, seemingly for the love of it. These people seem to have no conscience at all. But in severely Neg-influenced and possessed people, conscience can be depressed to the point where it ceases to exist. Lack of conscience and remorse for wrongdoing are indicators of serious Neg contamination or possession.

Neg-Induced Accidents: While it's not pleasant to think about this, it's possible many accidents are caused by Negs. After all, they are capable of telepathically stimulating emotions and compulsions, and this could easily be used to cause accidents. In any potentially dangerous situation, a Neg influence can turn a near-miss into a direct hit, a risk into an actuality.

Once I witnessed a young boy and his older sister. She was walking him to school, dutifully holding his hand as they approached the light traffic in front of the school. I had noticed these two children on previous occasions. They would often fight noisily over him not wanting to hold her hand. This day they fought as usual, and the girl lost her grip.

He charged straight across the road without looking. She dived after him, but sadly, they were both run over. The boy died instantly, and his sister was terribly injured. Think how a sudden projected impulse might affect someone in a situation like this. The sudden compulsion the boy had to wrench himself away from his sister and charge across the road could easily have been Neg induced.

This type of accident is not limited to children. It can happen to anyone. Drivers can be distracted at just the wrong moment, or suddenly decide to take a chance and overtake on a bend, or to speed dangerously for the sheer thrill of it. A friend of mine was almost killed recently when he took his eyes off the road and bent to search for a tape on the floor of his vehicle. Traveling at high speed, his car left the bridge, became airborne, and buried itself in an embankment. There are many situations like this in which *momentary* distractions and impulses can lead to serious accidents. The question is *where* do the distractions and impulses come from?

I have survived many such near-misses myself, some as a child and some as an adult. Looking back, I see that it's quite possible Negs were involved. One such incident happened when I was eighteen and in the merchant navy. I was lying on my bunk reading when I suddenly had an urge for fresh air and sunshine. I knelt on my bunk, swung the porthole in, and put my head out. Breathing deeply of the warm sea air, I heard a peculiar sound. I idly looked around for the source. I could hear the ancient steam winch on the stern heaving, but that was not the sound I sought.

Suddenly, a terrible fear swept over me. Call it intuition or blind luck. I threw myself backwards into my cabin hard. In panic, my world went into slow motion. As I fell backwards, a roaring noise erupted as a heavy steel wire slipped off the bolt-head it was caught under (at sea level, this was twenty feet below my port-hole) and ripped up the side of the ship. It tore a chunk of hair from my head in passing. I barely survived this. A hundredth-of-a-second delay would have cost me my head. I carefully poked my head out through the porthole again to survey the damage. The wire had ripped the paint from the ship's side and scraped my brass porthole mount back to bare metal.

If you look at the precise timing involved in these cases, including my own, it's very suspicious. I had been lying on my bunk for more than two hours, when I *suddenly* had the urge to stick my head out the porthole. About fifteen seconds later, the wire came loose and almost decapitated me. But I had a strong impulse to pull my head back in, a split second before the wire came loose.

I have lived through a dozen or more such freak near-misses. But something has always saved me at the last moment. Maybe it was my guardian angel that alerted me. Although, in my experience, angels will rarely intervene directly, I believe they do telepathically warn people at such times when, unbeknownst to them, their lives are in grave danger. Some people hear and react to these warnings, others do not. Sensitivity, and the heightened sense of intuition that comes with it, opens one to both positive and negative influences, which is why psychic sensitivity is a double-edged sword.

Realistically, not much can be done about momentary distractions, but something can be done about unsafe impulses, urges, and crazy ideas. Most people become more careful and thoughtful as they mature, and accident statistics reflect this. The younger a person is, the more likely he is to have accidents, and younger people are always more susceptible to Neg influences, especially children.

Forewarned is most definitely forearmed. Education is the best way to counter potentially dangerous Neg-related problems. Knowing that Negs can alter moods and cause spontaneous impulses, and recognizing the possibility of this when they occur, greatly improves the chances of weathering and surviving them intact.

PART III

Psychic Self-Defense Countermeasures: How to Protect Yourself against Unseen Spirit Influences

An Overview of Part III

Part III presents active and passive countermeasures, with explanatory sections and short tutorials given in support. It deals with important issues such as how intellect and willpower affect Neg susceptibility, and it examines some popular ways of dealing with bad spirits. We then consider the human energy body and Neg attachments and ways of protecting oneself against them and removing attachments. The relationships between Neg attachment points and certain types of skin blemishes are also discussed, along with a new way of treating these problems.

I provide instructions for identifying and neutralizing trauma memories (core images) and explain how these relate to Neg attachments. Following this, I offer advice on children and family Neg-related problems, and methods to deal with possession, exorcism, and self-exorcism methods.

Then, I review the use of applied metaphysics, showing various ways to use sacred symbols and words to defend against Neg attachments and manifestations, including an effective banishment ritual that anyone can use. Instructions on defending against mental attacks, and a ritual for self-exorcism, are also given, and part III closes with a discussion of the benefits of baptism.

11

Preliminary Discussion on Dealing with Neg-Related Problems

Strength of mind, visualized shields, white light barriers, visualized barriers, sending spirits to the light, the compassion method, and revoking Neg permission—all are popular ways of dealing with bad spirits. But how do these methods stand up in practice? This chapter discusses the ins and outs of some popular methods of psychic self-defense, and suggests it is sometimes better to not react to minor Neg disturbances.

Strength of Mind: Strength of mind will not, in itself, protect you from psychic attack and Neg-related problems. It's an invaluable asset, but will not alone generate immunity. However, combined with an understanding of the psychic attack and Neg problems, its defensive worth improves. No matter how strong a person may be inside, if one does not *recognize* a problem, one cannot deal with it. This is why Negs take great pains to hide their presence. People who do not believe in, and hence do not recognize, Neg activities are easy to interfere with, whereas aware people are a much more difficult proposition for Negs.

Visualized Shields: By far the most popular Neg countermeasure employed today is the visualized shield. One visualizes a thick shield of light, color, or glass surrounding oneself or someone else as a protective measure. It sounds good in theory, but unless this is supported by effective technique and regular effort, shields will be ineffective.

The biggest difficulty with shields is maintaining them over time. It takes time and effort to create and energize a shield. Most people will not take the trouble to create a shield until they need one, but putting this off until one comes under Neg attack is not a good idea. Visualized or imagined actions affect the astral dimension, where the human mind has strong creative abilities. If enough time and effort are put into the creation and maintenance of a shield, it will be durable.

There are many problems that arise with novices creating and maintaining effective personal shields. Anything created in the astral, especially by a human mind in its normal waking state, requires considerable effort to maintain in existence. As soon as the creative effort ceases, whatever has been created will begin to fade. To create something longer lasting you must employ a good technique, time, and effort. Trying to suddenly create an effective visualized shield in emergencies will have little or no effect.

The whole idea of a shield is preventive, to keep Negs away, but once an attack is in progress, it can be too late to create it, as the damage may already have been done. To avoid this, mystics and magical practitioners perform twice daily rituals and/or visualizations to maintain their shields.

White Light Barriers: When encountering the term *white light*, most people understand it as something that emanates from high-level spiritual planes. This white light exists, but is only perceived after long-term spiritual development and by those of advanced spirituality. In these cases, the white light will begin to surround one in the astral; however, the white light cannot be created or called down with simple visualization techniques, prayers, or wishful thinking.

White light is not a force, per se, that can be summoned, shaped, or directed. It simply manifests when conditions are right.

Usually, it's first seen in the mind's eye as a glow from above, illuminating the darkness behind one's closed eyes. This glow increases as spiritual progress is made. However, it will manifest more strongly (albeit temporarily) during high-level altered states of consciousness. This manifestation can be particularly strong during mystical experiences in which strong, tangible connections with one's higher self are realized. In effect, these consciousness-expanding events raise one to levels where the white light can be perceived as a tangible, all-pervading force.

Under these circumstances, the white light offers an impenetrable personal shield. When the white light is perceived within the mind's eye as flooding down from above, subtle energy radiations manifest, within which Negs cannot exist. If the person experiencing an internal white light manifestation gives contact healing to another person at that time, the healed person will be cleansed of Neg attachments and all possessing Negs evicted. I call this process deep healing. Performing deep healing takes courage, conviction, faith, and spiritual strength; if these elements are lacking, it should not be attempted.

The difficulty, of course, is with holding an exalted vibrational or mystical state strongly enough, and for long enough, to be effective. This is particularly difficult to do during direct Neg assaults, when one may be anxious, even shivering. When the white light manifests through a person, any Negs in the surrounding area will be driven back, or at the very least made extremely uncomfortable. If a suitable banishment is done with faith and conviction, it will be doubly effective. No Neg of any caliber can withstand such a positive onslaught.

Unfortunately, white light banishments and deep healing will not stop Negs from returning. Negs withdraw and wait for another time. Whether or not they will attempt to return depends on many factors, especially the reason they were there in the first place. Other countermeasures must be used to keep them away, and changes must be implemented to remove any weaknesses and other such lifestyle Neg attractors from the person in question.

Visualized Barriers: Visualized shields and barriers can be set in place and maintained to prevent Negs from entering an area or building. These are only effective if the person doing the visualizing has the skill required to not only create and maintain them, but to bless and connect them to suitable spiritual power sources. These are not a good short-term solution to Neg problems, especially for novices.

Apart from the skill required, a considerable amount of time and effort is necessary to create and maintain these barriers; if the maintenance is not kept up, they soon fade and become ineffective. This type of defensive measure is only mildly effective as a countermeasure. It's too late to try to erect barriers during strong Neg attacks, as they are already inside the perimeter a barrier would create. Therefore, these are generally of little use to most people.

Any type of visualized barrier or defensive shield is only as good as the person creating it. Most serious practitioners of magic create multi-layered barriers and use these as early warning systems. Ironically, a strong barrier system can also be interpreted as a challenge that can actually attract Negs. Because of this, if you start mounting visualized perimeter defenses, you should go all the way and back it up with other countermeasures.

Sending Spirits to the Light: Sending spirits to the light is a popular countermeasure. Much like visualizing a white light shield, this approach involves praying for help while visualizing the offending spirit as moving into a field or tunnel of white light. This method will only work when genuine lost earthbound spirits are involved.

This method also often involves calling upon God, angels, or good spirits to take errant spirits to the light. This method is usually ineffective in serious Neg-related situations as good spirits rarely intervene of their own accord. Good spirits may have the best of intentions, but expecting them to send off Negs is much like asking the average person to control a wild animal merely with his voice. Wild animals (and some domestic ones, for that matter) do not understand, or choose to ignore, verbal commands. The same seems true of Negs.

Compassion Method: The compassion method involves showing love and understanding towards troublesome spirits and asking them nicely to leave and/or go into the light. Again, this will only work with genuine lost earthbound spirits, which are rare in the cases of Neg problems. Projecting love, understanding, and compassion to Negs is ineffective because Negs do not understand these higher emotions. They have the emotional capacity of a praying mantis.

Showing love to Negs is not only ineffective, it can be used against you. Negs consider higher emotions to be a weakness. They often take advantage of this and pretend remorse, thereby encouraging their targets to give them more love and understanding. But while victims are being loving and understanding, they are not fighting back or doing anything constructive that might interfere with Neg activities, and the Negs have the run of their space. Anger is more constructive than love when dealing with a psychic attack.

Revoking Permission: Some Negs require permission before they can significantly interfere in your life. This factor is illustrated by legends, like stories of vampires needing permission to enter homes. Once permission is given, even if obtusely or as a result of trickery, it can be difficult to revoke. This can be likened to how legal contracts, such as marriage, in the real world are often difficult to revoke.

The level of permission needed, and what Negs are capable of doing after getting it, varies a great deal. In the experience in which I became possessed, which I related earlier in this book, the Neg in question did not strike me until the moment I gave it permission. I gave it mental, not verbal, permission, which indicates the Neg was aware of my thoughts at that time. Therefore, I urge caution with what you think, as well as say aloud.

Sex and fear are the two main devices Negs use to gain access to a victim's inner sanctum during attacks. Sex and fear involve primal instinctive reactions. With sex comes physical surrender and emotional bonding; strong emotional bonds form between lovers during sexual union and are reinforced with each subsequent union. This may explain why some Negs approach humans through sex.

Fear produces the fight-or-flight reaction, which is a powerful instinct. But when fear reaches the point of terror, another deeper instinctive reaction occurs: surrender and submission. This is a plea for mercy. Victims open themselves to attackers physically and emotionally; it's a last resort in hopes of mercy. Many animals exhibit this same behavior—a dog rolls over, exposing its belly and throat as signs of submission.

Another way of describing how fear and sex are used by Negs is to say that eliciting these powerful reactions causes victims to open up their minds and drop defenses, providing a window through which Negs can penetrate.

Some Negs require permission to enter your space, so it's reasonable to suggest that at least some of them operate within guidelines. There seem to be unwritten conventions that constrain many higher-order Negs from using direct force to do or get what they want. Because of this, some Negs will obey direct orders, if commanded in the right way. Incidentally, this is the basis of ritual exorcism and banishment. Commanding Negs can give unpredictable results, but it is always worth a try.

To React or Not: When a Neg problem arises, a decision must be made. You must decide whether or not reacting is wise, and if so, what level of action is warranted. While a psychic attack can last hours or even years, the average campaign lasts about thirty days. Sometimes, if problems are mild and no direct attacks are taking place, it can be wise to do nothing but keep track of what is happening. Inaction can be fruitful, simply because action may exacerbate an otherwise mild situation.

If Neg manifestations are not severe, accompanied perhaps by occasional light poltergeist activity and atmospheres, and you decide on action, it's usually best to start with passive countermeasures. Apply these and wait to see what happens before doing anything else. This will often discourage whatever is happening without causing Negs to overreact.

However, if a direct psychic attack occurs, both active and passive countermeasures should be applied immediately. This should be done as far as possible without letting Negs know countermeasures are being used. If Negs suspect their presence is known and that countermeasures are aimed at them, problems could escalate.

It's an unwise practice to openly challenge and/or abuse Negs verbally or mentally. This could antagonize them to the point where they will retaliate instead of leaving. The idea behind countermeasures is to make life difficult for Negs. Make the home atmosphere as uncomfortable for Negs as possible, but do not antagonize them. This will encourage Negs to vacate peacefully, leaving your home and family alone. As said previously, it's not wise to let Negs know that you know about them. They may stop trying to hide their presence, and their manifestations will be much less subtle.

1 2

First Steps in Psychic Self-Defense

An understanding of the energy body is important as Negs seek to attach themselves to it in a variety of ways, thus providing the mechanism for Neg parasitism, influence, and even possession. Just as there are different types of energy within the energy body, Neg attachments may affect the host in different ways, physically, emotionally, mentally, and psychically.

Despite this, we are not rendered helpless. The use of body-awareness actions disrupts the energy body substance, and serves as a countermeasure by interfering with Neg activity. Consequently, the establishment of Neg connections and the draining of one's energy from these may be prevented.

Employing the Energy Body

The energy body (also called the etheric body) is a complex structure that can be likened to a subtle reflection of a system in which every part of the physical body is represented. The substance of the energy body is not scientifically recognized. However, metaphysically speaking, this is the substance that binds the physical with the nonphysical, the solid with the spiritual.

At an underlying level, energy in the energy body and its systems is raw and undifferentiated. Its general function is to perform work at the subtle/spiritual level of existence. This energy system is complex, comprised of qualitatively different types of energy associated with energy "organs" called chakras (of which there are at least seven); these create, transduce, and store the different energies.

These energies are discrete at the chakra level and support functional attributes such as health, vitality, sex, emotion, communication, perception, and psychic intuition. At a systemic level, these energies interact and combine to form the more powerful kundalini, which provides spiritual power and transcendental enlightenment.

This chapter shows how the mind and the sense of touch (body-awareness actions) can be used to disrupt Neg interference and protect the energy body. It shows how to clear and strengthen your mind, how to increase your willpower, how to erect mental blocks, and why shifting your attention away from Neg disturbances can disempower them. This chapter also deals with meditation and prayer skills and getting advice from psychics on how to handle Neg-related problems. In addition, I'll show you some ways you can do this for yourself.

Body-Awareness Actions to Counter Neg Interference

This section teaches you how to manipulate the energy body with body-awareness actions, rather than with less-effective visualization techniques. Body-awareness techniques are useful in disrupting energy body interference. Surprisingly, it does not take much body awareness effort to seriously hinder Neg activity.

A body-awareness action causes what I call an attention-induced bioelectrical event in the energy body. This can be likened to a wave passing through it, like passing a magnet over a plate of iron filings, which disturbs and reorganizes the filings. One might, for example, draw a design in the iron filings (a Neg attachment device), but by passing a magnet over it (body-awareness action) the design is removed.

The most common symptoms of energy body interference are needle-like pricking and jabbing, plus localized tingling and buzzing sensations. These can happen anywhere in the body, but are especially common in the feet and legs. This phenomenon may be related to the acupuncture model of energy manipulation in which even a small pricking sensation in one's ear could indicate changes in one's energy body circuitry. In acupuncture, this renders physical healing effects.

Small energy-feeding Negs usually work at night. Small means they are at the bottom of the Neg food chain. They are about as intelligent and dangerous as mosquitoes. However, it's difficult to tell the difference between significant and insignificant Negs through energy body disturbance sensations. Therefore, it's wise to treat all energy body interference in the same way and to apply body-awareness countermeasures as a matter of course.

Your body's center of awareness is normally focused between your eyes, but it does not have to stay there. It can be moved and focused on any part of the physical body, an important skill that is easily learned. Combined with other techniques, this enables you to make a direct stimulation of your own energy body circuitry. You will find that there are many benefits derived from using this new skill. While the manipulation of body awareness serves as a good general "Neg repellant," it can also be used to heal and develop the energy body. This effectively boosts physical and emotional health and vitality, and can even enhance psychic abilities (see *Astral Dynamics* and/or my online book *NEW Energy Ways*).

In the following exercises, you don't have to achieve deep levels of physical relaxation or be in the trance state. Light relaxation is adequate. Close your eyes, take a few deep breaths, and allow your mind to wind down and settle for a few moments, then begin. I suggest you do not lie down or use a bed unless you have to. Wear loose clothing, sit in a chair with your shoes off, place a cushion under your feet, and do not cross your legs. Following these recommendations makes body-awareness techniques easier to learn.

In the body-awareness exercises, lightly scratch or rub specified body parts as necessary. This is an aid that highlights and targets specific areas of your physical body; body awareness can then be focused more easily and accurately. Use a small stick if you have difficulty reaching some parts of your body. Scratching and rubbing are not necessary once you become used to the technique and can target an area with body awareness alone; for most people, this does not take long.

Body-Awareness Exercise: Lightly scratch the skin of your left knee with your fingernails to highlight it in your attention. Do this just hard enough to leave a slight tingling sensation there after you stop scratching. Close your eyes and *feel* for this tingling area with your body awareness. Become intensely aware of that area and focus on it (this becomes a focal point). Highlight it with your body awareness until it stands out. Focus on the target area and forget about the rest of your body for a moment.

Now, move your knee slightly, feel for the whole of your knee, and become aware of it as a joint. Feel its outline and shape, get the *feel* of it with your body awareness, so that your center of body awareness is now focused entirely in your left knee.

Shift your point of awareness to your right knee, scratching it first to highlight it. Feel its shape with your body awareness. Your center of body awareness is now focused entirely in your right knee. Shift your point of awareness to your right big toe. Scratch it on top of the large joint where it joins your foot. Wiggle your big toe to help you get the feel of it so you can zero in on it with your body awareness. Feel the tingle on top of it, then feel its shape with your body awareness. Your center of body awareness is now focused entirely in your right big toe. Shift your body awareness to several other parts of your body (anywhere you like) highlighting them first by light scratching. Feel these areas as you target them with your new sense of mobile body awareness.

Repeat these two body-awareness exercises, but this time do them without scratching. Try to do this with your eyes closed so you focus with body awareness only; but use your eyes if you need to. As with scratching, the use of eyes for targeting should be done away with once you can do it with body awareness alone.

Body-Awareness Sensitivity: Moving your focal point of body awareness from one point to another, for example, from finger tip to elbow, has the effect of stimulating the area in between the two.

When first learning to move a point of body awareness through the surface of your body, it helps if you trace pathways along the skin with your fingertips or a paintbrush; this will highlight the path your point of body awareness will take. This also maps the pathway in your mind, making it easier to follow with body awareness alone. You may lightly scratch a small pathway on the skin with your fingernails or a ruler to highlight it more strongly. Follow the slight tingling sensation this leaves behind on your skin with your body awareness.

Wider energy pathways, such as the full width of your forearm, can be stroked repeatedly with a hand or a broad paintbrush. You can do this by yourself or have your partner do it for you as you follow the sensations caused by this touch with your focal point of body awareness.

To start with, trace a pathway from the base of your left thumb along the sensitive inside of your arm and up to your left shoulder. Close your eyes and concentrate on the *feel* of the brush or fingers moving along the surface of your skin. Ignore the hand that is doing the brushing and concentrate solely on its touch. Repeatedly stroke this pathway, from thumb to shoulder and back to your thumb again, following this with your body awareness until you have a good feel for the action.

Repeat the previous exercise with your right arm. Next, trace and follow a path from your left big toe, up over your foot to your ankle, up the outside of your shin to your kneecap, and on up the outside of your thigh to your left hip joint; then back down to the same big toe again. Repeat the previous exercise with your right leg.

Practice this technique until you can trace a pathway to anywhere on your body with a point of body awareness alone, feeling your way along the surface of your skin without having to follow a manually highlighted pathway. Rub, scratch, and highlight for as long as necessary while learning this technique.

The relevance of this new skill to practical psychic self-defense is twofold. First, your energy body will become more sensitive as a result of body-awareness exercises, and this will allow you to be more aware of Neg interference if, and when, it occurs. Second, you will be able to impede any Neg activity by stimulating and raising energy throughout your body.

Body Awareness Hands: If a focal point of body awareness is a difficult technique to manage, you might like to feel an imaginary pair of hands making contact with various parts of your body. In this way, your awareness hands become tools to mobilize body awareness and stimulate your energy body. Remember that the energy body is a reflection of the physical, so that in this respect awareness hands are actually etheric extensions you use to stimulate other parts of the energy body. This is the same as using your physical hands to scratch or rub down any part of your physical body. Awareness hands should be used as if they are connected to flexible and extendible arms so that any part of your body can be reached and stimulated.

With practice, the movement of awareness hands over your body directly contacts and stimulates the energy body and elicits a tingling sensation. Just as you can be aware of your physical body by touching any part of it, you can also be aware of your energy body by touching it with your awareness hands.

It is important to note that awareness of anything is due to a contrast between it and something else. We see objects because of light reflecting off their forms; light is contrasted with darkness, and an object is contrasted with empty space. In this way, we can feel and thus be aware of an object by contrasting its form with our form, especially with the form of our hands.

Body awareness becomes much more sensitized with practice, in the same way a blind person refines her sense of touch by continually using it in the place of vision. Eventually, you will feel the outline of your body using your awareness alone, and this will cause a sense of resistance to be felt that you can use to stimulate parts of the energy body. You can also extend this ability to be aware of the entire body at one time, and this has the effect of energizing your whole being and allows greater detection and eradication of any Neg interference, if it is present. To do this, you can start by feeling the whole of your hand and spread this awareness to incorporate more of your body. With practice, you will be able to feel the whole body instantaneously.

I invented this technique to help congenitally blind people (blind since birth) perform energy body stimulation and OBE exit exercises. Traditionally, visualization was used for such practices, but this is impossible for people born blind. Body-awareness–based actions proved so successful that I have used and taught it exclusively since.

Body-Awareness Exercise #1—Brushing Action: Move your point of awareness back and forth along the skin as if brushing that area with a paintbrush. Vary the size and depth of this body-awareness brush to suit the task at hand. For example, when brushing a foot, have the brush width cover the full width of the foot.

Body-Awareness Exercise #2—Sponging Action: Imagine and feel that your awareness hands are holding a large sponge and that they are sponging water (energy) upwards through the area worked on. This is primarily used for raising energy through the whole of a limb or body part. If sponging through a leg, feel as if that whole leg were being sponged on the inside, as if you are moving a large invisible sponge through the whole of the leg to make water (energy) move upwards through its length.

Split Body-Awareness Actions: Body-awareness actions can be split to cover two areas at the same time. For example, you can brush both feet or both legs simultaneously. An effective split body-awareness exercise is to brush both hands simultaneously. Using a deep, wide brushing action, brush the palms of both hands from fingertips to wrist, back and forth, for a minute or so. Then, use the sponging action from fingertips to shoulders, sponging through the whole of both arms simultaneously.

Another exercise is to brush both feet, back and forth from toes to heels, for one minute or so. Then, using the sponging action, sponge both legs simultaneously, from toes to hips, back and forth, for one minute or so. You cannot overdo these exercises.

These exercises can cause noticeable physical sensations, especially in the hands and feet and inside the shin and thigh bones. A deep tingling, surging feeling like rushing water is common; it may be felt all through the legs, especially in the shin bones. This can continue for several minutes or more after the sponging action has ceased. Although it can be uncomfortable, this is a good sign and no harm will result. The sensation means that energy blockages have been cleared and large amounts of energy are flowing up your legs and into your energy body storage areas.

Body-Awareness Countermeasures

You now have the basic techniques required for disrupting Neg interference and attachments. You can vary the brushing and sponging actions in scope, intensity, depth, and speed to counter any type of energy body interference. A good rule of thumb for an effective awareness brushing or sponging action is about one second per sweep for the length of the limb.

This is an effective countermeasure, as Negs seem to require certain conditions to operate within, as the physical environment is usually dark and quiet when Neg interference occurs. Negs also seem to require a *quiet* human energy body to operate upon, so that if you raise energy with body awareness you are effectively creating a distortion, which is a hindrance to Negs. This is analogous to the conditions required for a pilot to land his plane. With stormy weather, the pilot's landing is far from smooth, if he can find the runway at all. In this case, the pilot would have to stay above the clouds or find another place to land.

If you feel symptoms that are possibly Neg-related, such as localized pricking or buzzing, or anything unusual, brush or sponge that area with body-awareness actions. Continue this until the unwanted sensations cease. Note that body-awareness actions will often cause strong buzzing and tingling sensations, although they will not usually cause pricking and jabbing sensations (as if someone were jabbing you with a needle or sharp object).

Keep this firmly in mind after you use the body-awareness actions. Do not be alarmed if your feet and legs buzz and tingle after you have stopped your body-awareness actions. Compared with Neg interference, actions caused by body awareness are usually more widespread, filling a whole foot or leg rather than just a small area.

Exercises for Clearing and Strengthening the Mind

A clear, strong, balanced mind is an enormous asset during any type of psychic attack. Control over the content and actions of one's thoughts helps counter the telepathically broadcast hypnotic thoughts and compulsions common to most Neg attacks. Developing the ability to clear your mind strengthens it and gives you the tools to erect mental blocks, that is, barriers to mental influence from Negs. For example, you might repeat a mantra (a repetitive phrase) or prayer to occupy the mind, to reduce Neg influences.

Some of these exercises may seem difficult, but taming the mind is not difficult to do with regular practice. Take them in easy stages and regular practice—you will make progress in a fairly short time.

The mind is always active while you are awake. It can be likened to a huge message-and-reminder pad whose function is to keep you aware of everything going on around you. It chatters away constantly, reminding you of everything, continuously stating and restating the obvious, even making witty comments about everything.

For example: "Is that the bus going by? Bread, I've got to get bread! Damn, my car's windshield is really dirty. The washer doesn't work. Maybe I'll wash it tonight! Why did he say that last night? What did she mean by that look?" This is called the internal dialogue. We don't always notice these thoughts and images as they constantly flutter through our minds. They serve a useful purpose in daily life by reminding us to do things, but they are a nuisance when you're trying to relax, to clear and focus your mind. It's like having someone constantly talking while you are trying to do serious work. You cannot focus completely unless you have mental peace and quiet.

This, in part, is why many people can concentrate better while listening to music. Listening to music does not require our attention, but it occupies the surface mind and deadens the internal dialogue, affording us better concentration. Most teenagers can study well with loud music blaring, but they cannot do the same in silence because of the incessant internal dialogue. Here is an exercise that will help quiet that internal chatter:

Breath-Awareness Thought Control: Center your attention on the process of breathing and use this to keep your mind clear. Feel the leading edge of each breath entering your body and filling your lungs, and then feel the leading edge of this leaving your body. Follow the breathing process with your mind, but do not think about it. Feel it and be aware of it. Let the feeling of breathing occupy your mind. This exercise is enough to occupy the surface mind and keep its rambling thoughts at bay.

It's easier to grasp and follow the leading edge of a breath than it is to keep track of the whole breath action. Feel the breath enter your nose and follow it as it moves through your nasal passages and throat, then spreads down into, and fills, the lungs. Then, feel the air in your lungs rising up through your throat and passing out through your mouth.

If you need more than this, count your breaths. Count up to ten breaths, numbering each as 1, 2, 3, and so on, and then start over. When you count each number, drag out the mentally spoken word over the whole of each breath. For example, follow the in breath carefully and then count (mentally) Onneeeee (one) for the entire out breath. Hold your mind clear during the next in breath and then count (mentally) Twwooooo (two) for the whole of the out breath.

While you hold your mind clear, surface thoughts will attempt to creep in. When this starts, quickly and firmly push them away before they take hold and complete their message. With practice, you will soon be able to detect thought pressure alone. Then, you can stop thoughts before they can form into mental words in your mind.

With a little practice, you will be able to hold your surface mind clear, like a blank slate. The pressure of thoughts wanting to start will continue for some time, even after you master the technique, but this will ease with regular practice. The following is an example of the process of subduing the pressure of thoughts seeking expression in your mind:

A surface thought:	"Damn, I forgot to drop off the dry cleaning . . ." "Damn, I forgot to drop off the dr . . ."
Becomes:	"Damn, I forgot to drop off . . ." "Damn, I forgot to . . ."
Getting better:	"Damn, I for . . ." "Damn, ? . . ." "D??? . . ."
Nearly got it:	"??? . . ."
Pressure of a thought about to start:	" . . . ??"
Lessening pressure:	" . . . ."
Almost there:	" . . ."
Perfect:	"?"

No pressure at all = clear surface mind

Do the thought control and breath-counting exercises daily for a few minutes or more at a time, during waiting and travel time, for instance. Although this can be frustrating in the early stages, with a little practice the surface mind will respond, and soon you will be able to hold it clear with little effort for extended periods. It can take time for your mind to get used to silence, but you will soon learn to love it. Once you have attained inner silence, you can think more profoundly and focus your mind one hundred percent on whatever you are doing.

In the early stages of mental training, if you can silence your surface mind for more than ten seconds you are doing well. This ability is progressive. Keep working at it and your original ten seconds will soon grow into twenty, then thirty, then a minute, then two minutes and more, getting easier all the time. Once you break the three-minute barrier, you will be able to hold your mind clear indefinitely.

Concentration Exercises

The next set of exercises is designed to improve your concentration and focus. They can be done any time and any place during the day, such as during travel and waiting time. Take a deep breath, relax a little, and begin, standing or sitting. At least one of these exercises should be done for a couple of minutes, several times each day. The more often they are done, the faster your concentration will improve.

Note that the exercises, if overdone, can cause eyestrain and tension headaches. If this happens, take a break, treat them as you would normal eyestrain or tension headache, and see a doctor if pain persists.

Single Object Awareness: Pick an object—a tree, chair, picture, cloud, anything—and stare at it gently but fixedly. Do not focus on any part, but let your eyes gently gaze upon the whole of it. Use your breath awareness to hold your mind clear. Hold this object in view as long as you can without shifting your gaze or allowing thoughts to start. Focus on this object to the exclusion of everything else. Feel the whole of the object and feel the image of it growing inside your mind as you gaze at it. Do not allow your eyes or forehead to tense up. Continue this for three minutes or for as long as you can.

When you end this exercise, close your eyes and cover them quickly with the palms of your hands, shutting out all light. Try to hold and follow the afterimage of the object in your mind's eye for as long as you can. Try to make this afterimage grow stronger. As the afterimage fades, hold the memory of it in your mind's eye, imagining the details in the same way as you would build and hold a fantasy.

As an alternative (or if you are non-sighted), hold an object in both hands and feel it, moving your fingers slightly over it. Any textured object will do. Feel its shape and texture, and fill your mind with the perception image this generates; feel this to the exclusion of all else. Do not think about how it feels; just *feel* it and let this feel occupy your mind. This will deter thoughts from starting.

Spot Focus: Pick a small speck or mark on a wall and focus gently but fixedly upon it. Hold your mind clear of all thoughts. Use breath awareness to hold your mind clear. If you concentrate and stare hard, an optical effect will occasionally cause your vision to darken. Your view will go dark around the edges, getting darker and closing in, until you may temporarily lose your sight. This is not harmful. Ignore this, or just blink it away without breaking your concentration. Your vision will return to normal as soon as you stop concentrating. Continue this exercise for three minutes, or as long as you can.

Afterimage Retention: Relax, calm your mind, and stare fixedly at any gentle light source, such as the moon, a candle, a low wattage light bulb, an open window. (Do not look at the Sun or any light source strong enough to damage your eyes.) Gaze gently but fixedly at the light for thirty seconds or more without shifting your gaze or changing focus, but blink when you have to. Do not focus directly on it; just gaze at it. Use breath awareness to hold your mind clear.

After doing this, close your eyes and cover them with the palms of your hands, shutting out all light. Hold and follow the glowing afterimage that has been generated in your mind's eye. Keep sight of this for as long as you can. Try to make it grow and last longer every time. If you use an open window, try to also retain the afterimage of the scene through the window and not just the light, using your imagination to recreate it. Manipulating the focus of your eyes behind closed eyelids will affect the afterimage. Play with this focus until you find what helps retain an afterimage the longest.

These exercises will improve your concentration and strength of mind, thus improving your resistance to Neg influences.

Attention Shifting and Mental Blocks

A useful countermeasure against the mental aspects of psychic attack is to shift your attention away from it. This creates a mental barrier that deflects the attack. Neg attacks are often hallmarked by unusual, obsessive thoughts and compulsions that undermine your sense of psychological integration. When these are experienced, erect a mental block by clearing your mind and holding it clear, and applying the other countermeasures as necessary.

Mental blocks can help counter other types of Neg attack. When Negs begin an attack, victims usually feel some kind of energy body sensation, such as a tingling in the spine. This can be widespread or localized to a small area of the back. If this causes distress and fear, a connection is made that can allow the Neg to escalate its interference into a direct psychic attack.

When the first symptoms of psychic attack are felt, force your attention away from what is happening, and employ countermeasures as necessary. Clear your mind, refuse to think about the Neg, and refuse to react to it. Focus your mind on something positive and uplifting. This will often break the connection and defuse the attack. But this mental stance should be held as long as necessary, even if the attack escalates. There is no sense in making things easy for Negs; making Negs work harder costs them energy, and the less energy Negs have, the weaker and shorter will be their attacks.

Benefits of Meditation in Defense Against Negs

Regular meditation is an enormous help to anyone prone to psychic attacks and interference. It clears, balances, and strengthens the mind, and increases the flow of energy into and through the energy body. This helps to naturally heal damaged areas of the energy body.

For most people, meditation is best done from a sitting position in a chair. A slight level of discomfort is preferable to sensory deprivation. Too much comfort promotes sleep, not meditation. This is the reason many people lose track of, and cannot remember, what happens during meditation. For a light version of meditation, you should practice the breath-awareness thought-control technique given earlier. Meditation can be done almost anywhere, even while commuting, but I do not advise meditation be practiced while driving, for obvious reasons.

Trance Meditation: If you continue with the breath-awareness meditation, you will find your body settling deeper into relaxation. When physical and mental relaxation reach a certain level, the trance state is entered (trance = mind awake + body asleep). Entry into the trance meditation state is heralded with a warm, cozy wave and a slight disassociation from reality. This happens briefly every night, just before you fall asleep. It's the perfect state for deep thinking, introspection, contemplation, and prayer. For an extra challenge, you might like to try this with your eyes open.

You may appear to feel paralyzed in trance, as you will experience very mild body/mind disassociation. The physical body will move if you concentrate and apply a little effort. Movements will be slow and cause tingling inside your limbs, but your body will still work fine; you can stand and walk slowly, if you practice and keep your mind clear. This will feel as if you are walking on huge, fluffy pillows.

The practice of holding the mind forcibly clear in meditation is an effective countermeasure against intrusive Neg thoughts and energies. Negs find it easy to slide in among a person's internal mental dialogue, hiding amidst the meaningless chatter of undisciplined minds. But if the surface mind is held clear through disciplined mental effort, there is no place for Negs to hide.

The Power of Prayer: Prayer is a profound act. Prayers are heard and acted upon in the same manner in which they are offered. If sincere, heartfelt prayers are not answered within a reasonable time, this does not mean they have fallen on deaf ears. We often ask for things that are not good for us or for others. We cannot see the big picture, so we have no way of knowing the reasons behind things like suffering and misfortune. Sometimes, you have to suffer to learn life's lessons and make spiritual progress. Relieving suffering might make us feel happier for the moment, but it may not be in accordance with divine plans.

Most people have only a vague idea how to pray. Praying is much like dictating a letter, aloud or mentally. Pray to whatever deity or aspect of God you believe in most. If you have a Christian background, you might like to use a prayer you know, for example, the Lord's Prayer or the Twenty-Third Psalm; you can add a few personal requests afterwards. The words used are not as important as the sincerity and clarity with which they are said.

If you do not know any formal prayers, or do not feel comfortable using them, just talk with God, or write him a letter. You could simply say: "Dear God, please forgive me for my sins, as I forgive all those who have sinned against me, and guide me and protect me from all evil, etc.," and follow this with more specific pleas for protection and help with whatever is troubling you. The clarity and heartfelt sincerity with which prayers are said empowers them. Rattling off words parrot-fashion has no value apart from occupying one's mind in a positive way.

The best advice I can give is similar to the advice Jesus gives in the Bible concerning the Lord's Prayer: Go somewhere private and quiet. The quietest and most private place imaginable is within your mind. Clear your mind and go within to talk with God. The deeper the meditation, the more powerful will be the prayers offered.

Prayers are also beneficial when used to occupy the mind and clear it of Neg influences. Prayer holds the mind centered and balanced during stressful times. This focuses the mind on a strong source of positive energy: God. For this purpose, memorize some formal prayers like those just suggested; other hymns and psalms can also be used for this purpose. They can be said or sung aloud, or offered internally as prayers. Everyone should pray before falling asleep. Even if just a few words are said, if they are sincere they will be heard. A person under psychic attack, or suffering Neg influences, is well advised to pray many times a day as this may alleviate the experience with the positive state of mind that prayer renders.

Advice from Psychics: It can be worthwhile for persons under psychic attack to seek the advice of a good psychic. A clear psychic reading can help you analyze the attacks by providing you with impressions and background information you may not be sensitive enough to pick up for yourself. Keep in mind that you usually get what you pay for in this respect, so it's best to find someone who is well-recommended, and beware of charlatans.

Messages in Bottles (MIBs): Another way of getting a feel for what is happening in the background of your life is to do what I call MIBs, or Messages in Bottles. This is a simple intuitive process that works along the same lines as many divination methods involving random choice and intuitive interpretation. Messages in Bottles will often provide you insights on look-and-feel for what is happening behind the scenes. This will not usually give you precise information, although sometimes it can surprise you by highlighting a theme.

MIBs are best done spontaneously and should not be overdone. Once a month is usually enough, but it does not hurt to play around with it. Here's how to do it:

Reach out and grab a dictionary or thesaurus. Without looking or thinking, bend it slightly and let the pages flicker through your fingers. Do this quickly, stopping anywhere and fingering a page. Again without looking, quickly place a fingertip on the page and hold it in place. Read the word or phrase your finger is pointing to. Write this down. Repeat the process nine times. Then, examine the words individually, in groups, and as a whole list. Mark any of the words that jog associations in you. Look for meaning in the pattern of words. If the word list you get makes no sense, hold the book, relax, close your eyes, think about your problem, ask a question, and repeat the MIB process.

An MIB can be done with anything: books, magazines, newspapers, etc. They give the best results when the urge to do it pops into your mind spontaneously. When this happens, use your intuition and quickly grab whatever intuitively attracts you. With MIBs, often it's not the single word the finger rests on, but the phrase or sentence surrounding it, or above or below it, that contains the message. Follow your intuition on this. Sometimes MIBs can be startlingly accurate and profound. When this happens, it's a fair indicator that strong forces are at work in your life. Positive messages indicate higher forces are at work; unpleasant messages indicate negative forces are at work.

My first experience with MIBs was accidental, but MIBs have saved my life on more than one occasion. For example, the time I was possessed, the piece of paper that stuck to my leg was, in essence, an MIB.

A few years before that event with the scrap of paper, I had a vision during my daily meditation. I was wide awake in the trance state. In this vision I saw myself walk into the room and stop next to a huge bookcase. The visionary me looked a few years older, with different hair and glasses. (At the time of this vision I did not need glasses and did not have the bookcase.) The visionary me took a large book from the top shelf, opened it, and began reading. He looked up in surprise, took a step back, and looked directly at me, before replacing the book, waving at me, and leaving the room. The vision ended.

A few years after that experience, several months after my possession, deliverance, and episode with the scrap of paper, I was preparing to meditate in my living room. I looked up at the new bookcase, a full wall unit a friend had just finished building. Then, I remembered the vision from years before. I looked it up in my journal and it all came back to me. I was even wearing the same clothes and had my hair the same way as I had seen in the vision. To amuse myself, I reenacted the whole vision to see if anything interesting would happen.

Putting on my new reading glasses (that part had already come true), I left the room and reentered it, walking to where I had seen myself standing in the vision. I reached up and took down a large book at random, a volume of *The Encyclopedia Britannica* on the top shelf. I opened the book at random and looked down at it. I was stunned. The name *Robert Bruce* shouted up at me: my name. I had accidentally opened it to the pages containing short biographies of all the famous Robert Bruces in history. This surprised me so much that I looked at where I had been sitting years earlier, and saw my past self briefly materialize there, staring intently at me. I replaced the book, waved at my past self, and left the room.

When friends visited later, I told them what had happened. Excited, I repeated my actions. I grabbed a book from the shelf, again at random, and opened it—to exactly the same page with all the Robert Bruces. I did this a dozen times in a row (never missing once) over the next few days. Then, as suddenly as it began, it stopped.

I have been unable to repeat this since, even though I now know the specific volume and the rough location of the pages. Now I have to use the index and find it the old-fashioned way. This particular MIB was a significant turning point in my life, giving me the courage to persevere and overcome many obstacles in my life (including Neg problems).

After this event, all the pieces came together and I had a realization: everything in this world is connected, including the past, the present, and the future. This concept is nothing new, but having it proven to myself beyond all doubt is breathtaking. It brought me a profound, experience-based understanding of how my life is connected with the universe. Life tries to pass messages to us, in any way, shape, or form available to it, but it's up to us to discover them. They are everywhere—in print, in the clouds, in methods of divination such as Tarot and Runes, in the events that happen to us, in the things people say and do to us, on TV, in the books we read, and most especially in our dreams.

Advice in Dreams: Advice can be gleaned through your dreams, yours and those of everyone around you. So it pays to listen when someone says, "I had a dream. . . ." It just might concern you. Keep a journal of all your significant dreams and visions. Dreams show elements of the past, present, and future, and they will guide you along life's rocky pathways.

Often, dream elements become meaningful in hindsight. A dream journal allows you to draw comparisons with other visions, dreams, and real-life events. The accuracy of this kind of prophetic dream analysis, based on identifiable personal dream symbology, works better over time. Much like with MIBs, life will start working through your dream journaling and analysis process the moment you begin using it.

Everyone's mind works differently when it comes to dreaming. Everyone has their own set of symbols and associations. Learned mental associations, and those set within us all by the collective consciousness, are used by the mind on subconscious levels to create and store dream memories. The mind uses these associations to interpret dream-causing energies, received from dimensional levels above and beyond our base level of consciousness and understanding. These energies, perceived in their pure form during dreams, must be translated into base-level format before they can be downloaded into the physical brain and stored as recallable memories.

Only through the process of recording and interpreting dreams over time can the peculiarities of your personal mental associations be identified. Long-term recording and analysis allow the identification of the symbolism and metaphorical imagery generated within dreams by the subconscious mind. Repeated patterns appear, and these show the forms, structures, and symbols unique to the individual. When the basic elements of these patterns become known, you can use that knowledge for personal dream interpretation with ever-improving accuracy.

Let me offer a general caution about the abstract nature of dreams and visions. Misunderstanding the nature of dream imagery, plus wishful-thinking and jumping to conclusions, can generate confusion and damage your life. The setting, sequence, players, symbols, actions, modifying elements, connections, sign posts, and date stamps within dreams are all meaningful aspects. Everything is symbolic and only experience, logic, intuition, and common sense teach you to interpret them. Until you gain experience, it's best to treat all dreams and visions, especially those in high-interest areas like relationships, money, fame, or death, with caution. Do not over-react to dream content in real life, until such time as you gain experience and insight into how *your* dreams and visions work.

The relevance of keeping a dream journal to psychic self-defense is that it can give indication of Neg activity in your life and the karmic forces belying the ordinariness of apparently mundane, everyday events. This understanding empowers you and indicates where your efforts are best invested, such as resolving a conflict to bring about peace.

Dreams are enigmatic and may indicate past, present, or future events in two distinct ways. A dream may signify an event that is apparently detrimental to your well-being, or, alternatively, an event that is beneficial to yourself or others, yet susceptible to Neg sabotage. Of course the total outcome, when all is said and done, may be a positive from a series of prior negative events. That is, trauma can have the effect of making you stronger and of increasing your level of awareness and introspection.

Introspection and Self-Analysis: Self-observation, introspection, and self-analysis are valuable tools for psychic self-defense.

They allow Neg influences to be identified and dealt with before they become strong enough to do damage. Early identification of problems allows countermeasures to be applied earlier, and more effectively, while Neg influences are still weak.

Self-observation involves observing your thoughts, motivations, actions, and reactions as they happen. This entails being mindful of what you think, feel, do, and say at all times. This may sound difficult, but it's easy with a little practice. It's a watchful state of mind, like promoting a part of yourself to become a quiet observer in the back of your mind. This observer watches and notes everything; it reminds you when you step out of line or act in unusual or wrong ways.

Neg influences are progressive, usually beginning subtly with telepathic, hypnotic, emotional broadcasts that stimulate mild urges and impulses. For example, with no Neg stimulation you may feel mildly jealous if your partner dances with another person, but give it no further thought. However, with Neg stimulation this could grow into an unsettling condition that might plague you for weeks, even end up causing harm to your relationship and your life.

The same thing applies to natural urges and mild addictions, such as sex and alcohol. One may be naturally inclined to drink a couple of glasses of wine once a week and have sex every third day. But under Neg stimulation, you might begin drinking every night and craving sex every day. Your mind may fill with strangely powerful cravings and fantasies that feel as if they come from within you. These may come and go to begin with, but will grow in frequency and intensity if they are not identified and countered intelligently.

All compulsive and obsessive behavior starts this way. At first it is mild, but strangely compelling. Without realizing it, you start acting on these impulses every now and then. This may involve anything, such as frequent washing of hands; using pornography, drugs, or alcohol; touching things a certain number of times; lining things up neatly; doing and saying things out of character; or gossiping.

Introspection is the process of going within and examining your actions, reactions, thoughts, and motivations, taking an honest look at yourself and your life. In a way, introspection is analyzing notes taken during self-observation. Ideally, this should be done during a quiet time at the end of each day. Everything you have done and said should be examined for its content and motives. This does not take long and, in time, it becomes habitual. If you notice anything out of character, record this in a journal and work on countering it. This information may be useful later if you have to analyze a psychic attack and work out when it started and what its source is. This can also help you identify core images.

Simple meditation techniques, as given earlier, make introspection easier as your mind is clearer. This allows for a deeper, faster level of thinking. Sit, relax, clear your mind, and allow yourself to settle. Go through the events of your day and examine your actions, interactions, and motivations. This is about as private and personal as it gets, so be brutally honest and do not make excuses for yourself. Examine every human interaction for spiritual correctness. Ask these three questions: Was it honest? Was it necessary? Was it kind? The goal is to aim for a "yes" for every interaction.

When negative, unnatural, or out-of-character behavior is discovered, it's often enough to exert a little willpower and correct this in the future by not repeating it. Minor behavioral problems will often correct themselves once you become aware of them. If this does not work and they start becoming a problem, undertake a core image search (explained later in the book).

Strengthening Your Willpower: Strengthening willpower requires that you undertake a progressive course of self-discipline. The application of self-discipline to your body and life leads to self-control and self-mastery. This has enormous life benefits for anyone. Improved willpower is also invaluable when fighting Neg urges and compulsions.

Water Fasting: Any type of self-denial exercises the will. Fasting is difficult and is therefore a powerful method of increasing willpower. The stronger your will, the easier it is to resist Neg influences. It's best for a beginner to start with one full day of fasting, starting the night before and finishing the morning after the chosen day of fasting. Take nothing but pure water and lots of it, plus high quality vitamins. Build the length of the fast to three full days. Any longer than this can harm your health.

Water fasting can be difficult if you are working and need energy. Water fasting makes you tired, and you will find you'll need more sleep than usual. But you can water fast over a weekend, starting Friday (after lunch) and ending Sunday night or Monday morning. The mind can overcome low energy and tiredness, making this technique excellent for willpower training. Take at least a few days' break, eating normally between each water fast.

However, before fasting or modifying your diet in any way, consult a healthcare practitioner and insure this will not harm you. A variety of conditions, including diabetes, contraindicate water fasting and other types of fasting. In this case, other exercises must be used to the same ends. However, do not avoid water and juice fasting unless there are clear medical reasons for doing so.

Juice Fasting: Juice fasting is much easier than water fasting. It can also be sustained for much longer without overly weakening or tiring the physical body. Start with two complete days and take nothing but one quart each of fruit or vegetable juice. Make a fresh mix of whatever you like or of whatever is in season. Make fresh juice each morning, but keep a little juice handy for the first thing in the morning. Use only fresh, good quality produce for juicing. Ask at your natural foods outlet for booklets of juice recipes. Here are a couple of suggestions:

Basic Vegetable Juice: With a fruit and vegetable juicer, juice cabbages, carrots, celery, beetroot, tomatoes, and fresh parsley to make a good basic vegetable juice. The mixture should be two-fifths cabbage, two-fifths carrot, and one-fifth all the remaining ingredients. Add pepper, salt, and fresh herbs to taste.

Basic Fruit Juice: Use apple, orange, grape, and watermelon, in whatever quantities you prefer; add a dash of lemon juice.

Adjust these recipes to taste and tolerance, as well as to what is in season. Some people cannot take cabbage juice, for example. If you do not have a juicer already, get a high-quality model.

Freshly made juices are more satisfying and better for you. For maximum vitamin content, juice should be made daily and kept refrigerated in sealed glass containers. If you cannot make your own juice, buy the best quality pre-made juices you can afford.

Drink a 4-ounce glass of each type of juice and a glass of pure water first thing in the morning. Then, drink a glass of each type every hour or so; drink a small glass of each whenever you feel hungry or weak. Keep a few cartons of store-bought fruit and vegetable juice on hand for emergencies; take some with you when you go out so you are not tempted to eat.

Take multivitamins and extra vitamin B and soluble calcium. If your breath smells stale during a fast, a salt water mouth rinse helps. Carry a small picnic saltshaker; shake some salt onto your tongue and rinse your mouth with water. If your lips dry and crack, cut down on the quantity of citrus in your fruit juice and remember to rinse your mouth and lips with water after drinking juice. A good lip balm also helps.

If you smoke, and/or drink coffee or tea, be careful with them during water and juice fasting. They will get absorbed far more rapidly into your system while you are fasting. If you have them first thing in the morning, they can cause nausea, sweating, or rapid heartbeat. Try a weaker brew or strength of these substances. No alcohol or recreational drugs should be consumed during a fast, as these weaken your will, loosen inhibitions, and intensify your hunger.

For extended fasting (more than three days) take a mineral–salts rehydration sports drink several times a day; this is especially recommended during water fasting. This will help keep your electrolyte balance healthy and help overcome many potential fasting problems. If in doubt or worried by this, consult a medical doctor for advice.

Water and juice fasting purge the body of waste matter and lift its subtle energy levels. Purgatives and enemas can also be used to rid the body of waste matter more quickly during the early stages of a fast. If you are inexperienced with these approaches, consult a health therapist, yoga instructor, or medical doctor for competent instruction. Uninformed experimentation is not advised.

In general, for willpower training, pick something easy and achievable to begin with. Do not bite off more than you can chew. It takes time to develop willpower "muscles." Do one thing at a time and do it well; build on this success and you will become progressively stronger. This will provide you with the tools necessary to succeed with larger, more difficult goals. Boosted willpower will help you to resist Neg influences and has the effect of making you an unattractive target.

Substance Fasting: Another way of developing self-discipline is through substance fasting. Pick some things you like to consume and deny yourself these substances for a set period of time. If you have an addiction (say to caffeine, nicotine, or alcohol), abstinence may put you under stress. If this is the case, limit your intake in a disciplined way, cutting down on the chosen substance by fifty percent. Continue this for a set time, say three days, as with any other fast.

A good way to use this device is to pick three days a week, or every second day, and continue this fast on those days for the long term. This is valuable for boosting your willpower, as well as weaning yourself off undesirable addictions. A strict, healthy, calorie controlled-diet is also a valuable willpower exercise, but it is more suitable for long-term training.

13

Energy Body Attachments: How to Undo Their Causes and Effects

Would it surprise you if I said energy body attachments can cause skin blemishes? The look of incredulity that is probably on your face would mirror my own when I discovered this phenomenon. It involves a strange procedure I have been tinkering with for years. This highlights the relationship between certain types of skin blemishes and Neg attachment points. These attachments can be broken by removing the skin blemishes themselves with nothing more than a ballpoint pen.

I discovered this method by accident. Years ago, my then–three-year-old son had a large strawberry birthmark (called a nevus), about three-quarters of an inch across on his upper forehead. He was born with this. At that time, I was experimenting with ways to remove skin blemishes but without success. On a whim one day, I marked this birthmark with a cross, drawn with a blue ballpoint pen.

A week or so later the ink had faded, gradually having washed off in showers. However, when the ink was finally gone, something extraordinary appeared in its place. The ink cross had caused a bleached-white cross to form on the birthmark. Closer examination showed the swelling and redness of the blemish had faded from under the ink, leaving a clear white indented cross. This cross was also a little crooked, following the outline of the original ink cross exactly.

In earlier times, suspected witches were given a physical examination before any other proceedings were carried out. Witch examiners searched them for physical evidence to prove the suspects were witches by looking for certain types of skin blemishes, in particular, gristly tumors and hard areas of skin. These were of the type that would not bleed if a needle were inserted. Such a mark was said to be the Devil's Mark *(Stigmata Diabolis)*, the Devil's Seal *(Sigillum Diabolis)*, or Witch's Marks; this last type included protruding tumors at which demons were said to suckle. The discovery of such tumors and blemishes was considered the definitive proof, at the time, of being a witch, and justified torture and sentence of death, regardless of other evidence.

The theory of certain types of skin growths being indicative of Neg attachments seems consistent across various cultures and religions. I was unsuccessful with my efforts to obtain comment on this matter from the Vatican's demonologists. However, I speculate that knowledge of the relationship between Negs and skin growths (in particular granulomas, which are hard gristly lumps that when pierced with a long needle cause no pain and do not bleed) was obtained from the personal experience of church exorcists. They would have had to be blind not to notice the direct relationship between demonic possession and granulomas, especially as these marks appear at the instant of possession and burst at the instant of exorcism.

I also speculate that the modern Vatican still holds these views because they still perform demonic exorcisms today. These skin symptoms were involved with my own possession and release, and with the demonic possession and exorcism of many others I have helped, so I support this theory through my multiple observations and experiences.

The concept was supported in Judaism by the Kabbalist Rabbi Moshe Zaccuto (1625–1697) who wrote in his work, *Igerret*

H'Ramaz: "One of the primary ways to tell if a person has a negative entity attached to them is if there is a growth anywhere on their body." Another more modern Jewish view was put forward by Dovber Pinson in his book, *Reincarnation and Judaism*. Pinson revealed that the Hebrew word for a negative entity, *Dybbuk*, literally translates as "attached." He writes: "When a person is possessed by a dybbuk . . . he feels something external to his own existence now present, inhabiting and functioning within his body."

Types of Blemishes Associated with Neg Attachments

My experiments indicate a wide variety of lumps, tumors, and skin anomalies, even rough or hard patches of skin, can be related to Neg attachments. However, the exact type of blemish does not seem that important. Most are simple skin anomalies related to insignificant non-threatening energy body attachments. One can liken most of these to the barnacles on a ship's hull in that they are of no real significance or threat to the ship (in this case, the body) itself.

My theory of skin blemishes is based on how the mechanism of physical diseases and disorders are caused by energy body dysfunctions and aberrations. Science has a profound knowledge of chemical and biological causative factors underlying human diseases and disorders, but which comes first: physical symptoms or energy causes?

In my experience, disease first manifests in the energy body. Signs of disease appear in the aura (the field of subtle energy body radiations visible to clairvoyants) long before any physical symptoms appear. In one case, I viewed a woman's aura and I noticed a dark, murky-green patch covering the right side of her head; it was shot through with red and orange sparks. Three days later, this woman developed an acute infection in her right ear. This infection responded to antibiotics and slowly healed over the next two weeks, but the signs in her aura took another month to fade.

While I have only scratched the surface with my studies in this area, they indicate that a wide variety of common skin anomalies can result from Neg energy body attachments. The most significant are the seemingly harmless, benign, gristly tumors called granulomas. These first appear as soft lumps or blisters and slowly harden over a few weeks.

The only way to discover the significance of a skin anomaly is to test it by applying the treatment method (description follows) and observe how the skin problem reacts. In a sense, the treatment is also a diagnosis. If a skin anomaly containing a Neg energy body attachment is treated, changes and side effects will indicate its significance. Warts do not seem to respond well to this treatment, but as I have not had the opportunity to work on many, perhaps a longer treatment time is needed.

Neg attachment points affect the physical body in much the same way as do acupuncture needles when inserted in the skin. These points interfere with the flow of subtle energies within the human energy body (connecting, disconnecting, or redirecting the energy currents) which in turn affects the physiology of the physical body. A single energy body attachment may cause a single skin blemish or a network of interconnected skin blemishes.

Skin blemishes seem to be linked with core images. But it's difficult to identify relationships between particular blemishes and the core images that may be their root. However, a combination of ink diagrams, body-awareness actions, and core image removal seems the most effective way of removing them.

The underlying theory of skin blemish removal is simple. Any Neg-related energy body attachment point will contain a subtle energy filament. The energy of this filament is unnatural to the human energy body and causes a disturbance at the site of attachment; this in turn affects biological processes on and within the human body, such as skin, flesh, muscle, organs, bone, etc. Energy body attachment points can thus cause a wide variety of physical abnormalities.

An ink line drawn on the skin causes subtle energies to flow along it. An ink diagram enclosed within a circle attracts subtle energy, creating a small vortex of concentrated subtle energy. This concentration of energy interferes with energy body attachments and in time disconnects them. The reverse may also apply in that ink diagrams may block or shield subtle energies from skin blemishes, thereby "starving" Neg attachments. However, I think this less likely than the previous scenario. An ink design clearly interferes with the subtle energies associated with any type of Neg energy body attachment. The energy body eventually rejects the attachment and heals that area of the energy body. The physical body then rejects the biological aberration (the skin blemish) and rebuilds itself according to its natural template.

In the early days of my experimenting with this method, the possibility was raised by some of my volunteers that maybe I was personally affecting the skin blemish removal process. It was considered possible that I was carrying out an unusual type of spiritual healing, so that it was not the ink diagrams, per se, that were causing the phenomenon in question, but me.

A young woman undertook to prove this factor one way or another for herself. Without telling me, she began treating a large, black, flat mole (a third of an inch in diameter) on her stomach that had been there all her life. Four weeks after she began this experiment, I received an excited phone call from her. She had just peeled the mole off while taking a shower; this bled a little afterwards, but healed quickly to the usual white color. The next day, she showed me the place where the mole had been. The white color faded over the course of a year and left no scar in its wake. The point here is that the woman removed this mole with no help from me, thus disproving the suggestion that I, and not the technique, was the specific source of the healing.

Regardless of type, not all skin blemishes will respond in exactly the same way. For example, two people may start treating similar moles at the same time using the same blue ink diagram. One person will have a good response and remove his mole in a reasonable length of time while the treatment will have no effect on the other person's mole. It seems logical then that blue ink diagrams may only affect a particular range of Neg energy body attachments.

The types that are affected may involve energies that are easily interfered with by the subtle energy body stimulation caused by *blue* ink diagrams. The color and composition of the ink used thus may be responsible for these variations, affecting success rates accordingly, so if a skin blemish does not begin responding in a reasonable length of time, some experimentation with color and ink composition and alternative designs may be in order.

Treating and removing some types and patterns of skin blemishes may affect some health and disease conditions. Again, little is known about this factor. In any event all medical conditions, especially diabetes, should be closely monitored during mole removal treatments.

I removed a number of small, gristly skin tumors (granuloma type) from my body using a combination of ink diagrams and rapid body-awareness actions. These tumors carried significant Neg attachments. It was interesting to see how they responded under treatment.

While relaxing and using rapid body-awareness actions on a small lump on my right hip, I felt a noticeable stinging sensation coming from it. Then, I felt some faint stinging lines connecting this with several similar small lumps on my right side, back of neck, elbow, lower back, left knee, and right big toe. It was clear these were connected and possibly were a network of attachments.

Another interesting observation I made was when a gristly lump begins to respond, it will often flare up, becoming painful and infected, even sometimes erupting, before shrinking and dying. It may shrink and grow back several times during the removal process. Sometimes a new gristly lump will appear next to one being treated, as it begins to die; other times a new lump will appear on the opposite side of the body instead. For example, if a lump over the right kidney is being treated and it begins responding, a new one might appear over the left kidney.

New lumps generally begin as small watery blisters, growing into small boils with hard, gristly centers. These soon grow into hard, gristly lumps under the skin, identical to the one that was removed. If the new lump is treated, when it responds, often the old lump will begin growing back. But each time a lump is removed, it grows back slightly smaller, weaker and is more easily removed. Eventually, if you keep working on them, they die off and go away completely.

While removing the gristly lumps from myself and treating them with rapid body-awareness actions during trance meditation, I found spontaneous core imagery appearing in my mind's eye. Treating this imagery as it appeared significantly affected the gristly lumps and aided in their removal. Due to the peculiar way granuloma-type lumps respond to ink diagram treatments, they seem to support more intense Neg attachments than other types of skin blemishes. So removing any type of gristly lump generally requires a combination of ink diagram treatment and daily rapid body-awareness brushing. It's wise to have gristly lumps checked by a doctor, and to have them surgically removed if they grow too big.

Skin Blemish Removal Method

Here is the method I developed for treating and removing skin blemishes. This is the simplest and most effective method I've found to date.

Use a blue or black ballpoint pen, but experiment with other inks and colors if you like. Clean the skin area with skin cleanser or soap to remove skin oils. Draw a simple geometric design (see following section) clearly over the blemish. Leave it on the skin for as long as it takes, and touch it up or reapply as necessary, as it wears or washes away.

With moles, gristly tumors, and other distinct blemishes, the design should be approximately double the size of the blemish and centered over it. If treating indistinct areas, such as a rough area of skin or a group of blemishes, the design does not have to be much larger than the area being treated. Body-awareness actions can be combined with the use of ink diagrams to enhance this method. Body-awareness actions weaken energy body attachments, as do ink diagrams.

In my early days of working with this method, I believed I had discovered a new form of natural magic and that the symbols themselves were affecting the skin blemishes. But after trying many different symbols and designs, I found little difference in results. However, I am as yet still undecided on this matter.

Geometric Design or Symbol: The type of geometric design or symbol used does not seem that important. I have tried a variety of designs and symbols and found little difference among them. The neatness of a design does have some effect, but even a roughly drawn design will often work well. I have tried the pentagram, Star of David, and other designs, and all seem to work equally well. I settled on using an equally limbed cross within a circle with the cross touching the circle at all four points.

Open designs (ones not enclosed by circles) do not seem to work as well as designs enclosed within circles. In some cases, only skin bleaching will occur under the ink, especially with nevus and other skin pigmentation anomalies. Open designs seem to act only on the areas covered by the ink, but when enclosed within a circle, the entire area is affected.

The Effect of Ink and Color: I have experimented with different types of inks, dyes, and colors, but blue ballpoint ink seems to work best. Black and violet also work fairly well, but red ink seems less effective. It's possible the ink itself is causing these strange effects, as the type of ink used is important. I have tried dye pens and applying blotches of ink over skin blemishes with poor results. However, it seems more likely that the combination of ink, color, and geometric design all contribute to the result.

Time Factor: The time factor involved with skin blemish removal is important. Approximately fifty percent of treatable skin blemishes will begin responding within a week or two of treatment. Keep in mind, though, that the time factor is an unpredictable variable. Some skin blemishes respond very quickly, often causing immediate side effects, and will begin to change noticeably within forty-eight hours. However, some take several weeks or more before they begin responding.

As the time factor is so unpredictable, it's difficult to say exactly how a blemish will react and how long it will take to respond, but as a rule of thumb, most treatable blemishes begin changing noticeably within fourteen days.

My early experiments with more than thirty men, women, and children (ages three to seventy) showed a fifty percent success rate, that is, a total clearing up of the blemish. I also removed twenty or more skin blemishes from my body, including moles, freckles, small gristly tumors, and lumps. Only three of my volunteers showed no response at all to the ink diagram method. Given the success in treating other similar types of skin blemishes, it's possible that if treatment were continued long enough these would also have shown good results. The most stubborn blemish I have ever treated on my body took six months before it responded.

How Skin Blemishes Respond to Treatment

Blemishes respond in a variety of ways. A typical mole, of the type with a large hair in its center, will usually begin changing within forty-eight hours. The change is barely noticeable at first, but in an average of two to four weeks of removal time, it will slowly dry and change into a scab; it will eventually fall off or can be peeled off.

Once a mole begins to change and dry, its edges should be lightly scratched with fingernails during bathing. This will show its progress and indicate when it has changed into a scab or is ready for peeling off. Do not try to peel it off before it's ready. When the edge begins to lift, it can usually be peeled off like a minor scab. This will usually bleed slightly, so antiseptic and wound dressing should be applied as necessary.

After a mole has been removed, it will heal to white with no tan or pigmentation depending on natural skin color. In the majority of cases, it will leave no discernible scar tissue; however, this area of skin may take several months to pigment and tan properly so it matches the rest of the body. Peeling off a dead mole can leave a slight scar if peeled off too early.

I have only had one case where a successfully removed mole began growing back, twelve years after its removal. What was originally (before removal) a large, dark-brown raised mole with a large hair in its middle, a quarter-inch across, recently showed up as a pale, flat area of slightly discolored skin, the same shape and size as the original mole. However, this is barely visible to the eye and is not growing, darkening, or spreading. It may just be scar tissue showing up with increased age, resulting from peeling it off too soon.

Mild Side-Effects: Side-effects caused by the skin blemish removal process are varied and unpredictable, but considering the simple, non-intrusive method being used, according to medical science today, there should not be any side effects at all. My experiments indicate that less than twenty percent of people using the skin blemish removal method will experience noticeable side effects, and in most cases, when side effects occur, these will be mild and of short duration. The most common side effects, in order of predominance, are nausea, stomach pain, vomiting, diarrhea, fever, and anxiety. In most cases, symptoms either will be worse at night or will occur only at night.

One might think the side effects in question could be psychosomatic—caused by suggestion. However, many of my volunteers were not told about any possible side effects, yet still experienced predictable side effects at the same rate as others who were told of them. Several volunteers were not even told the purpose of the small designs I drew on them. I told them it was an experimental form of acupressure, using the tip of a pen to treat health problems, and that the ink diagram was only for my reference to remind me of the area I had worked on. I did not say I was attempting to remove skin blemishes. The results were the same as with subjects who were told the true purpose of the ink designs.

Stronger Side-Effects: Stronger side effects are rare. According to my experiments, less than five percent of all subjects will experience anything more than mild, temporary discomfort. In one case, a young white male was stricken with sudden, severe nausea, followed by vomiting and diarrhea, within thirty seconds of applying a blue ink diagram to a dark mole on the side of his neck. After an hour, during which he was in distress, I washed off the ink diagram, and all symptoms disappeared within a few minutes.

In another case, a dark-skinned Burmese male was instructed to touch up two diagrams I had drawn over small, raised moles on the side of his forehead. He had carried these moles since birth. There were no immediate symptoms, but I checked him two weeks later. He had been stricken with unexplainable nocturnal nausea, vomiting and diarrhea, and anxiety attacks every night for the week after his moles were first marked. He suspected the diagrams had something to do with these symptoms and had removed them so he could sleep. One of the treated moles fell off in the process.

In general, stronger side effects seem to occur in subjects when moles in the head and neck area are marked. This is also more noticeable with children.

Reprisals by Psychic Attack: Removing skin blemishes related to significant Neg energy body attachment points may precipitate some level of psychic attack. It's logical to suggest that any interference with energy attachment points could disturb the Negs attached to them. Stronger side effects, including psychic attacks and influences, are then more likely to occur. However, such attacks are usually short-lived. In cases like this, the Negs are already active in a person's life, so the skin blemish removal process merely brings Neg-related problems to the surface.

Precautions for Treating Children

Great caution should be used when treating children, especially very young ones, with the skin blemish removal method. Children should be monitored day and night after treatment, as the occurrence of moderate-to-severe side effects in children appears more frequent than with adults. I have seen several occurrences of strong side effects, including high fevers. However, no fitting from fever has ever occurred in my test subjects, and no child was ever harmed by these experiments.

High fever can cause convulsions and even brain damage. If fever begins to increase and analgesics fail to reduce it, thoroughly remove all ink designs. Treat the fever as a normal illness, and immediately give the child a cool shower or bath to reduce body temperature rapidly. If an ink design is causing a fever, once it's removed the fever should begin dropping immediately. It is wise to call a doctor or ambulance or take the child to the hospital as soon as the fever starts to spike.

With children, as with adults, stronger side effects are more common when treating blemishes on the head and neck. In one case, while treating a four-year-old girl with a large strawberry birthmark on her forehead, I found that her side effects varied enormously. The ink design was applied in the morning, but no side effects were apparent until sundown. She then experienced all the symptoms of food poisoning: stomach pain, nausea, diarrhea, vomiting, and high fever. The fever rose quickly until it was past the level that normally causes febrile convulsions.

The girl lay limply on her bed, semi-conscious with a high fever. An ambulance had already been called. The girl had been given a large dose of analgesic an hour earlier, several cool baths, plus cold cloths and ice packs, but nothing helped. Then, I removed the ink diagram with skin toner. All symptoms disappeared within five minutes. By the time the ambulance arrived, she was sitting up in bed playing, with no symptoms of illness at all. The paramedics checked the girl, shook their heads, and left, leaving the girl at home.

The next evening was even more curious. The girl came down with the same symptoms as she did the night before, an hour after sundown. Once again, she was given analgesics, cool baths, ice packs, and once again, the ambulance was called. The ink design (a cross in a circle done in blue ink) had not been reapplied since its removal the previous night. This time, I reapplied the ink design, and once again, all the girl's symptoms vanished in a few minutes. Once again, the ambulance boys shook their heads and left empty-handed. I removed the ink diagram two hours later, but her illness and fever did not return.

The only conclusion I could draw from this experience was that the Neg associated with the girl's forehead birthmark was highly disturbed by the attempts to remove it. It seemed to be deliberately confounding my experiment. Because of this, and the danger to the girl, I discontinued treatment on her entirely. There was no recurrence of the peculiar nocturnal illness symptoms. Of all the volunteers I have experimented with, this was the only case in which anything this severe happened.

General Considerations on Blemish Treatment with Skin Diagrams

Skin Cancers: The effects of the ink diagram method on skin cancer, or on any type of potential skin cancer, are unknown. I do not advise using ink diagrams to treat skin cancers. If any doubt exists whether a mole or skin blemish might be dangerous, see a doctor and have it checked. Skin cancer is the most treatable and easily cured of all cancers, if diagnosed very early; but it's the most dangerous of all cancers if left unattended. Malignant skin cancer can kill in a matter of weeks. If benign moles and skin blemishes are removed, logically, the possibility that they might one day turn cancerous is also removed. Therefore, this method may have unknown positive side effects on health that only time will reveal.

Cosmetic Considerations: The skin blemish removal phenomenon has obvious cosmetic applications. Disfiguring skin blemishes, such as moles, can be removed for no other reason than to improve appearance. Some people may find it socially difficult to continue ink diagram treatment on a daily basis. This is especially so if the ink diagram is visible to other people, such as on the hand, face, or neck. Embarrassing questions are sure to be asked. If the ink diagrams are not understood, one may be classed as a strange person. There are a few ways of getting around this. Cover the diagrams with makeup or small adhesive bandages; only apply ink diagrams at night; wear more expansive clothing to conceal the diagrams.

Cautions to Observe: Keep a close check on all types of skin blemishes during treatment. While this has not happened to any of my volunteers, some types of moles can undergo malignant changes. The most likely scenario for this happening would be if an already malignant mole (unsuspected skin cancer) were to be treated. The result of treating cancerous moles with ink diagrams, body-awareness actions, and core image removal techniques are unknown at this time. However, if one already has a medically diagnosed cancerous mole or skin tumor, especially inoperable tumors, I do not think it would be damaging to apply an ink diagram to it. This may or may not affect it beneficially, but it would be wise to have it checked frequently by a doctor.

If a mole being treated with an ink diagram starts to spread, grow, or change suspiciously, have it checked immediately by a doctor. However, keep in mind that when a mole begins to respond, it will undergo some changes. It will either shrink and fade, or begin to shrink and dry out with the edges becoming rough to the touch.

Treating Base Chakra Attachments

While all Neg attachments are significant, those connected to the base or root chakra tend to be the most important. If blemishes are connected to this chakra, they may physically appear at any place, as the energy body is an interconnected unit. The connection itself may also have a sub-dermal (beneath the top layers of the skin) or non-apparent blemish that will only flare up with the onset of frequent body-awareness actions or when Neg activity is prevalent.

The importance of Neg connections to the base chakra is arguably due to the role of this energy center; it is related to sexuality and supplies raw vitality to the whole of the energy body. In my experience, general health and sexual thoughts and urges are often interfered with by Negs.

The base energy center or chakra is particularly vulnerable to Neg attachments. The surface of the base chakra is located between the anus and genitalia and supplies energy for the whole energy body. Base chakra Neg attachments can be the most troublesome of all, usually involving strong Neg connections; they can also be the most difficult to counter and remove.

Whether or not any type of skin blemish or skin condition is involved, if Neg involvement is suspected, the base center should be regularly treated with body-awareness actions. Rough skin, pimples, boils, and a variety of other minor skin conditions near the coccyx (tail bone) or anus, or between buttock cheeks, or on the sides of the hip joints, are all common symptoms of root center attachments. I find it good practice to spend a little time brushing these areas daily with body awareness, such as while taking a shower or before sleep. Once familiar with the brushing technique, it only takes a small part of your attention to do this, like brushing your hair while watching TV.

The way to treat a suspected base center attachment is to use a wide, deep body-awareness brushing action. The first area to cover is from the lower back to the perineum. Repeatedly brush this area up and down with a wide, rapid, deep brushing action. By rapid, I mean one-quarter to one-half of a second in each direction. This can be done sitting, standing, or while lying down. Care should be taken not to involve the genitals in this action, as this may cause distracting arousal.

I recommend at least five to ten minutes of continual body-awareness action daily for early treatment sessions. This can be spread out over the day and you can make use of travel and waiting time for this purpose. Also spend a few minutes brushing any suspect lumps or blemishes in the hips, pelvis, lower back, and buttocks.

Skin blemishes or skin conditions near the site of any primary energy center (any of the other six major chakras) can also indicate possible Neg attachments. If suspected, treat these with suitable body-awareness actions, the same as you did with the base center treatment method given previously. A slice of raw garlic, or some fresh rosemary, wrapped in tissue paper, placed or taped near the area being treated, will also help weaken base center attachments (garlic contains sulfur, which is detrimental to Neg energies). Ink diagrams can also be used, if you can reach the affected area with a pen.

The most common side effects of treating primary energy center attachments are infections and boils. These can occur in the most peculiar places. Infections are more likely while treating base center attachments than any other area. Apart from my own experiences with this, two of my volunteers using body-awareness actions on base center attachments also developed nasty infections near the perineum and coccyx areas, requiring strong antibiotics to heal them. Because of this, I advise anyone working on possible base center attachments to take extra care. If an infection appears, I advise thorough cleaning of the area, seeking qualified medical help, and the early use of antibiotics.

1 4

Active Countermeasures against Negs

The next two chapters contain all the techniques in my anti-Neg repertoire. They represent a wide range of countermeasures, both active and passive, and all methods have been thoroughly field-tested. All will counter Neg activities and presences to some extent, depending on the circumstances and conditions under which they are used.

Active countermeasures are more aggressive than passive countermeasures, of course, and have a more immediate effect, but both types have their uses. It's up to users to decide which are most appropriate for a given situation. By using these methods, along with following the other methods and procedures given in this book, it will be possible for most people to withstand most levels of psychic attacks. At the least, your life will be improved and made more tolerable if you are a sufferer of severe or frequent Neg-related problems.

Your attitude can make all the difference during a psychic attack or while weathering Neg influences. A timid, defeatist attitude can make matters worse, encouraging Negs to greater efforts. Negs delight in fear and feed on the emotional energy it generates; it makes them stronger and bolder. It's difficult not to feel fear while facing supernatural problems, but you don't have to show it. Being brave does not mean no fear is felt; bravery means controlling your fear while continuing to function in a reasonably coherent manner.

Your attitude can make all the difference as to whether or not you ever experience psychic attacks or other Neg-related problems. Just as fear broadcasts energy that can attract Negs, a courageous attitude broadcasts energies that can repel them. Just as walking the streets of a modern city in real life, broadcasting a fearful, timid attitude will tend to attract human predators (muggers), a fearless attitude will repel them.

Tolerance should have no place in the hearts of people fighting Neg problems. Higher, positive emotions are incomprehensible to Negs. While a positive frame of mind is uplifting, I recommend "pissed-off" as a healthy attitude (especially if you lack the necessary bravery). This is far more productive and strengthening than being terrified. Resisting the adversity of Neg influences and attacks is a learning experience. By overcoming them you have the chance to become more than you were before.

Finding Fixed Core Images

We now move into the subject of core images—how to treat and cleanse them. Start a journal and record your progress through the core-image removal process. Apart from your progress notes, your journal may eventually contain lists of people and events, which in the past have affected you in negative ways. This will be useful for your current and future core-image work.

Fixed core images are found hiding behind real-life trauma memories. A trauma memory is the residual memory image of a bad life experience, real or imagined. It can result from anything, i.e., finding a spider in your bed as a child, accidents, injuries, deaths of loved ones, and emotional shocks. Any trauma memory provides a "surface" for Neg attachments to connect into you. Trauma memories create "holes" in the human psyche and Negs hide, take root, and operate from within these holes.

You are looking for the same thing any psychiatrist or clinical psychologist strives to uncover. Any traumatic event, real, imagined, or dreamed, will solidify itself into some level of memory. In time, these memories may erode and become lost, or exist as barely recallable mental imagery. This is especially so with childhood trauma memories. But as any psychologist knows, the power of this type of mental imagery can be immense, as are its effects on physical and mental health and the quality of one's life.

To identify fixed core images, spend some time recalling suspected past traumatic events and compile a list. While normal memory will suffice for most examples, deep introspection during meditation will yield better results. It's your choice whether you start from the present and work back, or whether you go back to your earliest memories and work forward to the present. Some people find a combination of both approaches suits them best.

Pushing your memory back as far as you can, list every traumatic or disturbing event you can remember. Rate the degree to which each event affected you at the time (on a scale of one to ten, ten being the worst) and how they affect you now. Losing a much-loved teddy bear at the age of five may seem unimportant to you as an adult, but the core image this had the potential to create then may be significant. The same applies to past relationships. In hindsight, one may be glad life worked out as it did, but past traumatic moments can still contain core images.

Apply the core-image cleansing technique (described on page 219) to every negative event on your list. To get good results, be thorough; spend at least a couple of weeks working on these daily to begin with; keep a journal of core-image work for your future reference. This is a distilling process that may uncover only a handful of significant core images. Transfer significant ones to a separate list and mark them for closer attention. More memories will surface as you progress, so add these to the appropriate lists.

Finding Recently Implanted Core Images: Aside from real-life trauma-related core images, you may find core imagery that has been recently "implanted" by Negs, such as during dreaming. Again, the experience itself doesn't necessarily need to be from real life. Core images will often show up among dream memories, as this is the outlet of the unconscious, so it is advisable to practice dream recall and keep a dream journal. Dream recall ability varies from person to person, but is not a difficult skill to learn or improve on.

Upon waking, sit on the bed (or wherever you feel comfortable) with closed eyes and relax. Gently clear your mind and hold it as you would if trying to remember something. Keep searching: fragments of dreams will begin to surface. When a fragment surfaces, lock onto it and pull back the rest of the memory by mentally replaying it over and over. If this does not work, keep searching until other fragments surface.

Dream fragments can lead to the recovery of more significant dream memories. The brain learns quickly and reinforces internal mechanisms to improve performance. For the rest of the morning keep a part of your mind searching for dream fragments. Mental associations sparked by mundane events will often trigger dream fragments. Note all disturbing or suspicious dream memories and transfer them to a "Suspect List" in your dream journal. Deal with these in the same way as fixed core images. Recurring dream imagery, for example, should be marked as suspect.

Another way core images can manifest is through obsessive thoughts. These are the kinds of thoughts that repeat to the point where they disturb normal thought and sleep processes. They cause obsessive worrying and brooding. In particular, mark any that contain elements of strong negative emotion for further treatment. Record any obsessive thought episodes and treat them in the same way as other potential sources of core images.

Finding Spontaneous Core Images: Many people experience some type of visual mental imagery during pre-sleep (this is called hypnagogic imagery) and everyone experiences mind's-eye imagery all the time; this is the stuff of imagination, fantasy, and reminiscence. While much of this type of imagery is meaningless, tag any suspicious images as potential core-image material.

Brief spontaneous mental imagery is more difficult to record and deal with in the same way as other types of core imagery, but the same basic technique is used to treat it, as described below. Spontaneous imagery is usually only of short duration, so action should be taken immediately, especially during pre-sleep.

Treating Spontaneous Sexual Imagery: Core image material will often manifest as immediate sexual fantasy. This can be triggered naturally by random thoughts, something seen on TV, an attractive stranger passing by—anything. All hormonal excesses aside, they can also occur unnaturally. For example, say a sexual fantasy pops into your head while doing the dishes or thinking about gardening, and there is no identifiable visual or mental stimulus to explain it. This is the most suspicious type of spontaneous fantasy. A Neg-induced compulsion should be considered possible here.

Of course, sexual imagery and urges are a natural part of life, but those related to core imagery and Neg influence are strange. The sign to watch for is when a spontaneous sexual scenario becomes mildly obsessive, with pressure mounting to physically act on the fantasy—to have sex or masturbate—especially if the fantasy is aberrant or out of character. This fantasy scenario should be noted in your journal as a suspect core image. This helps you to locate the root core image it sprang from.

This type of spontaneous core imagery is like a distorted echo of the root core image behind it. It can be treated immediately or during the next core-image treatment session. However, treatment may be difficult while it's still active in one's mind. Sometimes it's best to wait until later, when it is inactive, and treat it then.

Similarly, addictive urges and compulsions can be used to track down associated core images. For example, if you feel a strong urge to smoke, drink alcohol, or take drugs, feel for where this urge is located in your body. This is often localized in the solar plexus, stomach, or chest. Let this urge fill your mind and become an indistinct image behind your closed eyes. Reach out with your awareness hands, grab hold of it, and shrink it to postcard size, then treat this as if it were any other core image (see the core-image cleansing technique below).

Another way to uncover core images is to use afterimages. Get a picture of the subject or substance in question, for example, your brand of beer or cigarettes. Sit, relax, clear your mind, and prepare for a core-image treatment session. Under good light, stare fixedly at the picture for one minute, allowing the essence of how this makes you feel to fill your mind. Close your eyes; you will see an afterimage of the picture. Treat this afterimage as you would any other core image, as described below.

Core Image Cleansing Technique: The basic technique for treating core imagery is simple. Do this while relaxing or meditating with your eyes closed. It's slightly more effective when done in the trance state, but this is not mandatory. With a little practice anyone can do this well, even children.

1. Close your eyes, relax, and settle, using the breath-awareness technique for a minute or two.

2. Call up the mental imagery in question and relive or replay it as strongly as possible in your imagination. It's not necessary to see this visually; this is an exercise of constructive imagination. This is where you piece the core image together using something like fantasy, so that if a trauma memory is linked to a culpable core image, for example, you would remember and recreate the scene of the experience in question. You would plunge your self into the emotional and cognitive (thought process) state that you felt at the time.

   Thus, a holistic experience is regenerated, using external and internal cues. This will reconnect you with the energies that represent the core of the experience that are trapped within the unconscious, and which have been exploited by Negs to generate further core images.

   I'm sure by now you are beginning to appreciate just how insidious the attachment process is. Our deepest and darkest memories are used against us, memories we'd prefer not to think about, and this allows the core image and Neg attachment to remain without interference from the host.

3. Do all of this procedure with your eyes closed. From the experience you've recreated, condense it into a discrete package. To do this, look out at your internal field of view: the whole of the blank space you can see with your eyes closed—your mindscape. Hold the recreated experience in mind and place your body-awareness hands at the outer corners of this mindscape, corresponding to the outer sides of your eyes at the top of your

cheekbones (Performing this action with your real hands first will help you get the feel for this method). Now grab this mindscape with your body-awareness hands, and holding it as if it were a sheet of card, push it away from your eyes so that it becomes differentiated from the outer mindscape that lies behind it. Pushing this sheet of card away from you will have the effect of making it smaller and dissociated from the surrounding outer mindscape background.

Now you have a chunk of mind space that contains the essence of the memory in question, so that it becomes a visual-pictorial representation of the core image. Alternatively, you may find it easier to *transfer* the memory to the chunk of mind space, by calling up the memory and downloading it away from yourself and onto the chunk of mind space.

This is metaphysics in its truest form, where you are changing a memory of feeling, emotion, and an imagined scene into a visual mind space depiction. This prepares the memory image for subsequent manipulation and treatment.

4. Using your imagination and awareness hands, shrink the image to the size of a postcard, or smaller and freeze it in your mindscape. Accuracy is not necessary as long as its essence, the feel of it, is encapsulated in a package of mind space. This will produce a blurred, indistinct, pale shape as an afterimage. Holding the details after shrinking the image is not important.

5. Reach out with your awareness hands and imagine you are gripping the postcard shape firmly on either side. Turn the image over by pushing with one awareness hand and pulling with the other. If the image turns over easily and you sense nothing, this is a sign that no significant core images are attached to it. Rotate it several times to be sure. However, it's always a good idea to quickly slash and burn it with an imaginary sword and flaming torch that are held and used by your awareness hands, just in case. (Details of this technique follow.)

If the core image is difficult to turn over, this proves it is significant. Considerable effort may then be required to turn it over. Grit your mental teeth and exert as much force as necessary. Do not allow your physical body to tense up, as these are all imaginary actions, performed by your body awareness. Some people find it easier to tackle strong core images by peeling off layers or strips of it. Either method will produce good results if enough effort is applied.

Try your hardest, but if you fail, do not worry. Repeat attempts may be necessary to turn over strong core images. Play around with the focus of your mind and find ways of increasing the power of your awareness actions. Shifting the focus of your eyes behind closed eyelids will help you get a better grip on it. Each attempt will weaken the core image. If you fail the first time, work on it daily until it finally turns over.

6. After turning over the image, imagine you are holding a sword in one awareness hand and a large flaming torch in the other. Take a moment to bless the sword with the power of God: "In the name of Almighty God, let this sword be blessed with His divine power, Amen." Bless the flaming torch with the power of the Holy Spirit: "In the name of Almighty God, let this flaming torch be blessed with the divine power of the Holy Spirit, Amen." Hold the sword in your right hand if right-handed (or in your left if left-handed) and the torch in your other hand. Whether or not anything is revealed (seen or sensed) when the image is turned over, attack that area with your sword. Hack and slash at it for about a minute with your sword (longer if necessary) and then burn the area thoroughly with your flaming torch, imagining that the area is utterly incinerated.

7. If there was any sign of resistance while turning the image over and destroying it, further work can help with the healing process by sealing the weakness (or hole) it may have left behind. Using your imagination, create a sacred symbol of gas-blue fire, by drawing it clockwise with an awareness hand in your imagination. The color blue is traditionally more effective, as is a clockwise direction; both symbolize order and goodness. Use any sacred symbol that has meaning to you; the pentagram

is probably the most effective for this purpose. Sacred symbols should be traced clockwise three times and imagined to be as strong as possible. The resulting symbol should then be connected to what it represents: God, order, purity, or goodness, by blessing it in the same way as the sword and torch.

Although they can be considered optional, blessings and sacred symbols considerably increase the effectiveness of this technique. This is because the majority of Negs are offended and repulsed by these. Whether you believe in the effectiveness of these symbols and words or not, Negs are adversely affected by them, so it makes sense to use every weapon available when working against Negs.

In essence, identifying, turning, cleansing, and sealing core images allows you to focus on a particular area of your mind, an intangible area that contains the wound or hole in which a particular Neg is hiding, or through which it is operating. The attention and body-awareness actions used on these holes focus the power of your mind, like a magnifying glass focuses the sun's rays; it burns away the wound and then cauterizes it. In my years of exploring these matters, this is the only way I have found to come to grips with the roots of Neg-related attachments.

As mentioned often in this book, Negs interfere with and attack people while they are sleeping or when they are at their weakest. In a way, the core-image removal process reverses this. Now Negs are caught unawares, as it were, napping and defenseless. This technique is so new to them that they have no idea what to do to counter it because Negs are not good at adapting to change.

Looking Beneath Core Images: Sometimes, when a significant core image is turned, it will produce other mental imagery. You might, for example, see a twisted root-like structure, a circuit board, electrical wiring or pipes, or other strange symbolic structures, or you might see a large snake, a spider, or a demonic being. These might be animated and seem to be threatening or moving towards you. You may feel waves of revulsion and fear. This particular imagery is uncommon, but if it happens, this is the time for a little bravery. It can be unsettling, but know that you have the upper hand in this situation. Negs cannot hurt you during the core-image cleansing process; they can only try to scare you, and you can most assuredly hurt them. Use your sword and torch, but a banishment ritual is also appropriate here.

Regardless of what strange images, symbols, sensations, or beasties you see or feel, they signify Neg attachments, holes, or wounds in your mind and energy body. They should be slashed, burned, and sealed with a sacred symbol as a matter of course.

Morphing Spiders into Unicorns: Hypnagogic imagery is the name used to describe the visual patterns and images many people see during pre-sleep. Occasionally, disturbing images will be seen. This is especially likely during periods of psychic attack, when frightening faces and images will often manifest in the mind's eye, frightening you and disturbing your sleep. Regardless of its cause, here is a way to deal with disturbing hypnagogic imagery.

Treat disturbing hypnagogic imagery in the same way as any other core image, or you can creatively change the image into something else. Focus on an image and imagine it is morphing into something else. For example, if you see an astral spider, imagine this morphing into a unicorn. Imagine the shape of the unicorn as if it were already there, and concentrate on forcing the transformation. If more disturbing images appear, change them into unicorns as soon as they appear.

This method is an excellent way of shifting your attention away from the source of a psychic attack. This weakens and can even break the telepathic connection that allows it to occur. It's important not to allow yourself to react to disturbing imagery during and after the morphing procedure. Push the memory of what it was firmly out of your mind, and do not think about it. Focus on the unicorn and the beautiful ideals it represents. You might end up with a lot of unicorns, but this beats counting sheep!

Post-Treatment Maintenance: When a significant core image is destroyed, the influence and presence of the Negs associated with it will vanish. While this is a good thing, it can cause a variety of peculiar side effects. Most common is a temporary feeling of emptiness and depression. This is caused by the absence of the Neg presence and its motivational influences. This can last for a few days to a few weeks.

On a brighter note, the sense of emptiness caused by Neg eviction will slowly be supplanted by a filling in of more of yourself. This is empowering, and brings improved physical and psychological health and an increase in energy. There will also be a corresponding loss of negative behavioral traits, addictive urges, and whatever else unwholesome was associated with the ousted Neg.

Negs will sometimes attempt to reconnect after they have been ousted. They will either attempt to reconnect to their old core images, to use other existing ones, or to create new ones. They will also sometimes influence their victim's friends, families, and acquaintances to cause problems, thereby exerting pressure to cause unhappiness and disharmony. This can unbalance and weaken the person, making it easier for Negs to re-establish their attachments.

Treating the list of memory images that you've identified as potential core images can take time. How much will depend on how much time you spend on it, plus how many core images there are. The importance of this work cannot be overstated, and I advise you to do it carefully and thoroughly.

After all identifiable core images have been initially treated, you should have a list of all the major ones, including those that did not respond or took the most effort to treat. Call this list "Active." Go through it again, and make an "Active-2" list. This is a distilling process, designed to weed out the most significant and troublesome core images. When all core images on the Active lists have been successfully treated, keep the lists in a folder and use them for reference and periodic maintenance.

During this process, your dreams and intuition will begin telling you when new core images have been implanted. The subconscious mind learns quickly. As you are searching for core images, it will begin throwing these up to you in dream memories. The longer you do core-image work, the more this will happen and the better you will get at detecting them.

Analyzing Psychic Attack: The first task when dealing with psychic attack is to attempt to identify where it's coming from. If this can be determined, more can be done to counter the attack. If a human is identified as the likely source, much can be done to alleviate the situation. Here is a basic rule of thumb for identifying such a person:

1. Work out when the disturbance first started. List any disagreements or conflicts predating that time. For minor conflicts, going back one year is generally sufficient. However, it pays to include every major conflict you have had in your life that remains unresolved. There is no accounting for mental instability. Sometimes, for no apparent reason, people will start brooding and obsessing over something that happened many years ago. This can precipitate a psychic attack.

2. Make a list of everyone who could potentially be involved, including close family, business and social circles, competitors, and known enemies. Title this list "Suspects." Include anyone that might be annoyed with you, no matter who they are. Also, include any persons who may be in love or in lust with you, especially if this is unrequited.

3. Place four columns next to the list and grade people on a one (minor suspect) to ten (major suspect) scale. Indicate the person's personality strength and persuasive ability in the first column (1–10). Indicate the degree (1–10) to which each person might be angry or annoyed with you in the second column. In the third column, indicate the degree (1–10) each person is likely to brood. Add these and place the score out of 30 for each suspect in the fourth column. This will give you some idea of who might be involved.

Your list may contain a lot of seemingly trivial information, but some people are trivial. I have known people to unintentionally attack others over the most insignificant matters. The type of person you are looking for will have a strong personality, although he/she may not have good social skills. When in a bad mood or argued with, they will project an aura of persuasive uneasiness, often enough to fill a room. Sensitives will notice this immediately as a pressure in the chest, solar plexus, or stomach, and they may sometimes have difficulty breathing. This uneasy pressure can be apparent during any conversation, whether a disagreement is apparent or not.

Persons like this will be persuasive and controlling by nature, or they will try to be. They will have an energy draining effect, leaving sensitives tired and washed out after visits. Just being in the same room with them, or talking on the telephone with them, can be draining. It will be difficult to disagree with them over anything. They will be judgmental, unforgiving, and moody, and will tend to brood over any slight, real or imagined, no matter how insignificant.

The persons you are not looking for will be the opposite of this. However, be warned that many people put on personality masks and hide their true nature. Sensitives will always feel an uneasy pressure in the solar plexus when around them, so trust your intuition and solar plexus on these matters.

Whether or not a suspect is related to and/or ostensibly loves you is unimportant in terms of whether they can be an energy problem for you. I have known many parents to psychically attack their own children without knowing it. Such unintentional attacks can happen as children grow up and parents start losing control over them. I have also known many lovers and former lovers to attack each other unintentionally. Not surprisingly, family members are involved in a significant proportion of psychic attacks.

Using the Core Image Technique to Determine the Source of a Psychic Attack: There are two ways to use core-image work to identify the source of an attack.

1. During the core-image treatment process, if the image of anyone on your "Suspect" list appears beneath a turned core image, mark his/her name with the words "core image found." While this does not prove they are responsible for the current attack, if they are competitors or enemies it shows that a link

exists that could be contributing to the problem. If they are not already on your suspects list, add them to it and carefully examine your relationship with them.

2. Go through the core-image work preliminaries, relaxing and settling into the required state. Call up the current problem in memory. Relive or replay the strongest Neg influence or attack experienced so far. Encapsulate the essence or feeling of this memory in an imagined mental construction. Shrink this to postcard size, turn it over, and see what is beneath it. If you see something, note this and proceed with the slashing, burning, and sealing procedure. If you see nothing, reach out with your feelings, and see if you can pick up any intuitive clues about its origin, then proceed as with any other core image.

Breaking Links and Defusing the Source of the Attack: If the living human source of an attack can be identified, make a serious attempt to defuse the situation. This may entail swallowing your pride and apologizing even if you believe you are in the right. A telephone call or letter is the preferred way, as physical contact should be avoided. Circumstances will often not allow this, but if at all possible this course of action is most beneficial for neutralizing attacks.

After this, break off all contact with the suspected source of attacks. If this is impossible due to circumstances, at the very least stop all unnecessary contact. This will help defuse the situation, by not rekindling bad feelings that are causing attacks. If this advice is followed, most psychic attack problems involving a human source will subside fairly quickly.

If contact cannot be avoided, damage can be minimized by avoiding all hand and eye contact. The best way to do this, if you have to look "suspects" in the face, is to focus on the center of their brow and then shift your eyes slightly out of focus, rather than looking directly in their eyes. This is also an effective defense against people who tend to drain you of energy. If such persons accuse you of not looking at them properly, tell them you have eye strain. As avoiding handshaking is difficult, a false bandage slipped around two fingers is a believable ruse.

Victims of psychic attack, when the source becomes known, should completely forgive attackers. This is a powerful spiritual act that should not be overlooked, so think about this carefully. The victim must realize that attackers are fellow human beings and that, regardless of their actions and attitudes, they are what life has made them, just as we all are. Forgiveness also has the effect of protecting victims from any karmic backlash that might result from rebounding an attack onto the psychic aggressor, which often happens.

Often, without realizing it, victims of psychic attacks can be the cause of their own attacks. In real life, they might be angry and unforgiving towards their current psychic antagonists, thereby inadvertently attacking them. This has a rebound effect, causing people to defend themselves, intentionally or otherwise. Without the original bad feelings to spark a rebound attack, this would not happen.

With this in mind, when attempting to find the source of an attack, include not only those people who might hold bad feelings against you, but all those against whom you hold bad feelings as well.

If you cannot identify the source, start working through the most likely suspects on your list. Wherever possible, make amends, resolve issues or apologize. This may be difficult and out of character for you, but it's an effective way to neutralize attacks; this action can also help identify the source. Note the reaction of suspects when you contact them, and listen to what your intuition has to say.

Geographical Relocation: One of the wisest actions anyone can take during psychic attack or supernatural manifestation is geographical relocation. Move away from the area of disturbance as soon as possible. Negs do not travel well, so moving will avoid many potential problems. This action particularly applies to situations in which Neg problems are sensed when you enter a building, house, cemetery, shop, or any other public area.

Many people suffer heavy Neg-related sleep disturbances, but stay in their beds because they do not know any better. I always advise people to sleep in another room, or sleep on the couch in front of the TV, leaving a light on and the TV on low. Changing rooms, plus the extra light and sound from the TV, makes a difference; place a dark cloth over your eyes if you cannot sleep in the light.

If it follows you into the new room, leave the room and find somewhere to walk over running water, such as a water main or garden hose. If you cannot walk outside and do this (if you live in an apartment), a shower or bath will often do the trick. If this does not alleviate the problem, go for a drive in the car; this is another way of breaking attacks. You are sure to pass over many water mains during your drive.

If the attacks are bad and relocation fails to help you, sleep at a friend's home or stay at a motel. I know people who have slept in motor vehicles, garages, or in backyard tents for some days, thereby escaping serious Neg manifestations. A tent in the backyard (if you have one) circled by a garden hose with trickling water is an effective defense against most levels of attack.

If possible, try not to stay in the area, room, or house where manifestations are present or known to frequently occur. Try to avoid people who experience frequent Neg problems. If you can avoid these places and people, you avoid the possibility of being targeted and attacked by whatever Negs might be involved in the disturbance.

Running-Water Countermeasures: The practice of walking over running water as a countermeasure to Negs is not new. Most people have heard legends that witches, vampires, and demons cannot cross running water. Today, this is considered superstition, suitable for horror movies and fairy tales. But maybe it shouldn't be.

The ancient Celts and Druids knew the power of running water. For example, a Celtic healer's house had to be built over the top of a running stream of potable water. This may seem ridiculous to modern people, but if you take into account that running water repels Negs, it is logical. Sick people have low natural defenses and attract Negs, so recuperating in a house above running water would counter this. The proof that running water generates a strong subtle energy field is supported by water divining or dowsing. When a sensitive holding a dowsing rod passes over running water, she is noticeably affected by its emitted energy field.

Running water is the most powerful countermeasure I know. It breaks most direct attacks instantly. Most Negs cannot cross or even be near it. Just being close to running water or large bodies of potable water very quickly drains Negs of energy. All spirit entities, when manifesting strongly enough to affect the physical dimension, have subtle electromagnetic properties. The energy contained within a manifesting Neg can therefore be grounded and drained.

Negs manifesting close to the physical dimension, to the subtle energy field that covers the Earth, take on two-dimensional characteristics. They have limitations in this state; they cannot cross running water because this emits an energy field that resists and drains Negs of energy.

There are a few ways Negs can get around these limitations, but these take time and weaken them in the process. Some Negs cross running water by attaching to susceptible living beings (human or animal) and hitchhiking across; some cross it by sacrificing their energy, rebuilding strength on the other side. This is a lengthy procedure and I doubt Negs undertake it lightly. It would entail Negs shifting back to a powerless state in another dimension, then beginning the energy gathering process again.

Basic Water-Crossing Method: Running water is to be considered the first line of defense against any type of Neg attack. Running water is powerful against direct Neg attack as it forms a barrier between Neg and victim; but if the victim crosses back over the barrier, the attack can recommence.

The basic water-crossing method is to find some running water and cross over it as soon as possible after an attack begins. In cities and towns, water mains line every street; water pipes flow into houses and intersect roads every sixty feet or so in most towns and cities. Taking a short walk will thus usually do the trick; be sure to cross the road a couple of times to make sure. Crossing rivers and streams (aboveground or underground) will also work, as well as crossing oceans and lakes or paddling at the edge of a body of water. In my experience, the volume of running water is directly proportional to its effectiveness in combating Negs.

I lay a garden hose so it gushes water along the ground and then step over the water. I find this method more powerful if I step through the running water, wetting my feet slightly in the process, but maybe this is just a psychological benefit. The attack will be broken either way. If an attack recommences when crossing back over the hose, I walk in a circle and recross the hose several times, exiting on the far side. This seems to confound and weaken Negs. Negs seem to expend energy when their contact with victims is broken and each time they start a new attack. By repeatedly allowing their contact and breaking it again, I weaken them considerably.

If the attacking Neg still follows me, I lay the hose in a U-shape, enter the opening, and cross over the hose again. I then close the loop by throwing a section of hose over the open end of the loop to close it. This traps the Neg inside a loop of running water from which it cannot easily escape. I then slowly close the loop until all the space inside it is gone. A variation is to drag another section of hose over the loop, and/or to hose away the Neg by gushing water through it after closing the loop. A combination of these methods is probably best. Be careful not to touch the ground inside the closed loop with any part of your body. Trapped Negs are very dangerous and will attack viciously any chance they get. Still another way to trap a Neg is to stand inside a loop of waterless hose (thoroughly draining it first) and then to turn on the water and step out of the loop, thereby trapping the Neg.

These actions drain Negs of so much energy they are driven back into whatever black dimensional backwater they call home. The Neg in question thus is effectively negated for the time being. It may return another time, but this will take time and effort on its part, and it will think twice before attacking again. Negs are not good at adapting to change, so if an attack happens another time, repeat the entrapment method.

The Water Draining Method: An extension of these techniques is to place many coils of garden hose clockwise on the ground and turn on the water. Then, stand with your feet among the coils and close your eyes and relax. Imagine white light pouring into your head from above and filling your body; at the same time imagine black fluid draining from your feet into the ground. Continue this for several minutes or until the Neg pressure eases. Say a prayer or mantra to keep your mind clear when doing this. On one occasion, I used this technique and saw static throughout my mind space that resembled gushing water, instead of the horrible images that came when the attack started. This is the most effective defense against direct Neg attack I have to offer.

If none of these running-water methods are possible, a shower or bath will help. Negs are drained of energy by large amounts of potable water as well as by running water. Even a bucket of clean tap water next to the bed helps counter Negs, especially if you bless it or say a heartfelt prayer over it. Incidentally, crossing running water is still effective when done in high-rise apartments.

The Fire Alternative: Fire can also be used as a countermeasure and barrier against Negs. Like running water, fire generates energies that interfere with Negs. I have used this method when running water was not available, or on those rare occasions that it did not work. I have also used this in conjunction with crossing running water, as a kind of double whammy to rid myself of persistent Negs.

A couple of sheets of newspaper, set alight and dropped on the ground to burn, form an effective Neg barrier. As with a water hose, Negs can be trapped inside a ring of fire. If this ring is burned and filled with fire, or hosed away with water, trapped Negs are damaged, drained, and negated. When using the fire method, be careful not to set your clothes or the surrounding area alight. Keep a bucket of water or fire extinguisher handy in case of mishap.

Root Cleansing and Attachment Testing: Crossing running water and/or fire helps you discern whether an attacking Neg is attached to you or is trying to attach to you. If the attack is broken, this means the Neg involved was not firmly attached to you. But if the repulsion technique fails, the Neg can be deemed attached, indicating a preexisting condition, and other countermeasures will then be necessary.

A good rule of thumb for looking at Neg attachments is to consider that humans have energy roots, extending down through their feet and into the energy field that covers the surface of the Earth. As people move about on the surface, their energy roots create "furrows" in the energy field. Negs track people by following these furrows, and attack by latching onto their energy roots. Once energy root contact is made, the Neg extends part of itself up over the surface of its victim's energy body, and then begins the process of breaking through its natural defenses. This breaking-in process is what causes most of the unpleasant sensations and pains associated with a direct Neg attack.

If a Neg succeeds in breaking in, it will attach itself to a person. Once through the person's outer defenses, a Neg is both shielded and nurtured by its new host. It has gained basic hitchhiker status, which is a light form of overshadowing, but it is a tenuous state. Such a Neg may be able to withstand crossing running water and fire, but usually not. This depends a lot on the nature, strength, and experience of the Neg, the susceptibility of its new temporary host, and how well that person is shielded.

The running-water method will not remove firmly entrenched or possessing Negs, although it will certainly cause them problems, especially in cases of lengthy exposure. But if only weak or temporary attachments have been made, these methods will remove Negs completely. Sometimes several passes over running water are necessary to scrape off semi-attached Neg invaders. However, if symptoms of direct psychic attack are experienced, such as cold shivers, anxiety, or cramps, this indicates attacking Negs are not firmly attached. Logically, if they were, they would not need to continue attacking directly.

Hugging Shield Method: Another way of breaking Neg attacks is with what I call the hugging shield method. This should be tried if other methods fail or are impractical.

I discovered this method by accident during a strong Neg attack that would not break in the usual ways. This was just one episode in a series of attacks that had been going on for several days, and which resulted from helping another person and getting caught in their line of fire.

I was in a lot of pain with muscular cramps and bone-wracking shivers. It was night and I was outside, walking around my backyard growling in pain, trying to break the attack. It came on suddenly and continued half an hour. Two friends were present, a man and a woman, but they did not feel or sense anything. This is not unusual; direct attack is usually localized to the victim only.

I had tried crossing running water and fire, but the attacking Neg would not budge. I asked my friends to hug me from both sides. This method often works with children, so it was worth a try. The man hugged me from behind, but this had no effect, but when the woman joined in and hugged me from the front, the attack stopped instantly. A warm glow spread through me, partly from the cessation of pain and partly from the wonderful double hug. The attack broke and did not return that night.

The basic method is, while standing, to have two or more people encircle you with their arms and hug onto you from all sides. If the people doing the hugging are of mixed genders, the effectiveness of this technique is increased, possibly because a cross-gender energy circuit is created.

Energy Disruption Method: The body-awareness actions discussed earlier can be used to disrupt Neg interference anywhere in the body. Energy disruption should be used in conjunction with other countermeasures, but can be used as a stand-alone method. Body-awareness actions cause energy waves through the energy body, and these disrupt any kind of energy body interference.

The first step is to target the affected area with body awareness. Next, brush or sponge that area with whatever body-awareness action best suits it. If this area is a foot, use a brushing or sponging action, repeatedly drawing your body awareness through it. Continue the action until all Neg-related sensations cease. If the area of interference cannot be targeted or if the affected area is large or keeps changing, use larger body-awareness actions. For example, use the whole of a limb, the whole of your back, or the whole of your front body-awareness actions. These will cause widespread interference and counter the Neg problem.

Breaking a Sleep Paralysis: Sleep paralysis (also called waking paralysis) is similar to night terrors in that it occurs during non-REM (no rapid eye movement) sleep. This proves it's not caused solely by bad dreams although the dream mind is often involved. In fact, in my opinion, waking paralysis is usually caused by a fear conflict between the projected double (with an OBE in progress) and its physical body/mind. The physical body/mind is intimately connected with its projected astral double during an OBE. What is felt by one is felt by the other, particularly emotions.

Fear can reflect back and forth and compound, magnifying to the point where one or both aspects can become paralyzed, causing waking paralysis. Keeping your mind clear and refusing to be afraid during paralysis episodes help reduce this conflict. It is important to counter waking paralysis and fear, as this may be caused by an attacking Neg.

Paralysis is more likely to occur in certain resting and sleeping positions. Lying on the back, for example, tends to promote both OBE and waking paralysis for most people. It's worthwhile checking to see if your resting position is a factor and to avoid positions most likely to promote waking paralysis. When waking paralysis strikes a deeply relaxed but still awake person, or one trying to fall asleep, it starts with a noticeable falling sensation; you get a moment's warning, and this is the best time to fight it off.

Rolling out of bed quickly will stop it before it can take hold. Do not return to bed for ten minutes, or waking paralysis may start again. Overtiredness makes waking paralysis more likely, so catching up on your sleep helps reduce the chances of it happening. An empty stomach tends to increase the chances of waking paralysis, so try not to get hungry at night. I recommend a short walk to the refrigerator, as eating lessens the chances of it happening again.

To break sleep paralysis, the most direct approach is to concentrate on moving a single big toe. For some reason, a big toe is the easiest body part to re-animate during a waking paralysis episode. Once it moves, even slightly, waking paralysis ends instantly. To increase the effectiveness of this technique, use a body-awareness sponging action on the big toe while trying to move it.

Countering Obsessive Thoughts: Obsessive thoughts can happen at any time for no apparent reason. A line from a song, an advertising ditty, poem, snatch of dialogue, or anything similar may suddenly appear in the mind. It will repeat itself over and over, ad nauseam. This can also take the form of fantasy or memory images, rather than mentally spoken words.

The most common causes of obsessing thoughts, especially those containing tormenting dialogue and images, real or imaginary, are unresolved life conflicts. These may be related to core images; or your subconscious mind may simply be throwing up problems and demanding they be dealt with. Handle these problems intelligently and obsessive thought patterns will dissolve. But if you cannot deal with this alone, seek professional medical advice and treatment.

This is a frustrating problem and makes serious work or sleep virtually impossible. I have experienced this myself; I have seen people lose days of sleep from it. The following procedure can help overcome it:

Stage One: Hold up a fingertip at arms length and focus intently on it. Move this in a slow circle, about the size of a large dinner plate, while keeping your eyes intently focused on it. Repeat this several times with full concentration. This is very effective and can be used as a stand-alone method. It should be used whenever obsessive thoughts arise. Move on to the next stages only if obsessive thoughts continue.

Stage Two: Close your eyes, relax for a few moments, then encapsulate the thought pattern in your mind. Grab the essence of this thought as it's repeating. Feel your awareness hands reaching out and grabbing hold of an image, getting the essence of the problem thought. Shrink this and treat it as a normal core image, turning, slashing, and burning it, as per the method given earlier in this chapter.

Stage Three: Clear your mind through force of will, silencing the repetitive thoughts. Hold your mind clear while taking deep breaths for as long as you can. Whip your mind into temporary obedience; use breath awareness to help with this; physical relaxation is not required.

Stage Four: Replace the repeating thought pattern with another one. Use a snatch of song, poem, jingle, prayer, or affirmation. Repeat this several times, until the pressure of the original thought weakens. Then, change the replacement, also repeating it several times.

Stage Five: Continue stage three, using a string of replacements, repeating each several times. Make the last few replacements shorter, changing them frequently; use whatever words or phrases pop into your head; anything but the original.

Stage Six: Forcibly clear your mind, using breath awareness, and silence the final replacement. Hold your mind clear, for as long as you can. Finally, relax and allow your mind to return to normal thinking. Repeat stage one.

As a last resort, use headphones and play music to drown out problem thought patterns. This occupies the surface mind and encourages mental silence. Continue this for as long as needed, and sleep with the headphones on if necessary.

Obsessive, stressful thoughts are common during many types of psychic attacks. They are a fair indicator that core images are active or in the process of being telepathically implanted. This can happen while you are awake or asleep, and if you are asleep, they will usually wake you up. The main thing to watch for is when obsessive thoughts have no apparent psychological or real-life cause.

Energy Conversion Technique: Negative atmosphere problems and other supernatural manifestations can often be rectified with constructive imagination (visualization). Negative energy can be converted into positive energy.

For example, with your eyes open or closed (whatever works best for you), imagine a jet-black tennis ball floating in the middle of the room before you. Make the ball spin anti-clockwise and keep it spinning at all times in your mind's eye. As the ball spins, see it attracting black negative energy from the surrounding area and growing larger. See black clots of negative energy being ripped from your body and the room. Move the spinning black ball slowly around the room, gathering up all the negative energy. See it growing steadily in size. Once you consider it to be large enough (the size of a beach ball), reverse its direction and make it spin clockwise. Then, imagine it changing its color to brilliant white. Concentrate and keep the ball spinning clockwise as you change its color.

You should now have a large ball of brilliant white positive energy spinning clockwise in front of you. The last step is to explode the white ball, but it's a shame to waste all that positive energy. Imagine the ball exploding into the room, flinging bits and pieces of white energy everywhere, charging you and the room with positive energy.

Fumigating for Negs: There are a variety of methods for burning substances that will give off smoke that is offensive or damaging to Negs, or that change the atmosphere in beneficial ways. A censer is the most efficient method, and can be purchased from a church supplier or new-age shop.

Sulfur: The most effective substance for fumigation is sulfur. However, sulfur gives off poisonous gas when burned, so great care must be taken when using it. Close all windows in the room being treated. Remembering to hold your breath, add a small amount of sulfur powder (a teaspoon) to the glowing coals of the censer. Leave the room quickly, shutting the door behind you. Return to the room an hour later, and, holding your breath, extinguish the burning sulfur and open all windows. Still holding your breath, leave the room, close the door, and do not return for thirty minutes, or until poisonous fumes have aired away.

A whole house can be fumigated by burning a larger amount of sulfur, or by repeating the procedure in all rooms. All internal doors should be opened and all windows closed. Ignite the sulfur and leave the house for an hour or so, as you would if fumigating for insects. Hold your breath while opening the outer doors and leave the house again until it's safely aired. Take care to rest the censer on a safe, fireproof pad and remove all pet animals during fumigation.

Chili Pepper and Mustard Seed: The next most effective substances I have found are chili pepper and mustard seed. When burned, they emit a vicious smoke. Although it's not as dangerous as sulfur, take care to not breathe the smoke, especially if you are an asthmatic. This smoke has a violent effect on even the healthiest lungs, and stings the eyes and nose badly. A thick, damp towel held over the mouth and nose will filter most of it, but anything more than short exposure is not recommended.

Fresh chili peppers are best, but dried or powdered chili peppers can also be used. A censer can be used, or a small cast-iron fry pan with an insulated handle. Heat the pan well and throw in a handful of chopped chili peppers and/or mustard seeds. Copious amounts of smoke will soon be produced. Take this pan to a room and place it on a suitable heat-proof plate; close the room and leave it to fumigate for fifteen minutes. Then, enter the room, holding your breath, and extinguish if still giving off smoke. Then, air the room. You can walk through the house with the censer, entering every room and filling it with smoke, then leave the house until the smoke clears.

This smoke can also be used to remove Neg hitchhikers, in a variation of smudging. Ideally, the affected person stands outside the house, so the Neg is not released inside the home. Take the smoking fry pan and walk around the person several times, holding the pan close, moving it low and high, so his/her whole body is covered with smoke.

Garlic: If no chili peppers are available, use fresh garlic, peel and all. These can also be burned in a cast iron pan, and the smoke used in the same way as chili peppers. A tiny quantity of either ginger root or mint leaves can be added to any fumigant herb to boost its effectiveness; it's important not to use too much ginger or mint, or it will overpower the effectiveness of other herbs.

The Effect of Percussion and Noise: Percussion and noise are ancient methods of driving away ghosts and evil spirits. Gongs, drums, cymbals, bells, wind chimes, and firecrackers have long been used for this purpose by Eastern cultures. Loud noises affect any type of Neg manifestation; even clapping your hands or loudly banging pots and pans will have a detrimental effect on Negs. This approach breaks up astral lights and negative atmospheres, disturbing and disrupting Neg manifestations. This is especially effective while Negs are gathering energy and building up, which is their weakest moment. I have had a lot of success using this method, as have many of the people I have helped.

Fighting Negs During an Out-of-Body Experience: Astral combat is the traditional name given to combat engaged in during dreams and OBEs (astral projection). The principles of astral combat are simple: Anything created in the OBE or dream environment is relatively solid there because it's composed of the same basic substance as the environment itself. Thus, it is capable of directly affecting the contents of that environment. These same principles are used to create the tools used during the core-image treatment process, described earlier.

To create thought-form objects during OBEs or meditations, clear your mind and focus completely on the object being created. Construct and hold it with your imagination. See and feel the object as if it were already in existence. Hold its image firmly in mind while it forms. Will the object into existence and keep focused on it until it's fully formed. If the desired item tends to melt away quickly, more effort will be required to hold it in existence. In the beginning, keep created objects as simple as possible. Created objects—thought-forms—slowly become more solid and take less time and effort to create every time they are remade.

A good way of dealing with an OBE or dream hitchhiker is to bravely confront and/or attack it. Demand it leave immediately and threaten dire consequences if it refuses. If this does not work, create a sword or baseball bat and beat it until it leaves. The created weapon should be held firmly in your mind so it does not melt away while you use it. If this does not work, or if you are not up for a confrontation, denying its existence will sometimes work, although this generally takes longer. Ignore it and deny its existence; actively disbelieve in it and unmake it with your creative ability. Imagine and see its arms fading away and feel the rest of it fading out of existence. Alternatively, imagine it bursting into flames and burning away.

You can also use shape-shifting. The shape of the dreamer/projector can be changed to lose a hitchhiker. Small is usually more effective than big here, but both "sizes" should be tried. If you can hold the shape of a bee or wasp, you will often lose the hitchhiker in the process. The use of creative ability in this way alone is often enough to drive off a hitchhiker.

The strongest approach to driving away Neg hitchhikers is to banish them, using the sacred names of God and the angels, along with an appropriate sacred symbol. To do this its necessary to memorize a banishment ritual (given later).

The traditional approach to astral weaponry is for a projector to visualize and create a sword and armor. The armor offers protection and the sword is used for offense. When created, swords and armor should be blessed with the power of God before they are used; this will increase their effectiveness. Armor is created by imagining and feeling it on your body, and then by staying aware of its existence until it begins to set.

Energy bolts can also be created and launched at offending Negs and are imagined as exploding on contact. To use an energy bolt, construct with your imagination a glowing white ball of energy about the size of a golf ball. Feel some of your energy flowing into this as you create it. Make it appear in front of you and then launch it quickly at the target. Move the energy bolt with your mind as soon as it forms; feel, see, and imagine it as moving rapidly, expanding as it flies towards the target. See it explode sharply on impact. With a little practice, you can make energy bolts in a fraction of a second, and use this process to create a barrage. You can also create energy beams and flames to shoot from the tip of a sword; this technique, however, takes more concentration and practice than do bolts.

Creating complex images such as these can be difficult, so beginners should focus on one simple object at a time. Creating a single weapon like a sword or energy bolts is probably the easiest way to start. The distraction of creating and holding in shape multiple items may cause other created items to fade. If you can manage only to create a sword or baseball bat, use this on its own and do not attempt creating anything else for the present.

Warning: Never follow a Neg if it retreats, as it may lead you into a trap, a dimensional realm where it has more power and you have less.

Getting Outside Help: If nothing seems to help and if Neg-related problems continue, consult a competent psychic healer, shaman, white witch, or other serious practitioner of magic. They can often help with these matters, as can some priests and monks of any faith. Look in local new-age papers and magazines or on the Internet for advertisements for the services of someone in your area.

Obtaining a higher level of outside help than mentioned in the previous paragraph is difficult. The old saying "God helps those who help themselves" is apt here. It's wise to do what you can to overcome Neg-related problems for yourself. The reason for this relates to the reason why you have Neg problems in the first place. For example, the underlying reason behind serious Neg problems may be to push you into making lifestyle changes or exploring occult matters.

15

Passive Countermeasures against Negs

Passive and semi-passive countermeasures will affect your immediate environment, making it detrimental to Neg presences and activities. Many of these countermeasures can be left in place to provide a long-term deterrent against Negs. This chapter reviews a number of effective passive countermeasures.

Running-Water Barriers: Building on the principles of how water affects Negs, here are some long-term, passive and semi-passive applications using water as a deterrent.

As most Negs cannot cross running water, a perimeter barrier can be created to protect a room, or even a house, using thin plastic tubing. Any type of tubing can be used, even copper pipe, but clear oxygen tubing, PVC, or garden reticulation tubing is easily available and not difficult to use. To create a perimeter barrier, lay the tubing around the room on the floor next to walls; tuck it neatly under carpet edges, or tie or hold it in place with furniture. Once it's in place, connect one end of the tubing with a suitable adapter to a water tap and place the other end in a drain or outside to water a garden. Make sure the tubing overlaps.

For long-term use, you can make a simple water-recirculating unit out of a home-brewing keg, or a small aquarium, using a small submersible fishpond or aquarium pump to provide the necessary water flow. A submersible pump is preferable to any other type of pump because it is silent during operation.

Methods of Neg Containment: If you look at how residential streets are laid out, water mains follow the road and surround blocks of houses. Back gardens do not usually contain water mains and therefore provide access for free-roaming Negs that may be present within each block. Therefore, suburban homes are potentially exposed to hundreds of other homes and any Negs that may reside in them.

The same principle applies to city blocks and apartment buildings. While there are many water pipes in an apartment building, which is a bonus, usually these all enter on one side of the building, from the water main on the street; this leaves many gaps that can allow Negs free access to the interior. Therefore, any city apartment can potentially be exposed to every other apartment and building within that city block, and the Negs within them.

Given this, while running–water perimeter barriers do not offer a perfect defense, they are worthwhile as a local defense. This is especially so when one takes into account that many Neg problems originate within the home from Negs being carried in and deposited by visitors and family members. A home's front door should always carry some Neg-deterrent value.

Some Negs will get around the running-water barriers by using a type of remote projection, as discussed earlier. In this way, a Neg can project into, and manifest within, rooms protected by running-water perimeters; however, once a Neg does this, it is temporarily trapped. It cannot leave that area because it cannot cross the running–water perimeter barrier after it has built up enough energy to cause problems. If an attack begins within a protected room at night, moving to another room to sleep effectively leaves the Neg's activities contained in the protected room for a time. The Neg may repeat its remote attack method, but this requires it to start the build-up process again. Whatever it does will take time and weaken it in the process.

When Negs are trapped by running-water barriers, this is a

good opportunity for you to weaken them further by applying other passive countermeasures. At the very least, the main light should be left on, a radio or TV left playing on low, and some slices of garlic placed around the room. Negs need darkness and quiet in order to build up their charge. Deny them this, and their activities are severely hampered.

After coming under attack and leaving a protected room to sleep elsewhere, if the attack begins anew some time later, your returning to the protected room will often have the same effect, and provide you with a few more hours of Neg-free sleep. This weakens Negs and makes life difficult for them. This is not a perfect solution, but if you have serious Neg problems, this is preferable to doing nothing. I am confident that anyone can create a Neg-free protected area by combining this with other countermeasures.

Alternatively, if a Neg attack occurs inside an area protected by a running-water barrier, the barrier can be turned off for a short time to allow the attacking Neg to escape. The barrier should then be turned back on again after the area is clear and after other countermeasures have been applied, such as fumigation. Turn the perimeter barriers off for a while during the daytime, just in case any Negs have been trapped inside during the night. You do not want to collect Negs in your house; you want to expel them.

Artificial Telluric Springs: A telluric spring is a natural water spring or underground stream that contains a great deal of naturally generated positive energy. Telluric springs, such as the famous healing spring of Lourdes in France, are traditionally said to have magical healing properties. Bathing in the water of a telluric spring cleanses the body of negative energies. This can often result in miraculous cures of diseases caused by negative energies and Neg attachments. Long-term exposure to the energies of a telluric spring, such as by camping or sleeping above one, can rid you of serious Neg attachments, even possession. A key ingredient in my deliverance from possession (explained earlier in the book) was that after being guided to water, I camped for several days above a telluric spring. There are various ways of divining (such as dowsing) whether a spring or underground stream is telluric or not, but I suspect the key ingredient is that the water is in motion, as well as clean and drinkable, not brackish or tainted in any way.

Energies similar to a telluric spring can be created at home by extending the running–water perimeter barrier. Run the tubing around the bed so it overlaps, then lay many coils of tubing, in a overlapping clockwise fashion, on the floor beneath the bed. The more coils the better, but make sure there are no kinks. Check that water is flowing through the tubing; use a larger pump if flow is insufficient.

Many benefits derive from long-term use of an artificial telluric spring under your bed. Apart from built-in Neg protection, your continuous exposure to its positive energies may be beneficial to some health conditions, caused or exacerbated by Negs, and to the negative energy generated by their presence.

Feng Shui Fountains, or Japanese Water Sculptures: Feng shui water fountains are small indoor fountains designed to generate positive subtle energies. These can be purchased complete or as do-it-yourself kits; various stores and websites offer fountains and Japanese water sculptures for sale.

Any type of indoor fountain makes an excellent passive countermeasure. Ideally, a fountain should face the front door of the home or be in plain view near the front door. In this way, hitchhiking Negs are deterred from entering the home. This is similar in principle to why many churches have a font of holy water near their front door; many old churches also have a well or natural telluric spring close to their main entrance to deter Negs from entering the church. Add a small dash of holy water to fountain water daily to increase its effectiveness.

Repelling Negs with Salt: Table salt is well-known as a countermeasure against all kinds of Negs. Salt is made of crystals, and crystals absorb subtle energies. This effect can be increased if the salt is consecrated, much the same way as holy water is consecrated. Use salt as an alternative to the crossing-running-water method. Pour a thick line of salt on the ground and step over it.

Salt can also be used as a perimeter barrier; salt can be mixed with holy water to endow it with the water's properties. Salt barriers can sometimes be effective where water barriers fail, or where water methods are inconvenient. Doorways can be protected by pouring lines of salt across the doorsteps or under doormats. Windows can be protected by pouring lines of salt across the windowsills.

Another way to use salt is to place handfuls in small bottles, pots, or cloth bags, then place these about the home. To protect a room, place one pot at each cardinal point (north, south, east, and west). Salt countermeasures can be left in place, but salt should be swept up and/or changed once a week, or daily, if Neg problems are frequent.

Repelling with Holy Water: Holy water is water that has been cleansed and blessed in the name of God. This dramatically increases its effectiveness as a countermeasure. It also subtly changes it, making it detrimental to Neg energies. Holy water can be obtained freely from most churches, as there is normally a font of holy water next to the main entrance. If queried, say you need some to protect or cleanse your home. The containment bottle should be of sterile glass with a natural cork stopper.

Evaporating Consecrated Salt and Holy Water: Another method of countering negative atmospheres and Neg manifestations is to evaporate holy water that contains salt. Pour this mixture into saucers of water about the house and leave them to evaporate. To consecrate salt or water yourself, say a simple prayer over it to bless it; for more advanced techniques, consult books on magic.

Pots of Clean Water: One of the simplest countermeasures is to place a bucket of fresh water at the head and foot of your bed. Alternatively, place large bowls of water under or around your bed; change the water daily. Dashes of holy water and consecrated salt will increase the effectiveness, as will a blessing. Say a prayer over the water, asking that protective properties enter it.

Iron and Steel: Some Negs will not enter a home if a door or doorway, or the approach to it, is decorated with wrought iron or steel. An iron horseshoe (points facing up) or an iron crucifix (or other religious symbol) fixed to the inside or outside of a door is a good countermeasure. Wrought iron double spear points are also effective, as well as being attractive and unobtrusive; these can be attached to doorframes or inset into door surfaces.

Coal and Charcoal: Coal or charcoal can be used as passive countermeasures. They absorb gasses and pollutants, and they also absorb subtle negative energies, thereby draining and weakening Negs. Coal and charcoal contain high concentrations of carbon, much like diamonds but in a different form. They are used in much the same way as consecrated salt. Place them in bowls, bottles, or cloth bags under or around your bed, or around the room being protected. The four cardinal points (north, south, east, west) are the best positions for placement.

Coal can be left in place and changed once a week, but it should be changed daily if Neg problems are frequent. Used coal should not be burned for heat, but disposed of elsewhere. Traditionally it was buried or thrown into a river, but throwing it out with the trash is adequate.

A Garlic Repellant: Garlic is one of the great natural remedies and is a natural antibiotic, if taken in large enough doses. Garlic inactivates undesirable virulent microorganisms in the body, without harming the helpful ones. Apart from its medicinal value, garlic is reputed to have magical properties against evil spirits. In this guise, it is known, as are other substances and devices used similarly, as a ward. The truth is, apart from its pungent odor, garlic contains a high concentration of sulfur, and sulfur is highly detrimental to Neg energies. In fact, garlic is a powerful countermeasure against *all* types of Negs. I have used it and experimented with it for many years, and have thoroughly confirmed its efficacy. It is now one of my primary passive countermeasures. However, just placing a few bulbs of garlic around a room will have little effect; the sulfur-carrying odor must be released into the atmosphere.

Crisp, fresh cloves of red garlic are best. For a general deterrent, peel and slice a few cloves of garlic into thin rounds. Spread these over small plates, and position these near the head and foot of the bed, on bedside tables, or underneath the bed. Alternatively, place slices of garlic about the room on tables, counters, windowsills, and the tops of doorframes. Place slices of garlic under pillows and sheets and in amidst the bedding.

The amount of garlic used to treat a room depends on the severity of the Neg problem. As a general nocturnal deterrent, a few slices are adequate, but for more serious problems, several cloves can be used. The stronger the odor, the stronger the deterrent factor.

Used garlic should, ideally, be removed from the house in the morning and burned or buried, but realistically, flushing it down the toilet is adequate. Garlic should not be consumed after use as a ward, as it is reputed to absorb negative energies. While this is difficult to prove, it seems reasonable.

If the smell of garlic is offensive to you, but its use is still required, place a freshly crushed clove in a tissue held very close to your nose; take several deep inhalations. This will overload your sense of smell and make the smell of a garlic-treated room less noticeable to you. In any case, the smell of garlic in a treated room will soon lessen as the sense of smell tunes it out. Mix garlic with a tiny amount of ginger root or mint leaf to improve the smell. Ginger and mint are both activating herbs, increasing the potency of any herbs they are mixed with.

If you have an ongoing Neg problem, increase your daily internal consumption of garlic, taken fresh or in cooking, or in odorless capsule form if you do not like the smell and taste. When ingested regularly, garlic permeates the body and acts as a Neg deterrent.

Garlic also forms a more specific deterrent when applied directly to skin. This is particularly effective in countering nocturnal energy body interference. Apply garlic to the feet and hands by rubbing a peeled and broken clove over them. Alternatively, the garlic can be crushed and the juice used as a lotion. Take care to not get any garlic juice in the eyes or onto sensitive or broken skin, to avoid burns and blisters.

The feet are the most vulnerable areas and Negs always make a beeline for them. You can rub garlic juice into them, or slices of garlic can be wrapped in tissue and placed inside a pair of your socks. Garlic socks worn during sleep helps counter nocturnal Neg disturbances; the odor of garlic is intensified inside socks and its local effectiveness increased. Any area of the body can be treated in this way, with garlic juice or with slices attached to the body with surgical tape.

If garlic is to be taped to an area of sensitive skin, such as underarms, genitals, face, ears, or broken skin (it will blister sensitive skin), it's best wrapped in tissue paper first or used with a layer of plastic food wrap between it and the skin. Do not wrap garlic completely in plastic, as this blocks its fumes and defeats the purpose.

If your mouth is affected, chew or suck a small clove of garlic and do not brush your teeth afterwards. This will treat the whole mouth area. If you have never chewed raw garlic, be careful, as it's hotter than most people realize. The best way to eat a raw clove is to take small bites, chew quickly, and wash it down with water.

Garlic oil is a useful preparation. A tiny quantity of fresh ginger root or mint can be added to enhance its efficacy.

Thinly slice six to twelve medium-sized raw garlic cloves (depending on the size of the cloves and desired strength) and add to fourth-fifths of a pint of sunflower oil in a sterile glass jar. Seal tightly and leave to stand for ten to fourteen days; shake it daily. Strain the oil into a sterilized glass bottle, seal, and store in a cool, dark place. This oil can be used as an alternative to fresh garlic juice; it can also be used as a ward and applied to doorways to deter the entry of Negs, and to cleanse Neg-contaminated objects. Garlic oil, garlic juice, or even slices of fresh garlic, can be added to the water of a table-top oil burner, the type used to evaporate fragrant aromatherapy oils. This makes a general Neg deterrent. A few drops of fragrant oil will help mask the garlic smell.

Protective Herbs and Their Essential Oils: Sprinkling protective herbs around the home is a simple and effective countermeasure that helps counter most types of Neg problems. While not quite as effective as garlic, herbs are often more socially acceptable in terms of their odor.

Herbs and scents can be applied in a variety of ways: sprinkling, infusions, air sprays, potpourris, oil burners, joss sticks, perfumes, lotions and ointments, burned in charcoal censors. Using freshly cut herbs, flowers, and potted plants is a good way of applying scents to a room and of treating interior atmospheres. Living potted plants are best for long term protection. Good quality air-freshener sprays can also be a great help, and are excellent for treating negative atmospheres quickly.

Herbs, scents, and perfumes affect subtle energies and vibrations, thus changing and positively charging atmospheres. If applied to the physical body, with soaps, shampoos, body rinses, and herbal baths, they change the energy vibrations of the skin; if taken internally, they permeate the physical body and change its energy radiations. Here are some common useful herbs:

Wild Sage (mugwort): This herb is traditionally used for smudging and for fumigating areas to remove negative energies. Mugwort moxa sticks are available from Chinese herbalists.

Rosemary and Marjoram: These absorb negative energies and atmospheres, and raise positive vibrations and repel Negs. Rosemary bushes make an excellent countermeasure if planted near the main entry to a house; rosemary potted plants can also be placed near doorways and in bedrooms.

Clove and Cinnamon: These raise vibrations and repel Negs and they can be used as fumigation incense to banish Negs.

Fenugreek and Dill: These herbs erode negative energies, repel Negs, and attract good luck.

Thyme and Lemon Thyme: These repel psychic attacks, weaken Neg attachments, and protect against Neg attachments.

Citrus and Bergamot: These are good, all-round Neg repellents, promoting positive atmospheres.

Mint and Ginger: These are energizing, activating herbs that increase the efficiency of any herbs they are mixed with. However, use only tiny quantities or they will overpower the effectiveness of other herbs.

All herbs can be activated before use to enhance their protective properties. To activate, say a heartfelt prayer over them, stating what you want the herbs to do or to prevent from happening.

The simplest way to use them is to sprinkle some in the corner of every room. Sprinkle herbs around the outside of the home, or in entry points, to deter Negs from entering. They should be replaced when their smell fades; dispose of the old herbs and don't use them for cooking.

Atomizer Teas: Teas can be made from herbs in much the same way as normal tea, by soaking in boiling water, but herbal teas can be used in atomizing sprays and as a rinse to wash entry-ways, doors, doorsteps, and window frames to deter Negs from entering. Use teas to wash floors and walls to counter bad atmospheres and influences. Use teas as body and hair rinses after bathing, in place of herbal soaps and shampoos.

Religious Icons and Paraphernalia: Religious icons, pictures, ornaments, jewelry, or charms can be used as protective wards. Like symbols, these emit an energy inherent to the forces they represent. Many Negs find religious symbols, icons, and paraphernalia offensive and will not enter areas containing them; they will at least be made uncomfortable by them. This is especially so if these items have been blessed and connected with the forces they represent. If such items are loved and reverently cared for and what they represent is believed in with heartfelt sincerity, their effectiveness is greatly increased.

Light As a Countermeasure: Darkness makes it easier for Negs to build up and operate. It's difficult for Negs to make themselves felt and seen in well-lit conditions. Because of this, turning on main overhead lights is a good basic countermeasure. If it's hard to sleep with the lights on, cover your eyes with a roll of dark cloth. Children should always be given a nightlight or have the overhead light on if they have problems sleeping. Children are more sensitive than adults and will often sense things adults miss. The few pennies it costs to run a light bulb overnight is a small price to pay for a child's peace of mind and restful sleep.

Houses suffering frequent Neg atmospheres and manifestations often have cold spots. These are usually the quietest, darkest areas of a house, such as rarely used rooms, hallways, alcoves, cellars, or attics. Many Neg problems can be solved by opening curtains and blinds, installing brighter light bulbs or skylights, or by placing mirrors to reflect light into dark areas. Increasing the light in cold spots makes life more difficult for Negs that are otherwise using these spots to build up their energy, or to hide themselves during the daytime.

All Negs avoid strong light, especially sunlight because it weakens and drains them of energy. The photosensitive nature of ectoplasm is a good example of this. Ectoplasm is produced only in dark or very dim conditions, but never under strong white light or sunlight. Negs share the light-sensitive properties of ectoplasm, especially during visible manifestations and other such phenomena.

Sound and Music As Deterrents: Negs always seek dark, quiet places to build up in. Deny them this and their life is difficult. Add a repellent scent to a well-lit room and play a radio or TV softly, and it becomes an uncomfortable place for Negs.

Along these lines, music is a good general Neg deterrent. The type of music is important, but personal taste can be appeased. Even so, hard rock and heavy metal are not suitable. Any "feel-good" type popular music will help, but classical type music is by far the best. When played regularly it has a long-term positive effect on an environment. It could be said that the energies of classical music soak into the surrounding environment, and repel Negs by promoting a positive, wholesome, spiritual atmosphere.

For this purpose, the strongest audio countermeasures are Christmas carols, spiritual hymns, and children's nursery rhymes. They are linked (much like symbols and sacred names) to higher positive forces. The older and more well-known the carol or hymn, the more effective it will be. A parapsychologist researching the field of environmental exorcism (studying and stopping Neg manifestations) once told me: "A long-play tape of children's nursery rhymes drives most adults nuts in a few minutes; and the spooks . . . why they're outta here, man!"

It's best not to sleep in bedrooms with Neg activity until a positive atmosphere is restored. For long-term treatment, tune a radio to a classical station and play it day and night on a low volume. Open the curtains and windows during the day, and keep the overhead lights on all night. Fumigate the room and/or have fresh garlic or repellant herbs and scents placed in them daily. No matter how bad a negative atmosphere is, prolonged treatment will eventually restore it to a positive one.

These same types of music can also help those who hear disturbing, disembodied voices. Use headphones and keep the music playing continuously, even while sleeping. If you can hear them, they can hear what you hear. After a short time, the human mind tunes out repeated sounds and music, but Negs are unable to do this, making it an excellent countermeasure against their voices.

Wind Chimes: Wind chimes are excellent passive countermeasures. I recommend at least one wind chime for each suspected cold spot of supernatural activity in the home. Place one in or near each room of your house so it can catch occasional drafts of air and regularly tinkle. Also place them outside near windows. The level of noise they make can be adjusted by stuffing a little foam rubber into the wind chime tubes.

Old radios can be used for areas like cellars and attics where there may be no flow of air for wind chimes. These can be tuned to classical stations and left playing softly but permanently.

The Importance of Cleanliness: The old saying, "Cleanliness is next to Godliness" holds truth. Negs are less attracted to, and have more difficulty manifesting in, clean, well-aired buildings. I always advise a good spring-cleaning of the home when Neg problems first arise. It is also advisable to combine this with another passive countermeasure, such as using an herbal infusion, rosemary with holy water for example, as a final rinse for walls and floors. This will often solve Neg-related problems before they become significant.

Personal hygiene and the wearing of clean clothing are also important for the same reasons. Regular bathing clears away accumulated negative energy from the skin, along with dirt and oil. The absence of these increases the natural flow of energy body through the human body; this in itself is a good deterrent. Clean clothing and bedding, for these same reasons, also have positive affects. Tight clothing restricts natural energy flow, while loose, clean clothing promotes a greater flow. It is also advisable that you do not wear street footwear within the home, to avoid carrying in negative energies and contaminating the interior of the home.

I have also found that it's helpful to immediately change all your clothing (putting these in the wash) if you've just had a Neg experience of any kind, even a clearing. The energies of the Negs and your reaction to them is, as it were, imprinted on your clothing, and if you keep wearing them, it will remind your system of the bad energies and help magnetize the bad energies into returning.

The attitude you have while cleaning and bathing makes a difference. If cleaning dirt is all you hold in mind, this is all that will happen; but if you hold it in mind that you are also cleaning off negative energy (using your imagination to see dark energy washing away), then the cleansing is enhanced.

Protective Clothing: Clothing can be endowed with protective properties by way of an appropriate blessing or a prayer. Ideally, only freshly cleaned or new clothing should be blessed. Doing this whenever you get dressed is a good habit to get into for long term daily protection. Place potpourris of protective herbs in drawers and closets to endow clothing with their protective scents. Clothing and hats can also have sacred symbols sewn into them or drawn on their surfaces with essential oils.

Cleansing Contaminated Places and Objects: Secondhand objects can contain residual negative energy from previous owners and places, and these can provide targeting links that attract Negs to otherwise Neg-free areas. Clothing is not much of a problem as washing with detergent and a citrus-scented conditioner and a few days of airing outdoors are usually sufficient to remove negative energy. Dispose of badly contaminated clothing.

Wrap small items in plastic wrap and place in a suitable metal box (a cake or biscuit tin). Fill the tin with consecrated salt. The tin can be wrapped in plastic and buried in the ground or hidden for a few days. Repeat this process as necessary, until you sense the items are clean. If you sense an item is still contaminated after several treatments, dispose of it. Throw materials used for cleansing purposes in the trash.

Heavier items, however, need more attention. Line a cardboard box with newspaper and cover the newspaper with a thick layer of salt (half-an-inch); then cover the salt with more newspaper so items are not tarnished. Ordinary salt will work, but consecrated salt is best. Pack items into the box along with several big lumps of coal or charcoal. Seal and stand the box on the ground for three days, outside and under cover, on a balcony, or at least near an open window or door. Dispose of all these cleansing materials afterwards, but do not burn them in an indoor fireplace.

Most furniture can be decontaminated by a thorough cleansing, followed by rinsing and/or sprinkling them inside and out with protective herbs and holy water. Wipe wooden furniture with cleansing essential oils, then stand them (under cover) on the ground outside for a few days or on newspaper near an open window in the home. Fumigate furniture in a closed room with the sulfur or hot pepper method, as given earlier. Badly contaminated items should be disposed of.

Gemstones and Crystals: Certain gemstones and crystals have natural properties that offer protection against Neg influences. Their properties can be increased if they are blessed and endowed with the desired qualities. The more time you spend doing this and the more you treat and revere the stone as special, the more protective it will become.

Wearing a protective stone is not enough; it must be endowed with a vibrating field of force that will enclose and protect the whole body. To do this, relax and meditate, then hold the stone and imagine it vibrating at a high pitch. Imagine a field of light spreading out from the stone and enclosing your whole body. Holding this image in mind, proceed to bless the stone (using names of God and angels of choice), asking for it to be endowed with the desired qualities, such as repelling Negs and negative influences and energies.

Once it is endowed with protective properties, maintain the stone by remembering it during daily prayers and meditations as well as by repeating the preceding procedure at regular intervals. Do this on special days, such as the first day of spring, your birthday, Christmas, New Year's Day, etc., when you feel naturally energized, excited, and powerful, to increase its effectiveness.

Washing and blessing a protective gemstone regularly with holy water enhances its nature and its effectiveness as a personal ward. When not being worn, wrap your protective stones in silk and keep in a container made from protective woods (ash, yew, oak, cedar) or which contains shavings of one of these woods; the stones can also be sprinkled with protective herbs.

Which gemstones should you use? Amethyst, jade, diamond, tourmaline, rutilated quartz, double terminated crystal, smoky topaz, iron ore—these are popular protective stones. Also useful are flint (arrowhead-shaped flint in a pillowcase protects against dream invasion), obsidian, and petrified wood. The more valuable the stone you use for protection, the more you will value, revere, and care for it.

Medicine Bags and Charms: A medicine bag is a venerable Native American method of personal protection. In essence, a medicine bag is a small charm bag that contains sacred items and herbs; it becomes a magical charm and is usually hung around the neck or kept in one's pocket.

Christians have used something similar to medicine bags for hundreds of years. These include crosses, crucifixes, prayers, hymns, and copied-out verses from the Bible folded and wrapped into a small parcel hung around the neck. The Saint Christopher medal is probably the most well-known good luck charm; it is reputed to bestow protection and luck on travelers. Miniature Bibles are available, as are crosses and crucifixes, some of which have passages from the Bible that can be read through tiny lenses set in their centers. Good luck charms are still popular today. You will often see these advertised in magazines, generally accompanied by outrageous claims of good fortune.

No commercially produced good luck charm will have anything more than its natural energy, no matter what is claimed or how much it costs. However, a good luck charm that is revered and cared for by the owner increases in effectiveness. Any sacred or protective icon, or piece of sacred text, has natural energy because of its connection with higher forces. Widespread long-term belief in a sacred text (such as the Lord's Prayer) empowers it. These principles apply to all sacred symbols, names, and texts.

What items can you put in your medicine bag? You can collect special items, and the more special they are and the more effort that goes into collecting them, the more protective value these items will have for you. For example, a small weathered stone taken from a mountain peak you've climbed will have more value than a stone plucked from a beach; an eagle's feather taken from its nest after days of searching will have great value, as will a bear's claw, crocodile tooth, or hair from the mane of a lion or other animal. All of these items can be further empowered by blessing and visualizing connections with the forces they represent.

For example, connect an eagle feather with the great eagle spirit, and reverently ask this spirit to endow the feather with its protection to guard you. With imagination, you can sense this protection as a high-pitched, vibrating field of light, extending as a protective aura to cover your body. Imagine the eagle hovering above you, slowly descending and becoming a part of your protective field. Maintain this during meditations and prayers. When you store this feather, keep it in a box with an eagle engraved on it, or under a small statue of an eagle.

A homemade medicine bag is an excellent way to carry your personal protection with you. Make or acquire a small bag (or locket) of a suitable size. Fill this with miniature sacred items, such as names, texts, symbols, protective herbs, woods, stones, holy water, holy salt, or essential oils. Once it's full, bless the bag. Do not show anyone its contents, although it's fine to discuss the principles involved. Keeping it secret adds to its value and increases its effectiveness. Items can be blessed individually or in a group in the same way as you bless protective herbs and stones.

1 6

Countermeasures for Children

While I wish it otherwise, children are particularly vulnerable to Neg problems. Children have immature, inexperienced, easily frightened minds and soft energy body defenses. Fortunately, a lot more can be done for children than for most adults. If you catch Neg problems early, most childhood attachment and conditioning can be stopped from happening. This chapter contains advice for families suffering Neg problems with children, and it presents appropriate modifications to countermeasures given earlier in the book.

The Problem with Purity

The problem with purity is a matter often discussed in occult and spiritual circles. It is believed that if a person can attain a state of physical, mental, emotional, and spiritual purity, she can attain a state of grace, where she has a stronger connection with her higher self and with God. This is believed to be the ultimate protection against Negs. While this is a laudable and meritorious approach, my experience contradicts the efficacy of purity as a stand-alone countermeasure.

My primary reason is that I have seen children as young as nine months old suffering strong, direct psychic attacks. Babies and very young children live in states of physical, emotional, mental, and spiritual purity; they are not old enough to be any other way. However, babies still experience psychic attacks, and they usually suffer more than adults because they are so vulnerable. To Negs, babies, with their soft minds and few natural defenses, are a prime resource. Adults are more complex and difficult for Negs to work with.

Watching a baby under a direct Neg attack is heartrending. But most parents will not even entertain the idea their baby might be under attack by unseen forces. The main reason for this is denial. To believe otherwise threatens beliefs and personal security, so rather than face the possibility of being vulnerable and powerless, most parents slip into denial and reach for medication to mask the problem. Understandably, the subject of Negs is frightening, but much can be done to counter Negs and keep them away from children.

Most occult and spiritual teachers with whom I have discussed the matter of purity and children suffering Neg attacks cite karma—retribution for bad actions in past lives—as a prime factor. Many have advised me not to interfere or try to protect children, saying they must be allowed to suffer so as to overcome their karmic debts. However, while karma may be part of the equation, it neither helps nor explains the problem. It should not be used as an excuse to let children suffer alone and unaided. Much can be done to help them, and anyway, if a child received help, wouldn't this be a part of karma?

Detecting Neg Problems with Children

Diagnosis of Neg problems in children can be difficult. It's important to not leap to conclusions and think the worst just because a child has behavior problems. The golden rule is: Don't panic! We are all exposed to some degree or other to spirit influences, good and bad. Children are no different and these influences generally do them no real harm. They are a part of life and growing up. We may not like it, and may prefer denial, but in reality we all have to live with this.

To detect child Neg problems, the first signs to look for are sleep disturbances. These can range from pre-sleep problems, insomnia and unsettling dreams, to frequent sudden waking, nightmares and night terrors. Whenever a child experiences disturbed sleep, some action should be taken and passive countermeasures applied, just in case. Passive countermeasures do no harm; they are unobtrusive and easy to apply. They will stop the majority of minor Neg problems before they can escalate, which is good because the sooner Neg problems are countered, the easier they are to overcome.

Children, you will find, greatly appreciate anything that is done to ease their fears and counter their sleep problems. If done intelligently, using passive countermeasures will not spark unsettling imagination problems in children. Turning on a light and a radio, and maybe placing a few slices of garlic around a child's room (to keep away bad dreams) will not trouble their imagination. Taking a child outside and walking him over a hose gushing water on the ground (to wash away bad dreams) is a symbolic action children will understand. A child's feelings of security are always reinforced by positive adult actions like this.

As I mentioned earlier in the book, repeating nightmares and night terrors are the most significant symptoms of early Neg interference. Watch for sudden behavioral anomalies. If a normally kind child suddenly becomes cruel, or if a normally placid, cooperative child suddenly becomes hyperactive and stubborn, this may indicate Neg influences. It's not the behavior in itself but the sudden *changes* in behavior that can indicate Neg problems.

If children exhibit adult behavior, adult words, adult reactions, and attempts to manipulate others, behaviors that are too sophisticated for a child's age, these can indicate Neg influences. One of the most common Neg-related symptoms (for adults or children) is the urge *to control* others. Children under Neg influences often become bossy, controlling, and critical of others. They will often prefer to play with younger children because they are easier to manipulate. Their ability to withstand pain and punishment can also increase dramatically, as can their willingness to risk serious consequences. They will often have only a limited sense of right and wrong, honesty and dishonesty. Further, a fairly reliable indicator of Neg presences in children or adults are the effects they can have on sensitives. A sensitive's skin will prickle and crawl when Neg-contaminated people move close to them. Because of the strong empathic links, this reaction is particularly strong between mother and child.

Diagnosis of Negs is difficult, and you should never jump to conclusions. Most especially, never blame children for Neg-related problems. Children have no control over these matters. It all comes down to knowing your child and spotting unusual or sudden behavioral changes. Many of the phantom illnesses children suffer in the middle of the night are caused by Neg interference.

These are the kinds of headaches, earaches, stomachaches, and fevers children get that force parents to rush them to the hospital in the middle of the night. If this is a phantom ailment, the parents then find a happy, healthy child sitting beside them before they are halfway there. This is usually because running water, water mains, or underground streams have been crossed on the way to the hospital. The Neg interference has thus been disrupted, causing the phantom ailment that came with it to quickly disappear.

Children do change as they grow, and will experiment with changes in personality and behavior, but if you know your child, you will know what is normal and what is unusual, so trust your parental instincts to fill in the gaps here.

Keeping Watch for Neg Activities in Children

Some children have quiet nightmares and night terrors. Waking paralysis episodes, by nature, are also quiet affairs. When children come under Neg attack, it normally starts soon after they have fallen asleep; this can happen any time during the night, but it will normally occur during the first few hours of sleep.

The best way to keep tabs on this is to check your children a couple of times after they have fallen asleep. Take a small flashlight and check their eyes; observe their sleep body language. You should be able to tell if they are sleeping peacefully as they will look relaxed and blissful. If children are having nocturnal problems, they will be restless and tense, often moaning and moving in their sleep.

One indicator of Neg interference is open-eyed REM (rapid eye movement) sleep. If a child's eyes are wide open, eyeballs fluttering or moving about in all directions, this is a sign something is wrong. My experience indicates this is a type of sleep paralysis in which children are held awake in the trance state. This gives the appearance of sleep, and the physical body does rest, but the mind is kept active and denied proper REM sleep. Do not confuse this state with normal closed-eye REM, which is normal sleep behavior.

Open-eyed REM indicates Neg problems may have been underway for some time. Children may be undergoing psychological conditioning similar to brainwashing. If they are deprived of REM sleep, after a few days their minds will turn to mush, and this will expose them to Neg telepathic/hypnotic suggestions and influences. It is quite possible that normal dreaming can then be replaced with the reception of Neg-induced visual information and nightmares. Children will become tired, listless, and irritable, and they will be open to Neg influences during the daytime. Behavioral and personality changes will also usually be evident under these conditions.

When these symptoms are observed, children should be gently awakened. Walk or carry them over running water, then put them in your bed, preferably sleeping between both parents. This will afford some protection until the child's bedroom can be better prepared to counter Neg problems. Keep a close watch on your children once you observe open-eyed REM. The next day have a heart-to-heart talk with the children to see what information you can gather.

If taking children into the parents' bed is impossible, turn on the overhead light, leave a radio playing softly, and place sliced garlic around the child's bedroom. Rub some crushed garlic or garlic oil into the child's feet. These are the minimal countermeasures to apply; a prayer of protection for the child is also advisable.

Seeking Medical Help for Neg Problems in Children

As any parent knows, a normal, healthy child's mind is a very busy place. This is why Negs attack children during sleep and use a process designed to weaken their minds. Children are too difficult to telepathically, hypnotically influence otherwise. However, children's minds quickly weaken if they do not get enough sleep. The solution here is to make sure children get enough rest.

Drugs and herbs affect the interface between the human brain and its mind. Sleep medication changes the way the brain works, promoting deeper, more restful sleep. If children get proper rest, most Neg-related problems will cease or be significantly reduced. However, once a problem like this has been solved, children should be watched for recurrences as Negs do not usually give up easily.

If the sleep disturbances continue, consult a medical doctor and obtain sleep-inducing medication of the type that will help children stay asleep through the night. A pharmacist can also usually provide over-the-counter medication to help. I advise caution when explaining this problem to doctors. Sleep disturbances, nightmares and sleep terrors, listlessness and inability to focus, plus sudden behavioral changes, are classic symptoms of child abuse. Insofar as Neg-related abuse causes identical psychological symptoms to arise in children, you don't want doctors thinking you are abusing your children. Of course, you should be careful regarding the conclusions you draw on this matter. You should ascertain whether your child really is being abused, say, by another family member or friend.

Nothing happens without a reason, and as doctors generally don't believe in Neg-related problems, they will form conclusions according to their medical training. If this happens, it's unlikely you will get the necessary sleep medication at that time, not until the child has been examined by a child psychologist. Child welfare authorities and/or the police may also be brought in to investigate. This situation can cause serious problems for a family.

On the matter of child abuse, I do not disagree with the methods of doctors, child psychologists, and child welfare authorities, nor with their ways of identifying and handling genuine cases of child abuse. However, in the case of Neg-related problems, there are disagreements over what these symptoms indicate.

Behavioral Patterns to Watch For

Once a child's Neg problem has been identified, you may notice certain patterns. Affected children will often experience sudden mood swings and behavioral changes at predictable times. Prime times are when children are getting ready for something, e.g., school, bedtime, mealtimes. They may also throw uncharacteristic tantrums over particular things or at particular times.

I have seen hungry children fall into trance, change personality, and completely lose their appetite within seconds of sitting down to dinner. I have seen children throw hysterical tantrums at the same time every night. These types of problems are usually minor to start with, but will escalate and become habitual behavior if left unattended. Sudden changes like this are usually linked to particular triggers. Identifying the triggers and intelligently defusing the situations is the best way to handle this problem.

Here are details from some of the worst cases I have ever come across of child Neg problems. All these children had histories of sleep terrors and open-eyed REM.

- A bright, intelligent eight-year-old girl, happily watching TV with her siblings, is politely and gently asked to move a couple of inches so others can see the screen. She screams and throws herself on the floor and thrashes about; she tears her hair and scratches herself. This continues for several minutes before she staggers off, screaming and kicking walls and furniture on the way to her bedroom.

  Her tantrum continues for an hour until she falls asleep sobbing amidst the wreckage of her room. Her parents give her a cold shower and slap her to get her out of her hysterics, but nothing works. As these fits happen most nights between six and seven, the family has learned not to speak to her in the evenings, but this is difficult as she becomes obnoxious and pushy at these times.

- A nine-year-old boy decides he does not ever want to eat his dinner. Normally a great lover of his mother's cooking, he will now only eat cheese for dinner.

Attempts to force him to do otherwise result in violent tantrums; he has twice threatened his mother with a knife. If he is not given cheese he refuses to eat, fasting for days until his parents give in.

A year goes by with no change. Child psychologists and therapists do not help. The boy is steadily becoming uncontrollable and dangerous. He is expelled from school after school for violent behavior. He refuses to go to bed and falls asleep in front of the TV most nights. Any attempt to control him results in non-childlike extremes of temper and violence.

- A ten-year-old boy starts having mood swings and violent outbursts. They grow steadily worse. He tries to control everyone around him using adult methods way beyond his years. He threatens anyone he cannot control, including his parents, siblings, friends, and school teachers. Highly intelligent, he must be the center of attention at all times. He attacks a male teacher because the teacher interrupts his lengthy discourses in class. He gets expelled from yet another school. Everyone is afraid of him. His parents begin locking sharp knives away and locking their bedroom door at night. He fools a string of child psychologists and continually accuses his father of sexual abuse and brutality.

  After being punished one day, he bruises his face and damages his anus until it bleeds; then he goes to the police and tries to have his father arrested. The father is proven innocent. After his parents attempt to force the boy to clean his room one day, he slips concentrated insecticide into a bottle of soda and pours it out for the whole family, including his siblings. His mother becomes suspicious when she notices him smiling at her. She sniffs her drink. The police are called and the boy is taken away.

  He cannot see what he has done wrong. He is prescribed anti-psychotic medication, even though this condition is deemed "impossible" at his age. After a few months in a correctional facility he returns home, but he has no remorse for anything and cannot see what he has done wrong. He feels victimized.

These are extreme examples of the problem of Negs and children. The majority of children under Neg influences will not develop into monsters as these children did. This is especially so if parents understand what is happening and work against it. Parents have enormous influence over their children, more so than any Neg. If this influence is used wisely and countermeasures applied as necessary, the majority of Neg problems can be overcome; at the least, long-term damage can be minimized. Good parenting is thus a *crucial* factor in overcoming child Neg-related problems.

Countering Neg-Related Patterns

When Neg-related patterns are identified, it's important to counter them as soon as possible. The key is to change the situation. For example, have dinner an hour earlier; set aside more time to supervise children getting ready for school; change bedtimes and procedures so everything goes smoothly and problems do not arise.

Mealtimes are especially important for family communication and bonding. Always turn off the TV and radio during this time. Use this time to talk and exchange stories and solve problems together as a family. For some families, the evening meal is the only time when the family is together, so take advantage of this and use the time to improve family connections and harmony.

Mealtimes and the time while the child gets ready for school are prime moments for Neg interference. Disruption here can ruin the day. Parents are usually rushed, trying to get everything done on time, not paying attention. Children sense this. Many children will misbehave just to get more attention, but this is normal. However, Negs will use these natural urges for attention and *push* them, often to extremes. This can cause a meltdown in family unity and feed negative atmospheres, making it easier for Negs to operate.

Watching TV and videos can trigger Neg influences. As this is a passive activity that does not require much mental activity, many children slip into trancelike states while watching. If they are prone to Neg influences, this can open them to overshadowing and behavioral changes will follow. This is easily fixed. Turn off the TV and put on music the children like. Dance and sing with them. All children love to sing and dance. Read a story, go for a walk, play a game, get some energy going that requires attention, family activity, and togetherness. Stimulate the child's mind in a positive way.

I have used these simple methods in families seriously affected by Negs. These actions lift the atmospheres and improve harmony quickly. The positive atmosphere of a home builds up over time and provides a natural shield around the family home and its members. Ideally, no harsh words or arguments should ever be made inside the family home. Go outside to settle disputes. Arguing inside the home erodes the wholesome family atmosphere, filling it with negative energy.

Communicating with Children About Their Neg Problems

When Neg problems surface in families, children often have no idea what to do or who to tell. Typically, parents go into denial and accuse children of making it all up. Children are often coerced into pretending it's not happening (even if it is) and not to bother parents with their "fantasies." It's all in your mind, or it's only a bad dream—these are standard explanations. For sleep disturbances, children are usually told to think happy thoughts, and they are often blamed for not doing this correctly if they still cannot sleep.

But it's hard to think happy thoughts when a Neg presence is sensed or if a manifestation is taking place under your bed or in the closet. Children are often aware they are experiencing real phenomena, but are generally not sure of the cause. Denial is the safe way out, but it will not make Neg problems go away. It will only drive them underground, forcing children to suffer in silence, unaided and misunderstood. This can be psychologically damaging in the long term.

Here are the observations of psychologist Benjamin Bruce, who is experienced with Neg-related matters:

> The problems that children face are far from predictable. Childhood trauma can have very different effects upon different children, and as they develop into adults there are infinite variables that compound this unpredictability. There are the effects of the individual differences in personality for every child, as well as the biological, psychosocial and environmental factors. The evidence given in this book would also highlight the parapsychological domain. With an analysis of this variable, an "X" factor of unseen influences, or Negs, we can appreciate a whole other dimension to childhood developmental problems. The following are alternative hypothetical scenarios resulting from either acknowledging this *X* factor or ignoring it.
>
> **Two scenarios:** A child exhibiting Neg-related problems is told by his parents that it's all in his mind and that he should *just be normal*. Regardless of this "great advice" the Neg phenomena may continue (while he tries to sleep, for example) to the detriment of the child's physical and psychological health. There is also an interaction between the environment (the Neg interference) and the child's individuality, the thoughts and actions that are particular to him. The child will soon realize that his experiences are either real, if he is intelligent, perceptive, and trusts his senses, or fictitious if he is unable to discriminate and has low self-esteem.
>
> The former scenario (a sense of real experience) will promote a feeling of isolation within the child, and he will

think that his life is special in some way. He may also lose respect for his parents and feel unloved, as they do nothing to protect him from the terrifying phenomena. The latter scenario (a sense of fictitious experience) will cause the child to feel derogated, with his reality undermined so that he starts to doubt all his perceptual experiences. This is worsened by the lack of quality sleep and the mental influence to commit strange or horrifying acts that may result from Neg interference. This creates a schism or rift in the psyche, where the child's private world becomes separated from the public world of "consensus reality." The child now believes he is abnormal and mentally deranged.

This abnormality can be exacerbated with derogatory labels from his family and peers such as "freak" or "weirdo," or with clinical labels such as "schizophrenic" if he is introduced to a professional. The latter scenario will also be compounded with any antipsychotic or sedative medication (or other treatment) received, and the side effects of this. Over time, both scenarios may lead to a similar outcome of delinquency and aberrant or criminal behavior as the child/adult seeks to fit in and attracts like-minded company: people with similar strange and erratic thought and behavior. The child/adult may even be institutionalized, especially if any aberrant and destructive urges are acted upon.

Conversely, when these experiences first began, the parent(s) could have been more sympathetic and investigative of the source of the problem and the possible presence of Negs. Indeed, it is possible that the child is suffering from mental illness or experiencing the negative effects of real-life problems, such as child abuse, but all possibilities should be explored. If parents are observant and open-minded, any serious Neg interference should become noticeable, if it exists. This often comes with multiple parasomnias (sleep and sleep-wake rhythm disorders) such as: sleep paralysis, nightmares, night terrors, night sweating, open-eyed REM, sleepwalking, head banging, head rolling, body rocking, bedwetting, sleep talking, and tooth grinding. Although these parasomnias may exist as simple childhood disorders in their own right, links with Neg activity are conceivable. This is especially so if multiple parasomnias are linked with disturbing atmospheres, poltergeist phenomena, and other strange nocturnal manifestations around the child. But one should be on guard not to become paranoid or to develop a witch-hunt mentality. This line of investigation must be conducted with *extreme* caution, in plain view of all the facts. Otherwise, a self-fulfilling prophecy could develop and come to fruition, which would counter the intention of genuinely helping suffering children.

If the child is aware that he is being taken seriously with a mind toward problem resolution, there will be less chance of the potential mental schism in the aforementioned scenario resulting, and the child will find his perceptions more trustworthy. His self-esteem and self-respect will improve, as will his love and respect for his parents. He will feel more comfortable with, and connected, to reality, even if reality is extended to include abnormal events. Along this line of thought, it is possible that many doctors and psychotherapists, and the institutions they work for, whilst having good intentions, are overly focused on preserving their current paradigm: their view of the world and the people in it.

It is important to note that an apparently irrational person (child or adult) always has a reason for acting or thinking in such a way. In this sense, all thought and behavior is fundamentally rational: an effect resulting from a cause. Thus, a person who is apparently "strange" on the outside should be respected and given the benefit of the doubt. It should be kept in mind that the behavioral or thought disturbance has a cause, and that this is the person's way of reacting and coping. It is thus unconstructive and unhelpful to fob the person off as being "irrational."

As well as validation of experience, the person must also be made accountable for their thoughts and actions, such as with the application of mental discipline, and help given accordingly. However, this does not mean that one should blame the victim, especially a child, for their Neg-related problems. But if this accountability does not occur, the person will not develop the necessary responsibility for his or her actions, and may actually "luxuriate" or wallow in their problems and not face reality. This can lead to other psychological disturbances from basic immaturity to complex personality disorders later in life.

Regarding parental tactics, remember that children are generally braver and more open than most people think. They appreciate candor as much as adults. But too many details are counterproductive, needlessly frightening them. Tell the children only the basics in such a way that it's easy for them to accept. The truth can be desensationalized and honest explanations given.

If Neg problems are apparent, tell your children that something will be done about them. A good way of handling this is to expand on the usual explanation that the problem is caused by their imagination. You can tell children that a person's imagination can sometimes cause problems for other people, that sometimes this can cause scary things to happen. Point out that these things can only scare them and not cause them bodily harm.

A non-threatening name can be given to Negs, such as Spooky, Ghostly, or Casper. Today, kids are fairly comfortable with the concept of harmless but scary cartoon monsters. If parents are matter-of-fact about this, children will respond positively; keep in mind that explanations like this should be given only if Neg problems are noticeable.

Getting children involved with countermeasures and understanding how they work helps distract them. This in turn helps demystify and desensationalize a frightening situation. Then, doing something positive about Neg problems promotes peace of mind for all concerned. A family united and grounded in truth is far stronger than a family divided by denial.

Attitude is important when dealing with family Neg problems. The information children can provide is invaluable, and they should be encouraged to report anything that disturbs them. Encourage children with Neg-related problems to talk about their dreams and experiences, good and bad. Recurrent dreams can help identify core images to work on. Merely talking about bad dreams and nocturnal experiences and sharing them with loving parents while being believed and supported is beneficial to any child's psychological well-being.

Body-Awareness Actions for Children

Children can be taught simple body-awareness actions to counter nocturnal Neg interference. I have taught children as young as three with good results. However, body-awareness actions will sometimes cause extensive tickling because children have very sensitive bodies. One group of four-, six-, and eight-year-olds collapsed in a giggling heap trying to scratch all their hands and feet at the same time after I showed them the body-awareness technique.

Teach children to use body-awareness actions on any part of their body where tingling, tickling, fuzziness, fluttering, pricking, jabbing, hot or cold spots, or other things out of the ordinary are felt. As a parent you do not have to say these sensations are caused by Negs. Explain that these sensations are related to other people's imaginations, which sometimes can cause strange sensations. Knowing body-awareness actions helps counter these strange sensations and gives children something with which to fight back.

Here is a simple procedure for teaching children body-awareness actions. This works best outdoors, where there is a breeze, or near a fan.

For hands, stand with eyes closed, hands at your sides and fingers wide. Raise your arms to your sides and *feel* the temperature and *texture* of air moving through the fingers of both hands.

Become aware of and concentrate on both hands (palms and fingers) using body awareness. Imagine the feel of a big paintbrush, brushing from fingertips to wrists, over and over.

Continue this for one minute, or as long as desired.

For feet, repeat the hand procedure with bare feet. Sit or lie down, close your eyes and focus on the temperature and texture of the air moving over your feet and through your toes. Imagine the feel of a big paintbrush, brushing from toes to heels, over and over.

Continue this for one minute, or as long as desired.

Core Image Work for Children

Children above the age of four or five can usually be taught to do their own core-image work. This can be desensationalized by explaining it in an unfrightening way. All children are good with imagination, so explain that the images they might see are not real but of their imagination. Tell them that getting rid of these images will help get rid of bad pieces of their imagination that might be causing bad dreams. Gently talk children through the core-image treatment process, until they are confident enough to do it solo. In this way, as a parent, you can direct the flow of events and boost your child's courage.

• First, talk children through a basic relaxation process with their eyes closed until they have settled.

• Have them take several deep breaths, then imagine they are slowly walking down twelve big steps or going down twelve floors in an elevator, one at a time.

- Next, identify a core image; this might come from bad dream experiences or a fearful presence sensed at night.

- Tell them to imagine the memory of a presence as a pale, featureless cloud.

- Shrink this to postcard size or smaller.

- Grab it with body-awareness hands and turn it over.

- Attack it with imaginary weapons: sword, baseball bat, or rocket launcher.

- Burn it with an imaginary torch, flame-thrower, or laser beam.

- Seal the hole left behind by imagining a sword-bearing guardian angel filling it.

Parents and children have strong emotional, telepathic bonds between them; this is especially strong between mother and child. Using these powerful links, as a parent you can connect with your children and treat their core images. It helps if children are asleep, or at least relaxed and quiet while you do this. You do not have to be in the same room, but the optimal situation for this is while holding and/or nursing your child.

- Begin the core-image treatment process as normal, but instead of using your own memories, use one your child has described to you. This might be from a bad dream your child has had.

- Call this image up in your imagination and treat it as you would treat one of your own core images.

- After exhausting what core images your child has told you, use your imagination to dig further, especially for babies of pre-language age.

- Visualize an image of your child as best you can.

- Imagine a dark shape, like a shadow of your child, splits off from the image; this shadow contains all the negative energy from within your child, all his problems encapsulated.

- Focus on the shadow copy of your child, then shrink it and treat it as you would any core image.

- After turning it over, destroying and burning the shadow copy, seal the hole it leaves. Imagine a hole left behind even if one is not actually seen.

- Imagine an angel or sacred symbol fills this space and stands guard.

- Pray and wish protective properties into this guardian.

Here is an alternative way to do it:

- Imagine the dark copy of your child begins to spin counter-clockwise.

- Imagine it growing in size, becoming a ball, ripping dark strips of black, negative energy from your child's true image.

- As the dark spinning ball grows, imagine your child's true image turning white.

- When the dark ball is large enough, and the true image pure white, focus on the black copy.

- Imagine the black copy turns brilliant-white and changes direction to spin clockwise.

- Merge and reintegrate the two images. Precision is not necessary; just do the best you can.

- While doing core-image treatment for children, be prepared for surprises. All sorts of images may spring up in your mind, especially if you have some interior visual ability. These images may be related to your child's problems or they may be related to *your* problems; they may also relate to problems shared by you and your child.

Case history: A mother was concerned about her six-year-old son's behavioral problems. She had been practicing meditation and core-image work for some time, and so decided to apply this to her son. While her son was taking a nap on the couch, she sat beside him and relaxed. She focused upon him, visualizing his image with all the thoughts and emotions she felt about him. As the image of her son appeared in her mind, she attempted to turn this image over to see what was behind his behavioral problems. The image would not budge, so she tried another method of tearing strips away from the surface of the image.

After several minutes of deep concentration, the image of her son vanished and the image of a beer bottle appeared instead. The mother was shocked as this was a particular brand of beer that she drank regularly, and she realized at that moment that her drinking problem was related to her son's problems. She attacked the image with the cleansing technique given earlier. She then set about changing her life. She gave up drinking and sought professional help for her alcoholism. In time, her son's behavior problems resolved, and her family life was greatly improved.

Effective Countermeasures for Children

Apply all countermeasures (given earlier in the book) as necessary to protect your children. However, here are a few modifications and some additional countermeasures particular to children's needs:

Crossing Running Water: Crossing running water is the first line of defense against Neg invasion. Use this immediately when you suspect a Neg problem. This is safe and cannot harm children. It's a powerful defense and should always be used before employing other active countermeasures.

Babies can be carried over running water. A garden hose gushing water along the ground is all that is required; a water main will also suffice. When using the hose method, I dangle babies and very small children by the arms and walk them through the running water itself, just touching their little feet in the water as I carry them across it. The running water approach (plus visualization method given earlier) is excellent for helping children. Parents can perform the visualization for babies, after placing them among the loops of coiled hose.

Normally, a direct Neg attack will cease the instant the afflicted person crosses running water. However, it should always be kept in mind that when an attack is broken in this way, the Neg responsible is likely to wait on the other side of the hose. Throwing a loop of hose over where the hose was crossed can trap the Neg and allow safe passage back into the home. If you cross water mains in the street or by car, when an attack is broken, return home via another route so the Neg is not picked up again on your way back.

Some people find it difficult to accept that something as simple as crossing running water can help children's night terrors and other nocturnal maladies. This is denial stemming from materialistic thought; it also involves fear of the implications inherent to accepting supernatural possibilities. I have gotten around this problem many times by telling parents white lies. I tell them that children sometimes develop excess static electricity and that walking them over running water removes it. I say this often cures night terrors and other sleep-related problems. I have had many parents praise me for this fabrication, but these same parents would never accept the possibility their children might have Neg problems.

In the Parents' Bed: Placing children between the parents in their bed is an effective countermeasure for most nocturnal Neg problems. The energy bodies of the parents enfold the children, and Negs have to go through the parents to get at the children. Some Negs may continue an attack under these unfavorable conditions, but this is rare. The most parents are likely to face are a few cold shivers and a negative atmosphere, which is preferable to having a child face it alone. If the attack continues, use basic countermeasures like turning on overhead lights, playing soft music or the TV, or placing garlic and other deterrent herbs around the bed. These will usually ease the situation.

Light, Music, and Noise: Many Neg-related children's problems can be overcome using light, music, and noise. Leave on overhead lights or night lights if children want them. You can play any music softly through the night, but nursery rhymes, Christmas carols, spiritual songs, or hymns are best.

If a child begins hearing voices and/or noises, place the source of music closer to the child. Use pillow speakers or headphones, if you wish. Small portable radios are also a good option, placed near or under the pillow. I have helped many adults and children overcome serious audio problems in this way.

Noise-making devices make a good active countermeasure, like those loud clattery things people spin around at football games. Drums and cymbals, trumpets, even pots and pans banged together—anything that makes loud, sharp noises—will help break up Neg atmospheres.

Get your children to alert you if they have a problem and are too scared to get out of bed. Give them whistles, with which they can call for help.

Making Changes to the Child's Room: When decorating a child's room, a bright, harmonious, non-frightening ambience should always be the goal. There should be no dark corners. Some children may think it's "cool" to have pictures of monsters on their walls, but these can trigger negative mental associations and cause nightmares, which Negs can use. Use bright pastel colors for walls and curtains; keep the room clean and tidy. This is no easy task, knowing children, but it's worth the effort to counter potential Neg problems.

Place pictures of angels, sacred symbols, wards, and religious icons around the child's room. Tell the child these things are special and will help ward off bad dreams, that the more they are believed in, the better they will work. Children generally love having these items around them.

Bedtime Prayers: Teach children to pray aloud for protection at bedtime. Explain that prayers help keep them safe. The Lord's

Prayer, for example, can be memorized by children and said every night. Or use this simple children's prayer:

> Now I lay me down to sleep,
> I pray the Lord my soul to keep;
> And if I die before I wake,
> I pray the Lord my soul to take.
> Amen.

Helping Infants with Neg Interference

It can be difficult to tell whether an infant is suffering Neg interference, but the usual symptom of direct Neg attack is a sudden, screaming tantrum. The baby goes rigid and does not respond to feeding, changing, or cuddling. In this case, having the baby cross running water as soon as possible is advisable. This will usually tell you whether the baby's problem is Neg-related or something physical, then you can take appropriate action.

Disturbed infant sleep can indicate lighter degrees of Neg interference. Babies are highly sensitive and do not settle well in negative atmospheres. Of course, a strong Neg presence is very unsettling for adults and babies alike. However, if a Neg presence is focused on or around a baby, parents may still sense nothing. If babies show any symptoms of being disturbed, even if they only have gas, are teething, or are generally unsettled, it does not hurt to carry them over running water just to be sure. Trust your parental intuition here.

Dietary disorders are another symptom of probable Neg involvement. If children stop eating, or develop allergies or peculiar tastes, this can indicate Neg interference. Sudden pain that results in screaming fits, strange infections that come on quickly, and repeated jerking and/or sudden frequent waking, as if the baby were being jabbed or pricked—these are other symptoms. If you suspect Neg interference, apply appropriate countermeasures immediately.

Because of the difficulties in discerning if babies are having Neg-related problems, install passive countermeasures as a matter of course. Neg-deterrent herbs and scents, religious icons, symbols and pictures, and other wards for doors and windows will do no harm and can make all the difference, stopping problems before they start.

Here are two excellent passive countermeasures for babies and children, especially useful in situations in which one parent will not allow any more-visible countermeasures:

• Rub garlic lotion or oil into children's feet at bedtime. This also helps counter night-sweating and night-fevers, and is a simple herbal remedy for these conditions.

• Draw sacred symbols on windows, doors, and walls, using garlic or essential oils.

Negs and the Life of the Family

The advice I offer here is fundamental to all Neg problems, psychic influences, and attacks involving groups of people. However, it mainly applies to families with serious ongoing Neg problems.

Finding the Family's Weak Link: A family is like a closed ecosystem. Neg influences and activities are magnified within it. Because of this, Neg strategies are more easily recognized. Families are interconnected with strong emotional and telepathic links. Non-verbal communications are sensed through these links. Negs use these connections to manipulate family members and turn them against one another. This creates widespread disharmony and unhappiness; it affects the home environment and generates negative energy. This is why the home atmosphere should be carefully nurtured. Positive energy can be generated through the expression of love, happiness, and compassion; laughter has a particularly strong positive affect.

However, if Negs succeed in forming an attachment with one family member, they will try to spread their influences to others through the close family connections. It does not matter whether all family members are sensitive or not; all are equally vulnerable to this influence.

Here is a typical example of how this works: Take one happy, loving family just before dinnertime. Some mothers call this the "Acid Hour." This is when arguments are most likely to break out. Mom is busy preparing dinner, Dad is trying to watch the news, and the children are hungry and squabbling—a recipe for disaster in anyone's book.

The Neg begins by influencing the most sensitive child (the one it has most influence over) into starting a loud argument with a sibling. Mom gets annoyed and the Neg switches its focus to her, pushing her to overreact. The father tries to quiet things down, already annoyed at having his quiet time interrupted. The Neg switches to him and pushes him to overreact. The Neg plays the family like puppets, one against the other, creating the worst possible argument. The mother, protecting her children, turns on her husband. A domestic argument ensues, and dinner burns on the stove.

The evening is ruined for everyone. No one is talking to anyone; everyone is angry, even the dog. The children have bad dreams and parents sleep in separate rooms. If no more attacks occur, it may take several days for the home atmosphere to restore itself. Imagine what happens to a family when this is a daily event.

I have watched Neg-besieged families go through scenarios like this many times. I have seen a cloud of black dots (like swarms of flies) moving from person to person, spreading discord wherever they touch down. If allowed to proceed unchecked, more serious Neg-related phenomena often follow.

"United we stand, divided we fall"—this is a good maxim for families with ongoing Neg problems. A family must work together to overcome these influences. Family connections can be made to work *for* the family unit instead of against it. Family members should learn to work together, recognizing and countering Neg influences as they arise. They should watch over, and warn, each other, and have procedures ready for dealing with Neg problems before they can spread.

Discipline Issues: Discipline is a matter for parents to consider. Many Neg problems can be overcome by applying appropriate levels of discipline to children. Neg influences are often just simple influences, and parents have far more influence over their children than Negs do.

Fear of consequences and punishment for wrong actions are powerful motivators for children. Think of this as providing a counter-pressure to nullify Neg influences and urges. Children will grow stronger every time they fight off a bad urge or idea. In time, with consistent discipline and good parenting, most Neg influences will fade into the background and disappear.

Controlling Adult Emotional Outbursts: Adults can defuse most Neg influences on children with common sense and good parenting skills. But this service must also be performed for the adults, too. In order to prevent outbursts, procedures must be established for recognizing and dealing with sudden negative urges and mood swings in adults.

Take anger, for example. Negs will empower this and cause explosive outbursts over trivial matters. Affected adults should take some time out before their annoyance turns to anger. They should, ideally, leave the house and return only when their emotions are back under control. If this is impossible, take time out on a balcony, in a bathroom, hallway, or bedroom; as circumstances permit, walk over running water.

There are two ways to gain control over adult outbursts. The first is self-imposed, in which the angry person voluntarily takes time out of the situation. The second is for his/her partner or another adult (or even a child) to recognize the problem and suggest a time-out be taken.

I recommend using a sports hand sign for "Time" to indicate when this action is necessary. Adults must program themselves to react to this sign without question. It's important this signal be nonverbal, as this lessens the chances of Negs catching on to what is happening; the less they know, the better. This procedure only works if adults commit to it beforehand, promising to respond to the "T" signal without question. If one adult refuses to commit, or does not want any part of it, the other adults and children must do their best to defuse the volatile situation. They must work around reluctant family members. In time, when those who resist see it working, they will usually join in.

It might sound strange, the idea of giving children the power of the "T" over adults, but it works. Children are very sensitive to adult moods and will usually be able to provide early warning of Neg influences. Adults know when they are getting angry, so this system is rarely abused by children. I have worked with children in many serious situations. They might laugh about it to begin with, but will always take the sign system to heart.

Adults are usually the ones to abuse the time-out system. Many times I have seen adults deny they are getting angry, and argue until moments later they explode over this very issue. Normally, this only has to happen a couple of times before they get the idea and start working with the family. The time out procedure is also beneficial when dealing with domestic situations in which negative emotions, conflicts, and arguments (not Negs) are an ongoing problem.

Adult Attachments: A good way to help prevent Neg problems in children is for parents to deal with their own Neg attachments. Parents may not realize they have Negs linked to them, as this is often difficult to ascertain. But if they exist, dealing with such problems can prevent them from being passed on to children. Most of children's Neg-related problems come from adults; often, the same Negs that trouble children also troubled their parents during their childhoods.

Changing the Home Situation: A good way to counter Neg influences when children are involved is to introduce changes, altering situations known to cause problems. Any situation in which members of a family are preoccupied, hungry, or bored, leads to a lessening of individual self-control, and a corresponding drop in family discipline and communication. Watch for symptoms of trouble and take spontaneous actions to defuse potentially volatile situations before they can take root and ruin family harmony.

It pays to be spontaneous and a little on the crazy side when countering situations open to Neg influences. Children love spontaneity. Family interactions are fairly predictable and Negs rely on this to generate stressful situations. Negs are not good at adapting to changes in human behavior patterns; therefore, counter family

Neg influences by making sudden changes to predictable patterns of family behavior.

There are many ways to change things and avoid seemingly inevitable outcomes based on the earlier family example. For example, Dad can turn off the TV and pay attention to the children, occupying them by chatting and playing. Or, Dad could finish cooking dinner while Mom occupies the children. One parent could take the children out for a game of ball or a short walk, walking the dog in the process.

Watch Less Television: One simple countermeasure is to watch less TV. Watching TV is counterproductive to family harmony when Negs are around. It provides an open invitation for Neg influences. Television turns a family unit into a loose-knit collection of preoccupied, semi-tranced individuals. In this state, family members are far more exposed to Neg influences than when interacting as a family unit, paying attention to, and communicating with, one another.

I have yet to see Negs bring down a happy family atmosphere when this advice has been applied. A strong positive atmosphere with spontaneity and humor can overcome any negative one. If you can generate and spread happiness and laughter among children, something like a humorous exorcism takes place, effectively driving Negs away.

To summarize, in a family prone to Neg influences, the best way to handle the Acid Hour is for the family to stop what it's doing and turn off all TVs, radios, and computers. Make dinnertime a special family event.

Limit Your Open Discussion of Negs: Most Negs can understand human speech and thoughts. So it is generally wise not to discuss Neg problems and countermeasures when one might be overheard. This includes discussing them around other people and children who might not understand, or who may overreact. Go for a walk or drive when having a serious discussion about these matters; talk in a neutral, Neg-free territory. If a Neg is attached to you or your partner, this cannot be helped. Walking or driving involves crossing many water mains (running water), and this will at least make things difficult for any Negs that might be trying to follow you.

With all Neg-related problems, be careful with whom you share information. Some people will pretend interest and concern only to laugh and ridicule you later. I have known many families to develop serious social problems because of this indiscretion. Some have been reported to child welfare departments and police for alleged child abuse. This is mainly because people have been concerned about what seems to them crazy ideas and cult-like religious beliefs as entertained by the parents.

This happened to me once while helping a Neg-besieged family. They had major Neg problems including strong, frequent phenomena. Four young children were involved, ages three to six. Two weeks later, my countermeasures were working and Neg problems were steadily decreasing. But both parents had been involved in a series of nasty arguments with their respective families over what they had been doing, after both had confided in their families and friends.

Among other things, their house now smelled faintly of garlic and incense; the TV was stored in the garage; classical music, Christmas carols, and nursery rhymes played all day and night; the family members went for walks, played games, told stories, sang and danced and played together; all children were on prescribed sleeping medication; and everyone went to bed tired and happy after evening prayers. In two weeks, I had transformed this home from a place where children burst into tears as the sun went down into a beehive of happy family activity. The Negs were still there, but they had been driven into the background and were steadily growing weaker. The children loved the changes.

Then, one morning at ten o'clock while I was visiting, two senior investigative psychologists from the child welfare department arrived. They had received complaints of child abuse involving black magic and drugs. The family was given two choices: allow these people access to carry out an investigation and observe the children and home environment, or have the children taken away immediately for observation and examination elsewhere. A police car was parked in the driveway. Of course, the parents chose the former option.

At a loss for words I took a gamble and chose honesty. I discussed the situation with the investigators for most of the day. I explained the problems, citing examples, explaining the logic behind the countermeasures, and showing the results. We told them just about everything; they were stunned by the enormity of what we said. This was especially so because, what with the flood of negative energy in the house (caused by the fear of possibly losing the children), there was now again enough supernatural phenomena for my case to be convincing. It intensified when the eldest child arrived home from school.

After a private discussion, the investigators reciprocated our honesty. They confided in us that both of them had encountered similar situations many times. However, this was the first time they had ever seen anything being done about it. They could not officially support what we were doing, but they applauded our efforts. Leaving, they said the only thing they could do to help was overrule the pending complaint and to reflect in their reports that the children were in no danger.

This event helped me overcome my doubts about what I had been doing. I was guided by intuition. I was as stunned by what they confided in me as they were by what I confided in them. But this is not unusual. Over the years since, I have shared information with other health professionals with similar results. However, very few will openly discuss these matters for fear of professional repercussions.

Keeping the Family Lifestyle Wholesome: The home and family lifestyle, its visitors and family associates, have a lot to do with whether or not Neg-related problems will arise. Consider your children's friends and playmates. Their exposure to Neg-carrying people is a common cause of child Neg problems. As any parent knows, bad company equals bad influences; children quickly pick up bad traits and habits, and Neg influences, from other children. Allowing children to associate with badly behaved, undisciplined children is an easy way for them to pick up Neg hitchhikers. Bad associations can be countered by good parental advice, discouraging the bad associations and encouraging the good ones, and teaching children to discern this difference for themselves.

It's more preferable for young children to learn how to choose friends wisely than it is for them to learn this the hard way later as teenagers or adults. Children should be shielded from any contact with disreputable, immoral people, especially those with emotional or mental problems.

People with lifestyle problems, such as alcohol and drug abuse, should also be avoided. Protect the family home from anyone that might bring negativity into it. Cultivate the home as a spiritual haven, free of disharmony and strife, as a sanctuary safe for children to live in.

1 7

Dealing with Possession and Exorcism

No matter how you phrase it, the words "possession" and "exorcism" generate horrific images of rotating heads with ghastly faces spewing gallons of pea soup over chanting priests. But possession is actually fairly commonplace, and it always has been. Only the most extreme cases attract enough attention to be investigated and reported by the media, and even then its rarely called possession. It's called rampaging, crazy people. Possession is rarely recognized for what it is, and some cases are so strange they are immediately swept under the carpet.

There are two distinct types of possession. The first is called "instant possession" that generally results from a possession attack of some kind or another. The Neg responsible may or may not already be attached to the person it attempts to possess. This is the most noticeable form of possession, as it comes with a sudden, marked personality change, as the Neg personality replaces the human personality. The degree of control the Neg has in this case depends upon its strength and experience. This can result in instant virtual puppetry.

The next type of possession is called "progressive possession." This results from the slow integration of a Neg personality with a human personality. The length of time this takes is highly variable. In can take many years, often starting in early childhood, or it can happen in a matter of days or weeks. Again, this depends on the strength and experience of the Neg involved, plus on the strengths and weaknesses of the living victim.

Sometimes, a mixture of "instant" and "progressive" possession can occur. This is illustrated by the possession I experienced which began with an "instant possession," but continued as a "progressive possession" as the Neg involved progressively gained more control over me.

The modern explanation for most cases of possession is that it is a mental breakdown and/or mental illness. While this is true in some cases, which came first: the possession or the mental illness? Strong Neg influences, especially possession, always cause some degree of mental aberration that can easily be mistaken for mental illness.

There are many subtle degrees of possession, but the majority of possessed people do not rampage and hurl pea soup. Most suffer a range of psychological and behavioral disorders with occasional overshadowing. There is a difference between persons suffering Neg urges and compulsions and persons suffering possession. The former resist their urges and compulsions, while the latter cannot resist them. In this chapter, we look at some steps you can take for cases of possession.

Preparing Yourself to Deal with the Problem

To begin with, apply all the advice and countermeasures given in this book. Do this more vigorously and diligently than for normal psychic self-defense. Unfortunately, there is no easy solution to possession. There are no pills, potions, or charms that will make this nightmare go away. Considerable effort and dedication are required. However, no problem comes without a solution.

Religious Exorcism: Can religious exorcism help you? Possession is an ancient and well-documented malady, extensively recorded in the religious books and texts of all races and cultures, such as the Bible. Because of this, some churches offer help, and various types of exorcists are available. This can be an easier way to overcome possession than doing it yourself. But it requires one to become a dedicated member of the church or faith in question for good long-term results. Doing it oneself can take hard work and dedication, as well as courage and fortitude.

Change Yourself: The basic principle behind ridding yourself of a possessing Neg is to change your situation, internally and externally. Possession, no matter how it happens, involves Negs breaking through personal defenses by exploiting weaknesses particular to the individual possessed. Through this process, Negs gain control over that individual.

Logically, the way to counter possession is to attack the situation on all fronts. Old habits must be broken and replaced with new, healthier, and more spiritual ones. Changes must be made to uplift and strengthen your spiritual vibrations. These must be taken to the point where you become too difficult for possessing Negs to control.

Most people wish they had the power to change certain things about themselves and become better people. But the will power necessary to make significant changes is often too difficult to muster and carry through for the long term. Sage advice and occult knowledge are a great help, but will not provide you with the necessary will power to make significant changes.

Nothing happens without a reason, not even psychic attack and possession. We may not like it, but sometimes the only way we can learn and make serious life changes is through hardship. Possession is a major life-changing hardship. It indicates that serious changes are urgently required, and that the problem will not ease until these changes are implemented. Most of us do not know what we are capable of until we face an emergency situation. Possession is an emergency situation. It might not kill you outright, but it can destroy your life all the same.

Avoid the Love-and-Light Approach: Contrary to the advice of many modern spiritual teachers, turning the other cheek, refusing to fight back, and sending loving thoughts to an attacking or possessing Neg is not productive and verges on the ridiculous. It is an ineffective approach when dealing with attacking and possessing Negs.

A channeled spirit once told me that I come under so many intense psychic attacks because I resist. It said my resistance was an open challenge and this, in itself, attracts and causes psychic attacks. I was told to stop resisting and love my enemy, and that the attacks would stop if I ceased my fiery resistance. I tried this once (I'll try just about anything once) and it almost got me killed. I suffered a lot more damage than I would have, had I countered the attack in my usual way. Submitting to an attack and sending loving thoughts, if anything, empowers attacking Negs.

The love-and-light approach does not work against attacking Negs. It's akin to walking timidly and inoffensively through a busy city at night, sending loving thoughts to everyone; while laudable, sooner or later this is going to get you mugged. At the very least, apply the rules of diplomacy to the love-and-light approach. Say, "Nice doggy," and pat with one hand, while your other hand searches for a suitable rock to throw.

Negs thrive on the love-and-light approach and use it to further their ends. They use these gentle spiritual beliefs against people. Negs play on these and often pretend to be misguided lost spirits, projecting seemingly harmless illusory forms to the perceptions of sensitives. But in truth they are just furthering their controls. Negs are masters of lies, trickery, and deception. A troublesome spirit, no matter what it pretends to be, should *never* be trusted further than one can throw it. Negs should never be given the benefit of the doubt.

Negs feed and thrive on fear because fear exposes weak points in humans that Negs then take advantage of. Showing a fearless attitude, even if you're trembling on the inside, is bravery. This is preferable to submission when facing a foe with no conception of love, mercy, and compassion. I prefer the old saying: "Praise the Lord and pass the ammunition." This is down-to-earth realism that is both pragmatic and spiritual.

A Review of Effective Countermeasures

Let's look now at several approaches you can take to counter or undo possession.

Altered States of Consciousness: Altered states of consciousness can provide some relief from possession. The difficulty is that an altered state is hard to hold onto for long. Everyone must eventually sleep, and the trance state (mind awake + body asleep) will not, in itself, block Neg telepathic, hypnotic influences any more than sleep will.

The roots of possession lie in the base level of consciousness, in the dimensional interface at that level, between the human brain/mind and their unseen spiritual reality. The base level is the normal level of consciousness during the waking state. This is the level where possession is occurring, where Negs have levels of control they should not have. Changing this level of consciousness alters the frequency of the dimensional interface. A higher frequency will disable Neg controls, but until the base level is permanently altered, symptoms of possession will continue.

There are many ways to raise your base level of consciousness permanently, but all take time and effort, usually years. This is best considered a long-term project. However, during crisis situations you can cover much ground in a short time, as your motivation to do so is high.

You can change your base level of consciousness through the application of rigorous physical, mental, and spiritual disciplines. The practices of self-observation and introspection, and daily trance meditation and prayer, must be undertaken rigorously. All aspects of your life should be examined; look for areas where improvements can be made. Apply self-discipline and exercise spiritual virtues in all aspects of your life.

Moving Energy: Temporarily heightened energy levels (physical, emotional, mental, and psychic) gained through intensive energy-raising and development practices, can be a two-edged sword for possessed or severely Neg-influenced people. Increased energy levels will promote higher and more spiritual levels of consciousness, but if done quickly, any changes in the base level of consciousness will be unstable, fluctuating through a series of highs and lows. While this will settle down eventually, the extra energy produced will also be used by Negs.

Increased energy levels will tend to cultivate psychic abilities, and this can further expose you to Neg influences and manifestations. For example, you might develop astral sight and hearing (clairvoyance and clairaudience). Negs will then potentially torment you through your newfound abilities and their associated weaknesses.

The Power of Understanding the Source of Your Problem: In my experience, a deciding factor in the healing process with all Neg-related problems, including possession, is when you are given a direction to face. Once you understand that your unnatural thoughts and urges come from *outside* you, a huge burden is lifted from you.

It is soul damaging to believe that sickeningly unnatural thoughts, fantasies, and compulsions come from inside you, from your own seemingly unhealthy mind. It's difficult to fight yourself. But once you realize that badness originates from Negs, you get a direction to face. Most people in this situation will fight bravely, often cheerfully, because finally they have something tangible to fight. I have helped many people suffering from Neg-related problems, plagued by unhealthy thoughts, fantasies, and urges. Once they realize where all this comes from, their spirits are uplifted and they are greatly relieved.

Resisting Obsessional Urges: Key elements of possession are abnormally strong urges and compulsions. These will be unusual, often unnatural, and/or out of character for you, and at times even wrongful and dangerous. Expect paranoia and guilt-producing thoughts, fantasies, urges, and a variety of anti-social urges. You may become violent, anxious, suspicious, argumentative, critical of others, and have a tendency to explode over trivial matters. It will be difficult to keep your emotions under control. As the battle heats up, a noticeable division will appear inside your mind between natural thoughts and needs and unnatural thoughts and wants. You will have to fight to appear reasonably normal on the outside, while your mind seethes unnaturally on the inside.

You may begin having blackouts, or false waking dreams, in which your mind switches off completely. At such times you will act without thinking, as if in a dream or OBE; such episodes might last for seconds or hours. For example, you might find yourself stealing out at night to spy on neighbors or to prowl the shadows.

Persons doing this have temporarily lost control of themselves. They could stop this if they fought back, but they feel weak and disoriented, as if dreaming. These episodes will become progressively stronger until the difference between your real life and your false dream life becomes vague and blunted. During these surreal episodes, your conscience, fear of consequences, and all the higher emotions are eclipsed.

What I've just described is part of the mental battle that comes with serious levels of possession. This is the first taste of the surreal world awaiting fully possessed persons, if the Neg control gets to the point where virtual puppetry becomes possible. The mental battleground of a possessed person is as bloody, confusing, and frightening as a war zone. At times, the struggle to stay in control is a matter of survival.

It can be difficult to distinguish *your* genuine desires, needs and wants from Neg-induced ones. To overcome this problem, great care should be taken until possession is under control. Carefully examine the nature of all inner urges before you act upon them.

If you suspect you have the potential for loss of self-control, never allow yourself to be put in situations involving risk and temptation. Actively avoid all situations where weaknesses and urges might be exploited. If, for example, you have suicidal or murderous urges, avoid driving and all other activities involving control over things that could be dangerous to yourself and to others.

Avoid driving and caring for children. Keep dangerous weapons like guns, knives, axes, drugs, and poisons securely under lock and key, and have another person hold the keys. In this way, risks are minimized. Avoid dangerous places, especially high places.

Avoid alcohol and recreational drugs like the plague if possession is suspected. While these substances can help promote relaxation and sleep, they also weaken and expose your mind to further Neg influences and controls. The last thing a possessed person needs is to have his self-control weakened.

Sexual urges often form a part of this battleground. If you find yourself becoming sexually drawn to another person, and this is an inappropriate, immoral, or wrongful attraction, then actively avoid that person. Never allow situations to occur where you might be left alone with that person. This is especially so if you begin to have obsessive sexual fantasies about this person.

At the grass-roots level of the psyche, there are only two ways to fight Neg-related thoughts, fantasies, and urges, and neither is easy. The obsessions can be forcibly replaced with something else, or the mind can be held clear forcibly. Both methods provide mental blocks and shift attention away from Neg telepathic, hypnotic broadcasts. However, this requires technique and practice. It's easier to replace unnatural thoughts than it is to forcibly clear them. For example, it's easier to occupy the mind reciting multiplication tables, prayers, or poetry than it is to forcibly hold it clear. This memorization process, in itself, helps a great deal. It also helps if what is being memorized is of interest to the person memorizing it. This exercises and strengthens the mind, which surely is the whole point here.

If you are not used to the memorization process, some effort will be required to wake up your mind. But take heart, the human brain is capable of doing anything if it's properly motivated and regularly exercised. Undertake to memorize spiritually meaningful texts on the same level as the influence, which means, if influences are obsessional, then your efforts to memorize text should also be obsessional. Meet force with force. In extreme cases, spend a great deal of time and effort doing this each day.

Pick texts that are appealing and interesting, but also spiritual. You may, for example, pick the soliloquies of Shakespeare, but also pick prayers and hymns for memorizing. Memorizing these adds to the contents of your conscious mind at the base level of consciousness. Once memorized, these will be carried forever inside the mind where they can affect the spiritual quality and frequency of your mind.

Memorization is not only valuable exercise for the mind, but it benefits the will and spirit. To counter Neg problems, you need discipline and exercise. The stronger a mind becomes, the more difficult it will be for Negs to influence it. A person with a strong, well-disciplined mind is a difficult proposition for any Neg; one will rarely ever be approached, let alone be taken, abused, corrupted, or possessed.

Pay Attention to Your Dreams: Dreams can provide you with helpful clues about Neg situations. Possession is about as serious as it gets, so take careful note of your dreams and the dreams of those around you. Dreams highlight core images, and can indicate the source of Neg attacks and influences. Ask questions of your dreams by programming yourself with affirmations before going to sleep.

Seeking Medical Advice: Medical and psychiatric treatment can provide invaluable help for possessed persons. While the scientific model does not allow for Neg-related problems, medical professionals can still provide assistance. Possession always causes some degree of mental instability, and many other health problems as well, such as infections and pain. Professional advice and drugs can help here.

Some drugs change how the brain works, which in turn affects how the mind interacts with unseen influences. Thus some drugs can block out Neg influences. However, a chemical barrier is best considered only a short-term solution. While drugs can alleviate many symptoms, they do not address the root of the problem: Neg possession. Prescribed drugs should therefore be used in conjunction with other countermeasures.

The effort involved in making changes to yourself and lifestyle cannot be avoided. Spiritual and mental exercises that promote self-control and increased spirituality, plus other countermeasures given here, significantly reduce Neg control levels if you seriously apply them. They do this by changing the internal circumstances that allow possession to occur. Enormous effort may still be required, but possession, in varying degrees, can be overcome, and accomplishing this is a life-changing experience in every way.

The Value of Praying: The value of prayer to help with possession cannot be underestimated. Regardless of your beliefs, prayer is a serious countermeasure against all Neg-related problems. This is especially so if prayers are memorized and recited regularly with reverence. Here are a few you might use: The Lord's Prayer; Psalms 23, 31, and 35.

Other bible prayers and psalms are suitable, as are those in the holy books of other religions. Prayers connect you with the higher forces they represent and have the power to get you much-needed help. The more special you make the saying of these prayers, and the more reverently you do it, the greater is their power to elicit divine help for you.

Prayer can be made into a powerful, meaningful devotional act. First, prepare a room by cleaning it, burning incense in it (frankincense or church incense), and blessing it. Take a ritual bath and dress in clean, loose clothing. Go to this room, sit, perform a relaxation exercise, then clear your mind and meditate. Form a clear intention for the purpose of the prayer or prayers about to be said. When your mind is clear and focused, say the prayers aloud or mentally. Feel and realize the meaning of every word. If you have not memorized these prayers, read them directly from the book you're using. Purchase a new bible or holy book for no other use than this. If you have memorized the prayers, hold the holy book while you say them. If possession is suspected, recite Psalm 31 three times a day with reverence; do this morning, noon, and night, if possible.

Help from Churches: Most churches offer some help to possessed persons. However, getting help can take time and effort. The Catholic Church is known to carry out exorcisms, but getting an official exorcism from it can take months, even years. Unless there are obvious Neg manifestations around a possessed person, help is unlikely to be forthcoming quickly, and help is even less likely to be offered to non-Catholics.

Some other religions are more likely to offer immediate help, such as the Assembly of God or Baptist churches, which will usually offer help quickly. Any charismatic, born-again type church will be helpful; in many of these, exorcisms are a daily event. Buddhist monks and other Eastern religious organizations can offer help, especially Tibetan Buddhists. The general rule here is that if one church refuses help or is ineffective, seek another.

If a possessed person gets real help, it's advisable one joins and becomes a sincere and active member of that church. All religions and churches provide a group mind effect that is highly protective of its individual members such that if you leave the church that has helped you, that church's protection will soon fade away.

Exorcism: Exorcism, as carried out by the Roman Catholic Church, is a lengthy, complex ritual that may have to be repeated many times. Some exorcisms performed at the Vatican have taken several years or more to rid people of demonic possession. Possessed people undergoing exorcism have been known to vomit fire, coal, and even feathers. Among other strange phenomena, holy water blistered skin and caused vomiting; glasses containing holy water have exploded when touched.

You might think these difficulties arise from a poor understanding of possession, or from ineffective techniques being used. But let me assure you that the Roman Catholic ritual is a powerful tool. The efficacy of any type of exorcism depends greatly on the exorcist. The difficulties involved with any exorcism also depend greatly on the type and strength of the possessing Neg. Many exorcists themselves have been possessed and released. This has the effect of strengthening faith and mind. When it comes to exorcism, strength of mind, experience, and faith are essential for success and survival.

Some new-age healers, psychics, shamans, and "white" witches can help. But again, experience is paramount. Just because a person calls himself an exorcist, shaman, or Druid high priest, or holds certificates, does not mean he has the *ability* to perform an exorcism. An inexperienced practitioner can easily make a bad situation worse. Therefore, check not only their credentials, but their experience in this work.

Due to the violent reaction exorcism often causes in possessed people, exorcism should never be attempted in a one-on-one situation. Adults especially must be restrained (carefully but securely tied up) before an exorcism can safely be performed. These are wise safety precautions considering the enraged superhuman strength some possessed people can exhibit during episodes of virtual puppetry.

Responsible practitioners of magic can also offer help. However, treating possession is no matter for novice or intermediate students. High levels of knowledge and skill are required. Any person not well-trained in the intricacies of high magic is risking not only her own life, but the lives of those she is trying to help. Knowledge, strength, and experience are everything here. Initiates of the Hermetic path, the authentic Rosicrucian School, or of the Golden Dawn can help. Among these people, usually the levels of knowledge and experience necessary to exorcise strong Negs are high. Unfortunately, because of the reclusive nature of their work, initiates never advertise their services.

Advice on Self-Exorcism: The process of ridding yourself of possession requires courage, dedication, and effort, but it can be done.

To begin with, extensive work should be done on core images and energy body attachment points on a daily basis to weaken them. Be continually on the lookout for new core images and attachment points; these are sure to appear as old ones are weakened and removed.

The ability to discipline and control yourself is paramount when fighting the urges and compulsions that come with possession. There are various methods of training and strengthening the will, but all of them involve strengthening a lazy mind. Any mind, no matter how weakened, cowed, or obsessed by Negs, can rally and overthrow its oppressor if it tries.

Self-discipline is different from strength of personality. Just because a person has great strength of personality does not mean he has self-control, self-discipline, or willpower (the ability for self-discipline). A person can be strong when dealing with other people, but weak in disciplining his own body, mind, and self. You must train and strengthen your will through a series of progressively demanding exercises until your mind becomes strong enough to control the physical body and ego. It must become strong enough to overcome Neg-related compulsions that are interfering with your mental and spiritual health.

The self-denial involved with fasting is excellent for strengthening willpower. Fasting also helps purify the mind and purge the physical body of toxins. A three-day fast will often stimulate enough willpower to throw off, at least temporarily, heavy Neg influences. Possessing Negs will sometimes withdraw after a person's exhibition of self-discipline and willpower.

Unfortunately, fasting can be a two-edged sword for possessed persons. Fasting increases energy body levels and enhances psychic abilities, and because of this, it can also increase exposure to Neg influences. Even so, self-denial is a primary weapon against possession. Some Negs will broadcast a compulsion to starve oneself, even to the point of causing death. Eat sensibly between fasting exercises and do not fall into the trap of starving yourself for weeks on end. This can cause physical damage. If you doubt you are fit enough to undertake any type of modified dietary regime, ask the opinion of a qualified medical doctor beforehand.

When people become possessed, life is telling them that change is urgently required. As a general rule, it is advisable to make radical, broad-spectrum, positive lifestyle changes, including diet and exercise. These may not cure your possession, but any positive changes will help you.

Never give up. Throw yourself into self-improvement in every way possible. The harder you work at this, the more difficult a target you will become. If you make the situation too difficult, Negs will often withdraw. Fighting back in this way not only occupies your mind, but positive improvements change your situation; they have a cumulative effect, physically, mentally, and spiritually.

The effort involved also has a side effect that encourages spiritual help and succor from above. The greater the effort involved, the more likely you are to attract benevolent spiritual attention. The saying "God helps those who help themselves" is true in cases of possession. Doing nothing is counterproductive, whereas doing something positive will make things difficult for the Negs concerned.

After Clearing Out the Negs: When possessing Negs are exorcised, sometimes they will go quietly and sometimes they will go kicking and screaming. When they go quietly, all Neg-related problems wind down and cease. The moment of disconnection usually causes a sudden feeling of upliftment and relief. However, if the Neg resists being ejected, disconnection can be followed by a short period of intense psychic attack as it tries to reattach. If this happens, no matter how painful and distressing, know that this will only last a few minutes at most. Weather it stoically until it passes.

The aftermath of a Neg removal can generate mixed emotions. Feelings of upliftment and happiness will often fade into hollow feelings, a sense of emptiness. The reason for this is that internal Neg influences and motivations that may have been present for a long time have suddenly disappeared. This will often cause some depression. It may take several days for this to ease, as your own mind and spirit expand to fill the hole left by the departing Neg. Positive thinking and concentrating on your health, well-being, and happiness will help. This is a good time to take some time out to spoil yourself. You may not have enjoyed your life for some time, so this is a good time to catch up.

A common post-possession side effect is increased sensitivity to Neg presences. It may be uncomfortable to be around people with strong Neg attachments, even though those people are not actually possessed. Sensations like goose bumps, hair prickling, and a sense of things being wrong are common. Close proximity to somebody with Neg problems can cause a noticeable cramping sensation in your back muscles.

Possession and Exorcism in Children

In the following pages, I offer observations and tests for you to determine if a child is suffering from possession. Follow these instructions carefully and do not modify them. Keep a notebook handy and record all observations; these will help you to explain the situation if expert help is called in.

During Sleep: Watch the child sleep and look for abnormal behavior, such as strange, repetitive hand or body movements, sleepwalking, and talking in her sleep. Try communicating with the child while she sleeps. Speak in a gentle voice to the child's left ear; record what happens. Does she respond to your voice? What kind of response is it: normal and child-like or did something other than the child respond?

Strange Marks: Search the child's body for strange marks, lumps, or small wounds. Do not let the child know what you're seeking. You can pretend you're looking for ringworm.

Food Obsessions: Has the child suddenly developed an obsession or aversion towards food, or for a particular type of food? If yes, suppress his consumption of that food and observe the reaction. Is it violent and unreasonable? Is it adult-level violent, beyond what you would expect from a child?

Sudden Illnesses: Do health changes occur in the child suddenly? Do they experience fevers that come and go quickly? Pain and illnesses that come and go quickly? Do these changes occur especially at night, with no reasonable medical explanations?

Holy Water Test: Give the child a drink containing a dash of holy water from a church. Do this in secret, pretending it's a regular drink. Observe what happens. Do not expect the child to start convulsing, screaming, and cursing God in a strange tongue. This would only happen in a high level of demonic possession, which is rare. Instead, observe if the child vomits or becomes ill afterwards, or refuses to drink the water, claiming it tastes bad. Note anything unusual.

Phenomena: Are any supernatural phenomena taking place? Combined with other factors, this can indicate that progressive possession is taking place. On its own, this symptom can be caused by the child's natural mediumistic ability (psychokinetic energy).

Things to Record: When did the phenomena start? Can this be associated with any change in the child? Was the child present during a paranormal manifestation? Does the child see or feel anything during such manifestations? How does he behave during manifestations? Is anyone in the house experiencing psychic attacks? Are there any strange odors in the house? Can these odors be related to any deceased persons?

Hypnosis Possession Test: Great care must be used when making this test to see if a possessing Neg is inside the child. This *must* be done by a competent adult. I strongly advise that this be done by a professional, such as a doctor, psychotherapist, psychiatrist, or clergyman. The person making this test *must* stay calm and controlled at all times. Make *no* attempt to exorcise a possessing Neg at this time if one is found. Ignoring this warning could cause full possession (equating to full-blown psychosis) to occur as a reaction. If possession is ascertained, seek expert help.

Sit the child in a comfortable chair, or lay the child down in bed. Have adult assistance nearby in case something goes wrong, or in case actual possession does occur. Tell the child to close his eyes and relax. Say you are going to play an imagination game. No matter what happens, always insist that this is just a game.

Tell the child to concentrate on his feet. Then, tell the child to imagine a blue energy going up from his feet to head, slowly and gently. Continue this for several minutes. Suggest that as the glowing energy moves up, his body is turning into air, becoming very light, and that soon he will feel no body weight. Do not be forceful, but use relaxing suggestions.

Tell the child to imagine he is flying, and instruct him to settle on a cloud. Suggest the child relax on the fluffy cloud and has a nap there while it floats through the sky. Get the child to imagine a floating sensation, the land below floating past, as he floats through the warm, sunny sky. Allow the child to fall asleep. At this point, achieving sleep should only take a couple of minutes. You can use a slow, relaxed countdown, or something else to help induce the child to sleep.

When a possessed person is hypnotized, the possessing entity will normally manifest, sometimes making itself known the moment the person enters the trance state. If it does not, it can be summoned. For example, say, "I call upon the being inside this person to come forward and speak to me." The name of the entity can be used if this is known. If this is unknown, be careful not to stimulate the child's imagination or an imaginary being may be created. To avoid this, when the child is in trance (past the falling-asleep stage), say, "I am now talking to the being that is causing harm to this child or family."

Talk as if to another person, not directly to the child. In this way, the child will not assume a personality induced by hypnotic suggestion. Look away from the child and talk in another direction, so the child does not sense he is being talked to.

If the child is possessed, the entity within will give some kind of response immediately. Sometimes, when a possessed person is put under hypnosis, he will have minor twitching convulsions, or make repetitive movements or hand gestures. Sometimes, these actions look as if someone were trying on new clothes and trying to settle into them. Such a person may wriggle and shrug and move about as if trying to make himself comfortable.

If the Neg manifests through the child's voice, you can question it. Be aware and cautious at this time. Ask its name, element, rank, purpose, and the length of time it plans to stay with the person its possessing. Record any answers given. However, if great care is not used it may become violent; it will always lie and deceive. It will never speak the truth unless it is commanded in the proper way.

The entity can be dismissed by saying: "Go to where you belong and come back when you are commanded to come." Then, gently talk the child out of trance until he is fully awake again. The child may remember, but do not explain what happened or why it was done. Say only that what happened was a game. After this, say a sincere prayer to God, asking for protection and help for yourself and the child. Do not try to exorcise the Neg at this time! Do not suggest it leave the child at this time!

If the response to the tests for possession are positive, begin searching for experienced help. Apply all countermeasures given in this book as necessary. Never allow inexperienced but well-meaning dabblers to attempt an exorcism, especially of a child. This could be likened to letting an automobile mechanic remove a child's appendix. Keep in mind that this situation is not the child's fault. He is an innocent victim and will need a great deal of support to get through this.

Summary of Useful Steps: Here is a summary of what you should do if possession is suspected:

• Make frequent, reverent prayers for help

• Undertake core-image work

• Work on energy body attachment points

• Memorize poetry, prose, prayers, and psalms

- Install the running-water perimeter barrier surrounding the bedroom

- Create and sleep over an artificial telluric spring

- Apply all advice and countermeasures herein as necessary

- Make significant, positive lifestyle changes

- Find help, from a church or experienced exorcist

- Never give up hope

In this chapter we have gone deep into the subject of possession, and how to deal with it by exorcism. We have seen how attitude, energy, and altered states can affect or be affected by possession; how to resist obsessional urges and some things that should be avoided; how symptoms and advice can appear in dreams; and how doctors, drugs, and churches can help. Possession, exorcists, exorcism, self-exorcism, and how children have special needs and considerations have also been discussed. In our next chapter we examine procedures, which have their roots in applied metaphysics, that can help you defend yourself against, and banish, troublesome Negs.

18

Sacred Symbols and Banishments
Effective against Negs

In this chapter we take a walk on the wild side of spiritual existence, and examine some methods of psychic self-defense that involve elements of applied metaphysics, which is to say, the practical application of magic. I have thoroughly tested these procedures and found them to be very effective. Combined with other methods and advice given herein, they will provide you with a formidable anti-Neg arsenal.

Sacred symbols, words, and actions can be combined to form rituals. Rituals form the basis of all magical and religious practices, which have existed for thousands of years in most, if not all, cultures and religions. Even simple prayers or the acts of touching wood or crossing your heart are rituals. In my experience, certain sacred symbols, words, and ritual actions can be used effectively as Neg countermeasures.

Sacred symbols can be said to generate the energies of what they visually represent. However, the effective use of sacred symbols as wards involves having some understanding of their meaning. This knowledge is the key to connecting them with their higher powers. The more that is known about what a symbol represents, and the more elaborate its creation and blessing, the more special and powerful it becomes. A simple geometric design can thus be transformed into a sacred symbol, which will be a repellent to all Negs. Let's review a few sacred symbols that can be used for psychic self-defense.

Sacred Symbols

The Circle: A circle has no beginning and no end. It thus represents infinity and the whole of creation, and the omnipotence of God without beginning or end. The circle is often represented in magical symbology by a snake devouring its own tail. When any symbol is enclosed within a circle, the meaning of the circle is added to that of the symbol enclosed within it; thereby greatly increasing its symbolic meaning and power (see figure 1).

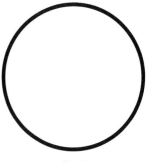

Fig. 1

The Pentagram: The most basic meaning of the pentagram is that it represents humanity. Its mathematical equivalent is number five, and it is related to divine law as well as the five elements: earth, air, fire, water, and spirit. When one point of a pentagram is on top, it represents light and goodness, but when two points are on top, it represents darkness and evil.

If you draw or affix a pentagram onto a vertical surface, such as a wall, door or window, one point should always point upwards. But if a pentagram is laid horizontally as a ward, such as in a doorway, it should have a single point directed into the house, with two points directed away from the house. If a pentagram is used on the floor or ground (apart from a doorway), its upper point should face east. When drawing a pentagram as a ward or banishment, always start from the bottom left point and draw it upwards and clockwise, as per the numbers in the diagram below (see figure 2).

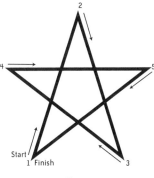

Fig. 2

The Tetragram: The Tetragram (an equal-limbed cross—also called the Kabbalistic, Gnostic, or solar cross) represents the dualism of all forces in the universe. According to the kabbalah, the vertical bar represents the masculine and active principle of creation, the sacred phallus, and the horizontal bar represents the feminine and passive principle of creation, the sacred uterus. The Tetragram also represents the Tetragrammaton, which is the four-character Hebrew name for God (*YHVH*). It also represents the four elements of the physical universe, fire, air, water, and earth; and the four magical elements, Azoth, Sulfur, Mercury, and Salt (see figure 3).

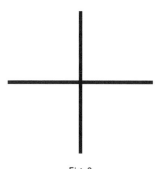

Fig. 3

Calvary Cross: The Calvary Cross is the symbol of Jesus Christ, the primordial roots of the Christian religion, and of redemption. It also represents the crucifixion of Jesus dying on the cross for the sins of humankind. If carrying a statue of Jesus, it is called a Crucifix, which is the primary symbol of the Catholic Church (see figure 4).

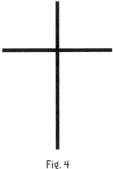

Fig. 4

The Hexagram: The six-pointed double triangle symbol represents the six days of creation, and wholeness of God and His perfect creation. It is also called the Star of David, the six-rayed star, or the Seal of Solomon. One triangle points upwards and symbolizes the forces of the Earth ascending into heaven, and one triangle points downwards and symbolizes the forces of heaven descending into the Earth. The linking of these triangles therefore symbolizes the link between heaven and earth, between non-physical and physical (see figure 5).

Fig. 5

There are various ways to make and use symbols as wards. The simplest way is to draw them on a paper or card, bless them, and tape them to walls. Light pastel colors are best for general protective use. However, some paper wards can attract awkward questions from human visitors. If this is a problem, tape wards to the backs of pictures already hanging on walls. Symbols can also be put under carpets, mattresses, doormats, or taped to the undersides of beds and furniture. Paper wards can also be framed and disguised as abstract art pieces.

Creating Wards: The effectiveness of symbolic wards is increased when they are created with care and attention to detail. All new materials should be acquired for this purpose: new paper, ink, and cutting and drawing instruments.

Simple wards can be made by placing objects, with blessed protective symbols drawn on their bottoms, around the home and garden. Household ornaments, rocks, and garden ornaments can have protective symbols drawn or painted on their undersides. Rock wards can be placed around the garden and along walkways leading to the home. Smooth river or beach stones are ideal. Painted ward stones can even be buried if desired. Furniture pieces can also have protective symbols drawn on their undersides, out of sight from prying eyes, or drawn in essential oils.

While it could be counterproductive to paint sacred symbols on the outside of one's home, as neighbors may misunderstand your intention, they can be drawn unobtrusively in pencil, chalk, or essential oils. If you are planning to repaint the home, blessed symbols can be drawn or painted on walls and eaves, door and window frames, covering all entrances. These can then be painted over without reducing their effectiveness. Likewise, symbols can also be drawn on internal walls and doors, and then painted over.

All symbols should be drawn upwards and clockwise from left to right. Neatness is important but not essential. Crude, hand-drawn symbols will suffice in most circumstances, especially if you draw them on household surfaces in chalk or essential oils. The imagined perfection of rough hand-drawn symbols, of the forces they symbolize and the blessings they are given, plus the value and reverence bestowed upon them, are more important than geometric perfection.

During strong Neg attacks, I have resorted to creating large wards of construction paper and attaching one to each cardinal point of bedroom walls. Luminous paint can be used to make them glow in the dark. They can also be splashed or traced over with Holy Water while blessing them. This extra attention makes them more special and increases their effectiveness.

I find the Tetragram (equal-limbed cross) within a circle attracts far less curiosity from visitors, and as a ward this is equally as effective as any other sacred symbol.

Blessing Symbols: After drawing or mounting a symbol, energize it by closing your eyes and praying over it. The simplest blessing would be: "I bless this symbol in the sacred names of Almighty God and Jesus Christ. May its holy power banish all evil spirits and forces. So shall it be. Amen."

Sacred Names

The most effective sacred words for banishment I have found in the Western world are the Names of God and His Angels that are given in the kabbalah. Just as symbols have some natural energy in their forms, sacred names also generate natural energy. Words and names of power can be spoken, or written and used in the same way as symbol type wards. The sincerity and confidence with which sacred words are written or spoken are important.

Unlike symbols, the sacred names of God and Angels do not require blessing before use, as long as they are spoken or written with reverent intent. Sacred words can be written on walls, doors, windows, and other items to deter Negs from entering. These can be written in chalk, pencil, or essential oils. A number of these names can also be written in a line, or in a circle, to create barriers. However, the area they are to be written on should be thoroughly cleansed and blessed first. All Negs are repelled by sacred names.

Sacred God Names: The Tetragrammaton is the Kabbalistic abbreviation for the primary, ineffable name of God (*YHVH*). This is made up of the four Hebrew characters of the sacred name, as read from right to left in the Hebrew way. These are often abbreviated in English to *YHVH* or *YHWH* (V and W are interchangeable) but the absolute correct pronunciation is a well-guarded mystery. It is said that if a mortal pronounced the actual true name of God, the earth would shake.

Each of the ten sacred names of God given in the kabbalah refers to a different aspect of God. The primary name of God is: YHVH (pronounced as *"Yud-Heh-Vahv-Heh"*). Some other sacred names of God from the kabbalah that are commonly used for banishment purposes are: Adonai (*"Ah-Doh-Nye"*) and Agla (*"Ah-Glah"*) and Eheih (*"Eh-Heh-Yeh"*). Because these names were originally written and spoken in Hebrew, and they have been extensively used in religious and magical ritual practices for thousands of years, they have become magically empowered. They are thus universally recognized by Negs for what they represent.

Latin has also been similarly empowered because of its extensive use in church ritual worship. Modern English, however, is a relatively young and thus less powerfully evocative magical language. Whilst there are other styles and languages of mysticism found throughout the world—Sanskrit, Australian Aboriginal, African, Arabic, Chinese, Native American, and Egyptian—I have found that the Hebrew Kabbalistic style is extremely effective for repelling and banishing Negs.

Banishment Rituals

The following is a greatly simplified version of the LBRP (Lesser Banishment Ritual of the Pentagram). For this, the pentagram is drawn in midair in a particular way, as follows: Extend your arm and point your index and middle fingers as a visualization drawing tip. Trace the pentagram symbol in front of you while you visualize a blue streak like gas flame trailing behind your moving finger. Start from your left hip and ascend in a straight line to a point in the air above your head, then down to your right hip, then diagonally up and left (adjacent your left shoulder), then horizontally right (adjacent your right shoulder), then diagonally down to finish at your left hip again (see figure 6).

Fig. 6

Always keep in mind that the essence of banishment involves giving a direct and authoritative command, in the name of God. It must therefore be performed and spoken in a reverent, forceful and commanding way. Practice this hand action until you can do it smoothly with a confident, purposeful sweeping action. Once you have learned this action, say the banishment words that follow whilst you make the sign of the pentagram, as described. Use a strong, deep, commanding voice, saying: *"I banish all evil spirits and influences from this place and command them never to return; in the name of the Father, the Son, and the Holy Spirit."*

The previous is the simplest banishment ritual possible. However, its power can be greatly increased by using sacred God names from the kabbalah. These Hebrew words should be spoken in a deep and commanding voice, vibrated from the back of your throat. With a little practice, you will find these can be spoken loudly or quietly, while still vibrating the power of the words effectively. Each God name should be spoken and vibrated in a drawn-out way, using one complete exhale for each. While making the sign of the pentagram, say *"I banish all evil spirits and influences from this place and command them to never return, by the most sacred and holy names of Almighty God, Yud-Heh-Vahv-Heh; Ah-Doh-Nye; Ah-Glah; and Eh-Heh-Yeh."*

While learning this procedure, you might find it easier to use only one God name, *Yud-Heh-Vahv-Heh,* to start with, and then to add the others as they are memorized. It helps if you write them on a small card and hold it in your free hand during the banishment.

This single banishment action can be used to dispel a single Neg manifestation or disturbance, if you know where it is in a room and can face it. This can also be done while you are lying in bed, to repel nocturnal attacks and interference. The banishment action can also be visualized and the words spoken only mentally, but this will significantly reduce its effect on Negs.

The banishment is more effective if it is done with hand actions and spoken commands; it is also more effective when it is repeated in all four quadrants of a room. This is necessary to completely clear a room of Neg influences. Here's how to do it:

Stand in the center of the room and face the east, relax for a few moments, and clear your mind. Then, concentrate and fill your mind with God's power and the intention of what you are about to do, which is to banish evil spirits and influences.

Before and after clearing a room with the following banishment, perform the following protective crossing ritual: (The more effective Hebrew words are given in parentheses. If used, these should be spoken so as to vibrate them in a drawn out way.) As you cross yourself, visualize a brilliant white cross forming inside of you, with each point extending to the edge of the universe. Touch your forehead with the fingers of your right hand, and say "For Thine" *(Ah-Tah)*; then move your hand over your genitals and say "Is The Kingdom" *(Mahl-Koot)*; then touch your right shoulder and say "The Power" *(Vih-G'boo-Rah)*; then touch your left shoulder and say "And The Glory" *(Vih-G'doo-Lah)*; then clasp hands together in center of your chest, as if in prayer, and say "Forever And Ever, Amen" *(Lih-Oh-Lahm, Ah-Men)*.

Perform the first pentagram banishment sign and words, visualizing blue fire flowing from fingertips. As you finish this, move your hand up to touch the center of the pentagram. Pause a moment, visualizing the pentagram hanging before you.

Keeping your arm extended, trace a line with your extended arm and pointed fingers as you move your body ninety degrees to the right, to the southern quadrant of the room, while visualizing a line of blue fire flowing from your fingertips. Repeat the banishment, then continue the line to the west and repeat the banishment, and then to the north and repeat the banishment.

After the final banishment pentagram and words, complete the circle by turning right to face the east again, moving your pointing fingers back to the middle of the first pentagram you drew there, to complete the circle. Visualize and feel these four connected pentagrams hanging in the air around you. Visualize them as being linked to each other and forming a circle around you, all in a gas blue flame color. Imagine this protective circle forming a wall of protection around you, with the pentagrams growing in size and filling and sealing the four quadrants of the room. Finish by crossing yourself again, as you did at the start.

A full banishment ritual should be done in every room of a house, if a serious Neg attack is in progress, or if you need to clear a whole house of Neg influences. You cannot overdo the banishment procedure and it will grow in power the more practiced at it you become.

The pentagram banishment method can also be applied to the core image removal procedure (given earlier) to banish Neg images and to seal core image holes. It can also be used during OBE and lucid dreams to repel Neg manifestations. The full LBRP is far more powerful than the simple version given above, but this is beyond the scope of this book. (See Kraig's excellent book *Modern Magick,* for full instructions).

Names of Angels

The names of angels can also be used as written or spoken words of protection and banishment. There are a great many angels listed in the Kabala and other holy books, but the following archangels are most commonly used for protection and banishment purposes: Raphael, lord of the East and of Air, Gabriel, lord of the West and of Water, Michael, lord of the South and of Fire, and Uriel, lord of the North and of Earth.

Direct Body Symbol Protection

Protective symbols and sacred names can be drawn directly on the body to repel psychic attacks. This method is particularly good for repelling energy draining Negs and defending against possession attacks, and for protecting against all Neg-related sleep or pre-sleep disturbances. This is also excellent for protecting children, babies, and invalids. Drawing on yourself might sound a little on the crazy side, but it is probably the most reliable and effective anti-Neg countermeasure I have found to date, especially when combined with the use of garlic. I have known several people who were so impressed with this method that they had their bodies tattooed with sacred symbols to give permanent protection. I have also known people to paint sacred symbols on their fingernails and toenails.

Maximum Protection: Using a pen, draw a pentagram on your brow (one point up) and an upright Calvary cross over your heart. Write the name of God (*Yud-Heh-Vahv-Heh*) in Hebrew characters on your solar plexus (see figure 7), and a tetragram cross over your navel. Write the name *Jesus* on the back of one hand and Christ on the back of the other. Draw a large tetragram cross within a circle on the top of each foot, and a large tetragram cross in the middle sole of each foot.

Fig. 7

Use a blue ballpoint or felt-tipped pen for this purpose. Wash your skin first to remove body oil and to make skin drawing easier. To draw circles neatly, use the bottom of a drinking glass as a template, and a ruler or similar guide for straight lines. As the most likely time for Neg attack is during the night, draw these in place each night and wash them each morning.

Everyday Protection: When psychic attack or Neg interference is possible but not a certainty, the minimum defense is to protect only the feet with symbols, as given above. The feet are the most vulnerable area of your energy body. Rubbing a broken clove of garlic into your feet will increase the level of protection.

Protective Clothing: This is a version of the previous approach that does not involve drawing on the skin. It can be done by embroidering or drawing on white clothing, such as pajamas or T-shirts, and white cotton socks and gloves. With this method, the symbols and names can be repeated on the rear of the pajama shirt. Continuing along these lines, a white sheet or bed cover can also be covered with sacred symbols and names. This can then be taken out to cover the bed and ward off Neg attacks at night and folded away from prying eyes during the daytime.

A good way of protecting babies with this method is to prepare a white one-piece jumpsuit, bed cap, mittens, and bed covers with sacred symbols and God names. Another idea is to find or make clothing with pictures of angels, and then to draw or embroider an archangel's name on each picture. Place pictures of angels containing the names of archangels around a baby's room. In this way, a baby's attire and sleeping environment can be made protective without being too obviously "weird" to curious onlookers.

Ritual Bathing

A ritual bath is an excellent way of reducing Neg influences and lessening the effects of psychic attacks. Taking a ritual bath and dressing in clean, oversized clothes also increases the power of any ritual done immediately afterwards.

Fill your bath with water, hot or cold. Throw in a handful of table salt and then bless the water by praying over it, asking for it to be endowed with spiritual cleansing properties to remove Neg influences. You can also add protective oils and/or herbs to the bath, and burn incense in the bathroom. Candlelight helps set a good atmosphere. Get in the bath and soak, clearing your mind and relaxing. Duck your head underwater several times. Say The Lord's Prayer and ask for protection and cleansing of all Neg influences.

Soak for five or ten minutes, visualizing dark fluid leaking from your body into the water. Then, remove the plug, but stay in the bath. Feel the water on your skin as its level drops, and visualize this is sucking all the darkness out of your body and washing it down the drain.

A variation ritual bathing can be done in the shower. Get under the shower and after washing feel the water running over your head and down over your body. Say The Lord's Prayer and ask for protection and cleansing of all bad influences. Imagine a brilliant-white light flowing into your head and filling your body, and black fluid leaking from your feet and flowing down the drain. Continue this for a few minutes or more. Repeat this every time you shower.

Mental Defenses: Versicles and Mantras

Versicles are short prayers or mantras that are repeated mentally or spoken aloud to ward off Neg influences and clear troubled minds. They must be said over and over, with no other thought in mind but the versicle so that it fills your mind. The first versicle can also be used as a method of self-exorcism, if combined with a ritual bath. It is said that no evil can harm the person who says this with pure faith and concentration.

> *May God be resurrected and His foes vanish.*
> *As wax melts before fire,*
> *As smoke disperses in wind,*
> *So may all who hate the Lord flee from His sight,*
> *And the just rejoice!*

This versicle was used by Christian saints to fight off mental attacks, disturbing thoughts, and temptations. The author is anonymous, but I found it in Mouni Shadou's excellent book, *Concentration.*

The following versicle was given to me by my mother. She heard it as a girl, many years ago, and used it all her life to ward off bad thoughts, influences, and temptations. The author is anonymous.

> *God and goodness alone*
> *Governs and guides me*
> *No other presence*
> *No other power.*

Self-Exorcism Ritual

The following is a Greek Orthodox exorcism ritual ideal for psychic self-defense or self-exorcism. This should be memorized and repeated several times, while taking a ritual bath. By memorizing this, you are placing it into your mind, which makes it more effective than if it is just read from a card.

"O, eternal God, who has redeemed the race of men from the captivity of the Devil, deliver your servant (your name) from all the workings of unclean spirits. Command the evil and impure spirits and demons to depart from the soul and body of your servant (your name) and not to remain nor hide in him. Let them be banished from this creation of your hands in your own holy Name and that of your only begotten Son and of your Life-Giving Spirit, so that, after being cleansed from all demonic influence, he may live godly, justly, and righteously and may be counted worthy to receive the Holy Mysteries of your only begotten Son and our God, with whom you are blessed and glorified together with the All-Holy and good and life-giving spirit now and ever and unto the ages of ages. Amen."

(From: "Exorcism for General Use", St. John Chrysostum [344-407 A.D.] from the Greek Orthodox *Book of Divine Offices [Euchologion]*, translated by Eusebius A. Stephanou.)

Egg Decoy Method:

This method removes many Neg types. An organic thing, such as an egg, is used as a decoy to attract and trap a troublesome Neg, so it can be removed and disposed of. For this you will need the following: a fresh egg; a small picture of yourself; a small lock of hair or spot of blood; some holy water and salt; a small nest box or cup.

Wash and dry the egg carefully, write your full name on its shell, and draw a sacred symbol on it, such as a cross. Glue or tape a lock of your hair to it (or a spot of blood), and affix your picture to the egg. Sprinkle this with a mixture of holy water and a little salt, then baptize it with your name as follows: (Make the sign of the cross over the egg with the pointing fingers of your right hand, wherever the sign + appears). Dip your fingers into the holy water, and say "I baptize you (your name) + in the name of the Father +, the Son +, and the Holy Spirit +, Amen +."

Place the egg in the box or cup and keep it close to your bed for seven days and nights. At least twice a day, perform the following visualization: Close your eyes and relax. Imagine the egg has a glowing aura and that this is expanding until it encloses your whole body. Imagine and feel that you and the egg are becoming one. Concentrate to make this feel as real as possible. Imagine all your problems passing into the egg as a black cloud.

On the eighth day, dispose of the egg somewhere far from your home during the daylight hours. Throw or break the egg into running water, including the picture of you. Alternatively, scratch a depression in the ground about the size of your hand, and pour a thick circle of salt around it. Break the egg, dropping the shell, hair and picture into the hole. Throw a handful of leaves over it, taking care not to disturb the circle of salt, and walk away.

The Baptism Ritual

Baptism is a sacred ritual that dedicates your spirit to God. This association brings you under God's spiritual protection. All religions have some kind of baptism rite for this purpose. Unfortunately, many people today do not baptize their children, thinking this is a meaningless, outdated exercise. This is understandable, but by all that I know, baptism is a very wise thing to do for yourself and your children. Think of baptism as an anti-Neg spiritual inoculation. While baptism does not provide perfect protection, it significantly reduces your chances of having serious Neg-related problems.

The essential difference between baptized and unbaptized people can be likened to the difference between holy water and ordinary tap water. Holy water is exorcized, blessed and dedicated to God, which turns it into a powerful holy symbol of purity. Holy water has a protective, cleansing spiritual glow that repels Negs in the same manner as sacred symbols and words. Plain tap water has only its natural properties.

Last Words on Dealing with Negs

Thank you for reading my book. It might sound strange for an author to say this, but I sincerely hope you never have any need for the advice I've offered. I also hope you have enjoyed our journey together through the darker realms of spiritual existence. The writing of this book has been an illuminating voyage of self-discovery for me.

Psychic attacks and other such unseen Neg-related problems are anything but simple. My ways of dealing with these things may go against popular opinion, but they are logical and practical, based on my wide range of field experience in these matters. While some of the subject matter I have dealt with may seem distasteful and even disturbing, it is always good to be prepared for any eventuality. Many people have likened this book to a fire ax, saying it should be kept in a glass-fronted case with the words in red: "In case of emergency, break glass!"

No single method or piece of advice I have given can offer a perfect defense against all psychic attack and Neg-related problems. But when combined and used intelligently, these will provide you with formidable anti-Neg capabilities. These will allow people with no occult knowledge to survive nearly any kind of psychic attack.

I recently had an argument with a well-read skeptic on the subject of possession. He grew hot under the collar when I presented my experience and views because, according to him (ostensibly citing the Vatican), only one in a hundred cases of demonic possession are ever found to be "genuine." My next question was: "What about these one-in-a-hundred genuine cases of demonic possessions you admit to?" For some reason my opponent suddenly lost the power of speech at this point. My reasoning here is that if only one in a hundred cases of apparent psychic attack, negative influence or possession is genuine, then this book's position is validated. While some people are more sensitive and therefore susceptible to these things, Neg events can happen to anyone.

Demons and angels and the host of greater and lesser spiritual beings between these two extremes, are ageless spiritual foes. They have been known by all of humankind down through the ages, albeit with many different names and cultural attributes. But essentially we are all looking in the same direction: we either see foul servants of Darkness or brave guardians of the Light. In our world, the conflict between good and evil rages on all fronts.

However, this book equips you with the knowledge needed to seriously hinder the activities of the unseen dark forces that plague our world today. The more people who resist and overthrow Neg influences, and the more children who grow up Neg-free, the better this world will be. In the fullness of time, this will make a big difference to the future of humankind.

Endnotes

Chapter 6

1. Body-Awareness actions involve using the sense of touch to manipulate the energy body and its subtle organs. Body-Awareness Hands are natural extensions of body awareness, using the sense of touch, in which you feel yourself using your arms and hands, but without actually moving your physical body. This has a strong effect on the energy body. Body-awareness hands are combined with visualization to destroy core images.

2. Astral feedback: This telepathic phenomenon can occur when two identical minds (the physical mind and its projected astral double's mind) connect during an OBE. This is nauseating as one mind reflects into the other, into infinity, like the infinity effect caused when two mirrors reflect into each other.

Bibliography

Amorth, Father Gabriele. 1999. *An Exorcist Tells His Story*. San Francisco: Ignatius Press.

Ashley, Leonard R. N. 1996. *The Complete Book of Devils and Demons*. Fort Lee, N.J.: Barricade Books.

———. 2000. *The Complete Book of Ghosts and Poltergeists*. Fort Lee, N.J.: Barricade Books.

———. 1997. *The Complete Book of Spells, Curses and Magical Recipes*. Fort Lee, N.J.: Barricade Books.

Barlow, David and V. Mark Durand. 1995. *Abnormal Psychology: An Integrative Approach* (Second edition). Pacific Grove: Brooks Cole.

Bruce, Robert. 1999. *Astral Dynamics*. Charlottesville: Hampton Roads. (www.astralpulse.com)

Butler, W.E. 1991. *Magic, Its Ritual, Power and Purpose*. London: Aquarian Press.

Clifford, Terry. 1990. *Tibetan Buddhist Medicine and Psychiatry: The Diamond Healing*. Boston: Red Wheel/Weiser.

Cooper, Jason D. 1994. *Esoteric Rune Magic*. St Paul: Llewellyn.

Cunningham, Scott. 1985. *Cunningham's Encyclopedia of Magical Herbs*. St Paul: Llewellyn.

Dagyab, Loden Sherap. 1995. *Buddhist Symbols in Tibetan Culture*, trans. Maurice Walshe. Boston: Wisdom Books.

Denning, Melita and Osborne Phillips. 1980. *Practical Guide to Psychic Self-Defense and Well-Being*. St. Paul: Llewellyn.

Dhonden, Yeshi. 2000. *Healing from the Source: The Science and Lore of Tibetan Medicine*, trans. B. Alan Wallace. Ithaca, N.Y.: Snow Lion.

Fiore, Edith. 1988. *The Unquiet Dead: A Psychologist Treats Spirit Possession*. New York: Ballantine.

Fortune, Dion. 1988. *Psychic Self-Defense*. Wellingborough, England: Aquarian Press.

Guirdham, Arthur. 1972. *Obsession: Psychic Forces and Evil in the Causation of Disease*. London: Neville Spearman Ltd.

Harish, Johari. 1987. *Chakras: Energy Centers of Transformation*. Rochester, Vermont: Inner Traditions.

Horne, James A. 1992. "Sleep and its Disorders in Children." *Journal of Child Psychology & Psychiatry & Allied Disciplines.* Volume 33 (3), pp. 473-487.

Horowitz, Mardi Jon. 1988. *An Introduction to PsychoDynamics: A New Synthesis.* New York: Basic Books.

Kardek, Allen. 1975 (First published in 1898). *The Spirits Book.* London: Psychic Press.

King James Bible. 1974. Chicago: Processing and Books Inc.

Kraig, Donald Michael. 2000. *Modern Magic: Eleven Lessons on the High Magical Arts.* St. Paul: Llewellyn.

Levi, Eliphas. 1972 (First published in 1896). *Transcendental Magic.* London: Rider.

MacNutt, Francis. 1995. *Deliverance from Evil Spirits: A Practical Manual.* Grand Rapids: Chosen Books.

Martin, Malachi. 1992. *Hostage to the Devil: The Possession and Exorcism of Five Americans.* New York: HarperSanFrancisco.

Mathers, S.L. MacGregor. 1974. *The Kabbalah Unveiled.* New York: Samuel Weiser.

Mathews, Caitlin and John. 1994. *The Encyclopaedia of Celtic Wisdom: A Celtic Shaman's Source Book.* Rockport, Massachusetts: Element Books.

McConnell, Brian. 1997. *The Possessed: True Tales of Demonic Possession.* London: Brockhampton Press.

Pinson, DovBer. 1999. *Reincarnation & Judaism: The Journey of the Soul.* Northvale, N. J.: Jason Aronson.

Rinpoche, Patrul. 1998. *The Words of My Perfect Teacher,* trans. Padmakara Translation Group. Boston: Shambhala.

Robbins, Rossel Hope. 1959. *The Encyclopedia of Witchcraft and Demonology.* New York: Crown.

Roberts, Jane. 1972. *Seth Speaks: The Eternal Validity of the Soul.* Upper Saddle River, N. J.: Prentice-Hall.

Rosnow, Ralph L and Rosenthal, Robert. 1997. *People Studying People: Artifacts and Ethics in Behavioral Research.* New York: W.H. Freeman & Co.

Sadhu, Mouni. 1985. *Concentration: A Guide to Mental Mastery.* Hollywood, CA.: Wilshire Books.

Sambhava, Padma. 1994. *The Tibetan Book of the Dead,* trans. Robert A.Thurman. New York: Bantam Doubleday Dell.

Shapiro, Francine. 1995. *Eye Movement Desensitization and Reprocessing: Basic Principles, Protocols, and Procedures.* New York: Guilford Press.

Stores, Gregory. 1998. "Sleep Paralysis and Hallucinosis." *Behavioural Neurology.* Volume 11 (2), pp. 109–112, ISSN 0953-4180.

Weitzenhoffer, Andre M. 1989. *The Practice of Hypnotism: Volume 1—Traditional and Semi-Traditional Techniques and Phenomenology.* New York: John Wiley & Sons.

Whyte, Maxwell H. A. 1992. *A Manual on Exorcism.* New Kensington, PA.: Whitaker House.

*For more information, articles, updates, and interactive forums, dedicated to metaphysical, spiritual, OBE, and psychic self-defence related matters, please see the author's homepage—The Astral Pulse—at www.astralpulse.com.

Index

About the Author

Robert Bruce is the author of *Astral Dynamics,* one of the most popular and comprehensive how-to books for out-of-body exploration on the market, with more than 13,000 copies sold. For nearly three decades, Bruce has been an active scholar and explorer of metaphysical subjects including psychic abilities, out-of-body experience, human and Earth energies, healing, occult criminality, and mysticism. Since 1992, he has provided a free consulting service to the global internet community from his web site *The Astral Pulse,* www.astralpulse.com. Bruce wishes all his readers a hearty "G'Day!" from his home in Australia.

Hampton Roads Publishing Company

. . . for the evolving human spirit

Hampton Roads Publishing Company
publishes books on a variety of subjects,
including metaphysics, health, integrative medicine,
visionary fiction, and other related topics.

For a copy of our latest catalog, call toll-free
(800) 766-8009, or send your name and address to:

Hampton Roads Publishing Company, Inc.
1125 Stoney Ridge Road
Charlottesville, VA 22902

e-mail: hrpc@hrpub.com
www.hrpub.com